"This new work by Suzanne Cremen challenges us to stretch our imagination and consider new perspectives on the making of career and vocation through calling. The pathway to this new understanding is through a reconsideration of basic principles and concepts from depth psychology. While one might question some of the underlying assumptions, this is a journey that is well worth the effort! The book is creative, stimulating and well written. It also has broad application to many of our current psychological and ecological challenges."

– **Norman Amundson, PhD**, Professor Emeritus, University of British Columbia, Canada, author of *Active Engagement, Essential Elements of Career Counseling, The Physics of Living, Career Pathways* and *Guiding Circles*

"The achievement of Suzanne Cremen's book is to bring into conjunction two areas of study which had not previously been linked with confident knowledge and understanding of both. Traditionally, vocational or career advice focused on the practical matter of finding and improving the individual's employment in the material world. In contrast, analytical psychology tended to concentrate on the state and development of the individual's psyche, so that the inner or non-ordinary world takes priority. This book, in addition to being authoritative, is a delight to read, advancing a rational case with the passion due in explorations of the psyche. Dr Cremen reaches out tactfully to her readers with an impressive blend of analytical rigour and enthusiastic commitment to her topic."

– **John Izod, PhD**, Emeritus Professor, University of Stirling, UK, author of *Cinema as Therapy: Grief and Transformational Film* and *Screen, Culture, Psyche*

"Many people struggle deeply with allowing and listening to the deeper call of the psyche in relation to work and career path. Suzanne Cremen writes on the subject of vocation in a way that is clearly connected to her own vocation. Her passion for the subject is evident. Her work demonstrates strong scholarship and engaging writing. A distinctive feature of this book is the gripping, raw and honest examples of individuals' descents into their personal nekyias which opened them to new life and vocational paths. Adding weight is that the author is willing to tell her own story. Exercises at the end of each chapter help the reader to take the ideas further and personalise them. Highly recommended for anyone who suspects there is much more to life and work than traditional outdated modes of career and success."

— **Ana Mozol, PhD**, Depth Psychoanalyst, author of *A Re-Visioning of Love: Dark Feminine Rising*, and Founder and Director of Dreamwork Theatre Inc. in Vancouver, Canada

"*From Career to Calling* is engaging, alive, filled with clear explanations of concepts used, stories that illustrate the issues at hand and a vulnerability from the author in sharing her own stories. The book is grounded, drawing on more orthodox career guidance foundations, but goes deeper, bridging into the field of depth psychology. It is also distinctive, bringing theory, concepts and story together in a way that is rich, practically helpful and challenging. As we enter an age of anxiety around the future of work, this timely book is profoundly relevant. I couldn't put it down."

— **Peter Westoby, PhD**, Associate Professor in Social Science and Community Development, QUT, Australia, and author of *Soul, Community and Social Change*

"Many readers will discover new hope with this book: for the professional, something akin to 'this new process will really help Client X', and for the layperson, 'At last, here is a new way of understanding myself and the work that I am called to do'. The author's personal accounts, extensive excerpts from interviewees, the pertinent reflective exercises and the depth of academic rigour make this a robust and engaging resource."

— **Michelle Mearns**, Career Transition Coach, New Zealand

From Career to Calling

Finding and following an authentic calling challenges us to bridge the intuitive, soulful and the hard-edged, material dimensions of everyday life. *From Career to Calling: A Depth Psychology Guide to Soul-Making Work in Darkening Times* opens new avenues for vocational exploration and career inquiry in an imaginative way.

This unique book draws on insights from the field of Jungian and archetypal psychology to reimagine our attitudes and approaches to work, money, vocational guidance and career development. As people find themselves disillusioned with or disenfranchised from capitalist notions of work and career, Suzanne Cremen's interdisciplinary approach illuminates how a creative, meaningful and influential work-life can emerge from attending to the archetypal basis of experience. Interweaving elements of her own journey, Cremen connects individual experience with the collective in an original way, spotlighting depression in the legal profession, marginalization of the feminine principle in work environments and how understanding the roots of our cultural complexes can spark personal callings which facilitate collective transformation.

Blending compelling real-life stories with robust scholarly analysis and reflective activities, this book will help practitioners support individuals to develop a sense of their soul's calling and offer guidance on creating an authentic vocational life within the constraints of the contemporary era. Additionally, it will be invaluable to those in career transition, re-discovering their purpose at the end of a career, or commencing work-life.

Suzanne Cremen worked in over 25 occupations including lawyer, screenwriter, conference producer, publisher and career counsellor before earning her PhD in depth psychology. She serves as faculty at Pacifica Graduate Institute (USA) and founded the Life Artistry Centre for Archetype, Imagination and Vocation (Australia), where she teaches and consults.

From Career to Calling

A Depth Psychology Guide to Soul-Making Work in Darkening Times

Suzanne Cremen

Routledge
Taylor & Francis Group

LONDON AND NEW YORK

First published 2020
by Routledge
2 Park Square, Milton Park, Abingdon, Oxon OX14 4RN

and by Routledge
52 Vanderbilt Avenue, New York, NY 10017

Routledge is an imprint of the Taylor & Francis Group, an informa business

British Library Cataloguing-in-Publication Data
A catalogue record for this book is available from the British Library

Library of Congress Cataloging-in-Publication Data
A catalog record for this book has been requested

ISBN: 978-0-367-44450-1 (hbk)
ISBN: 978-0-367-44451-8 (pbk)
ISBN: 978-1-003-00983-2 (ebk)

Typeset in Times New Roman
by Apex CoVantage, LLC

Dedicated to the ancestors, whose lives led us to this moment, and to the more-than-human world, especially to those species whose existence now depends upon human beings heeding a deeper calling.

Contents

x *Contents*

Figures

Acknowledgements

By far the person who has played the greatest role in helping me to bring this work into the world has been my husband, James H Davidson. From visioning and strategizing along the way, to being a sounding board for ideas and expression, to proofreading the text and attending to the regular myriad demands of home and life that someone needs to take care of if a book is to be written. . . . Thank you, James, for backing me all the way with this, and for believing in me and in the value of this work.

To those magnificent souls whose stories and insights appear under pseudonyms in this book to bring theory to life and as a beacon lighting the way for others – I remained deeply honoured and appreciative of your willingness to participate in the interview process with me. The stories you generously shared were ultimately so much richer and more complex than I have been able to include here. Thank you for entrusting me to weave what I can of your words and lives into this book in service to the topic of vocation and calling.

The research which led to this book was supported by a La Trobe University Postgraduate Research Scholarship and an Australian Postgraduate Award. Travel to conduct the interviews was funded by a La Trobe University Internal Research Grant. Thank you, Australia, for still making higher education accessible and affordable.

There are many intellectual forebears and teachers whose work I draw upon in the course of this book, especially those in the depth psychological tradition. One scholar and teacher who has been particularly instrumental in extending my understanding and appreciation of the ideas of CG Jung and James Hillman has been Glen Slater. I am indebted to Glen too for his role in shepherding me through the PhD process, and for his ongoing friendship, collegial support and teaching at the Life Artistry Centre on his visits to Australia.

My gratitude to Safron Rossi and to Keiron Le Grice for their practical and timely support to bring this work to publication.

I would also like to acknowledge James Hollis, John Izod, Terrie Waddell, Alexandra Fidyk and the editor and reviewers of the *International Journal for Educational and Vocational Guidance* for their constructive and critical comments on previous versions of this material, which shaped it in certain directions. Several paragraphs in Chapters 5 and 6 are extracted from my article "Vocation as psyche's call: a depth psychological perspective on the emergence of calling through symptoms at midlife", published in the *International Journal for Educational and Vocational Guidance* (Cremen 2019).

On a continent with a general paucity of forums to discuss Jungian and archetypal psychology, I have enjoyed the collegiality and friendship of the good folk on the committees of the CG Jung Societies of Queensland and Melbourne – particularly Marie Makinson and Diane Rockloff, who kept in touch with hospitality and an understanding ear at key stages during my writing of this work.

Thank you to my students at Pacifica Graduate Institute and the Life Artistry Centre. Through our engagement in every course, I engage with these ideas afresh. By bringing your own perspectives, questions, challenges, intelligence and insights to bear on the topic, you are instrumental in the evolution of this work.

To my friend Deb McNab, I am immensely grateful for your skilful professionalism and generosity to create the diagrams in this book, and for your good humour and patience as I endlessly tweaked them.

A special thank you to my mother Eleanor and to my 'sister' Liane Norman for their unwavering love and encouragement during both the peaks and the vales of my personal journey.

Lastly, it would be remiss of me not to remember my dear canine companions, past and present – Jonge, Trixie, Hero and Africa. Each faithfully kept their place beside my chair throughout the many years in which I studied and wrote. Our afternoon walks together have been my simplest pleasure, clearing the mind and restoring the soul; I have shared the happiest parts of each day with you.

Preface

> *So this is the call, then, to be oneself, as a service to the whole of nature and to succeeding generations who depend on us to become ourselves.*
> – James Hollis, *Tracking the Gods* (1995, p. 143)

The mythologist Joseph Campbell famously recommended to people that they follow their bliss. Which is a great idea – if you can find it. At other times, we know our path because it's that thing that simply won't let us be until we do it.

For me, that thing has been to write this book. When I began writing this book fifteen years ago, it arose from decades of wrestling with my own vocational frustration. What was the deeper psycho-spiritual basis of my life? What was my purpose, my calling? Could I fulfil this purpose within employment in organisational life? What did my personal struggles with these questions indicate, if anything, about the collective issues of our time?

By my early thirties, I had earned three university degrees and worked my way through over twenty different occupations. Not just different jobs, but entirely different *occupations*. That somewhat embarrassingly long list included lawyer, college teacher, screenwriter, professional services marketer, editor, lexicographer, conference producer, new product developer, business development manager, publisher, and producer of Australia's first National Children's Summit at Parliament House. In each role, I applied myself to the best of my abilities and was duly commended for my work. Yet after a couple of years at the most in each position, something inside me simply could no longer suffer working where it did not feel that I was truly meant to be.

At the age of thirty-three, I met my husband, a visionary man who was ready to brave the quest with me for a more fulfilling life than either of us had been able to find or make in the corporate world. I resigned from my role as publisher with a multinational publishing house in the harbourside city of Sydney, which had always been my home. We jumped in the car and drove north. Guided by synchronicities and intuitive responses to people and places, we made a tree change to a bohemian rural community on the Sunshine Coast hinterland of Queensland.

After years of suburban and organisational life, living in closer relationship with nature for twelve years was a healing balm for the psyche. Our five-acre property, which we named Pilgrims' Retreat, cost less than a small apartment in Sydney, so the mortgage stress was reduced. For the first time in my life, I was growing my own food and drinking and washing only with the rainwater we caught and conserved. Our empathic connections with the seasons, the trees, the land and the matrix of plant, insect and animal worlds deepened. At dusk one full moon, the moment when the women's circle I convened was due to start, a mother koala with baby clinging to her back unexpectedly arrived to scratch at the door of my studio. There were enchanted moments like this when it seemed as if we were living in a more fluid relationship of balance and dialogue with the more-than-human world. Later we discovered that this region was sacred for thousands of years to the Gubbi Gubbi people. It was the place of the triennial Bunya Gatherings, to which the tribes from South-East Queensland would come to conduct ceremonies and business and feast on the nuts of the sacred bunya trees. I do not wish to give the misleading impression that life and work became easy or devoid of worries and challenges here. It did not. Nevertheless, this was a nurturing and magical place to reconnect with qualities and potential inherent to our original, indigenous selves, beyond family or societal conditioning.

There were few employers in the region from whom we could earn an income, so to survive, it was necessary to create our own work. We took risks and worked hard to grow a small home-based scholarly and professional publishing company, eventually exporting books and journals in print and online to over thirty countries. Publishing is a tough industry with slim margins, but our independent business was modestly profitable, enough to support ourselves and the families of the people who worked with us. Best of all, instead of being corporate serfs, we had reclaimed some sovereignty over our working lives. We felt blessed indeed to be able to work with authors from around the world on meaningful projects, while our dogs napped beside our desks and our two Dexter steers grazed peacefully on the verdant hillside, just as pretty as an advertisement for butter. For a time, we found ourselves cast as the 'downshifting' poster couple in the national media, embodying the dream of leaving the rat-race to get a life. I was, as Joseph Campbell famously encouraged his students, following my bliss. Although, as Campbell also warned, when you follow your bliss, there is always the possibility of a fiasco.

Due to the knack I demonstrated with career and life transitioning, people began asking if I could help them, too. I requalified as a Myers-Briggs accredited career counsellor for adults in midlife and opened a small private practice called Life Artistry, offering workshops teaching people how to find and transition to the work they loved. Along the way, I interviewed and collected stories from inspirational people who had left mainstream career paths to do courageous, creative and socially or environmentally beneficial things. I started writing a book, entitled

Career as a Journey of Spirit, and was working assiduously to fulfil what seemed almost like some divinely inspired plan.

That all unravelled in Spring 2007, when life, the gods, fate, the psyche – whatever you choose to call it – dealt me a devastating series of blows in a short period of time. A beloved close relative in my family became ill and died. A dear friend and colleague who was a spiritual leader in the Interfaith community suddenly committed suicide. I made the devastating discovery of my husband's affair with a woman we employed, the shock of which was further amplified by a deep betrayal by two longstanding, trusted friends. These concertinaed traumatic events meant that my world came crashing down (along with the global financial crisis which took a good portion of my savings with it). The disorientation, grief, anguish and betrayal I felt from these events cracked me apart. It was as if the first, and then the second, airplane had crashed into the Twin Towers of my psyche. Suddenly, all that I knew to be real had collapsed.

For the next ten years, the home page for my website simply said, "This site is under reconstruction". What that really meant was that *I* was under reconstruction.

I relate this background story because it leads to one of the central themes of this book: that when life as we know it falls apart, the experiences of shock and disorientation we suffer can be the very rite of passage which initiates us more deeply into a gnosis of the soul and into a sense of authentic vocation.

Over time, as recounted in the following chapters, the rupture in my psyche, and in the fabric of my life, was the catalyst for a more far-reaching path. Led by a combination of dreams, synchronicities and initiatory experiences that pulled me further down into life than I would have otherwise wanted to go, I eventually found my way to a graduate school in the United States which offered degree programs in the traditions of depth psychology.

What is **depth psychology**?[1] It is a discipline that acknowledges the continuous interaction of conscious and unconscious influences on human behaviour. Depth psychology values what the Swiss psychologist Carl Jung called the **collective unconscious** or the objective psyche – a realm which is beyond conscious knowledge and personal will – as a source of wisdom and guidance. This is a very different approach from that taken in mainstream, cognitive behavioural psychology. When I discovered depth psychology, I realised that this sensibility of the psyche was what I had been searching for all along but had found missing in mainstream university psychology programs. Depth psychology fascinated and appealed to me because of its psycho-spiritual, phenomenological, yet intellectually robust approach towards understanding the patterns of human experience. I realised that I had already been inadvertently introduced to this field through some of my favourite books, particularly those by the archetypal psychologist Thomas Moore. To deepen our understanding of the psyche's processes, depth psychology draws on insights from the humanities, mythology, the arts, indigenous traditions and the natural world. It offers an appreciation of imagination, intuition and feeling as ways of knowing – and moreover, a reverence for mystery and for ineffable qualities too often exiled from academia, such as soulfulness. Originating in Europe and further developed in North America, depth psychology remains little known or understood in my home country of Australia. But once I discovered this existed as a formal discipline of inquiry, I saw it offered a significant perspective previously missing in my education. I knew I had to follow it.

Commuting across the Pacific Ocean to California for years, I undertook a Master's degree in Engaged Humanities and Mythological Studies, grounded in the traditions and scholarship of depth psychology. The subject matter was so illuminating, stimulating and therapeutic that, when the program finished, I immediately enrolled in a second Master's degree in Depth Psychology, specialising in Jungian and Archetypal Studies.

Throughout these programs, a constant theme to which I returned in various research papers was that of vocation. How do we hear our vocation, our calling? How do we follow it? And always, in the background, after the myriad occupational pathways I had tried to squeeze myself into: *what was my true vocation*? Until one day, a professor said to me, "You know, Suzanne, I think perhaps your vocation might be thinking and writing and talking about vocation". This observation helped me to recognise that an uncommon but authentic calling did indeed reside in my ongoing preoccupation with these questions. Later, I was awarded a scholarship to complete my PhD in Australia, on "A depth psychological approach to vocation and career".

Career as a journey of spirit – or of soul

So you have here a vastly more ruminated book than the one I originally endeavoured to write. There has been plenty of time to chew the cud. For a start, the title has changed, away from *Career as a Journey of Spirit*. Initially, the word 'spirit' seemed to encompass the desire I felt to write a book which explored and celebrated the importance of the intangible, non-material dimensions of working life. A refugee from the corporate world, I was preoccupied by the question of how our daily work might be in service to some deeper or higher meaning, beyond a paycheck or the bottom line. It seemed to me that this was essentially a spiritual question.

Spirituality is, of course, a notoriously difficult term to define. We know it has something to do with the search for meaning, purpose, integration and the possibility of personal transformation. Spirituality encompasses a sense of being connected to something 'beyond'; something transpersonal; something which *transcends* our mundane, everyday, material lives. People may variously feel this connection is to their higher Self, God, humanity, Nature, Gaia, the Universe – or to some other 'Ultimate Signifier'. While some people still experience spirituality in orthodox religion, many of us have questioned and departed from monotheistic religious traditions to seek or embody a spiritual connection through other pathways and practices – including through our work in the world.

What does it mean to think of one's career as a journey of spirit? The word 'spirit' derives from the Latin *spiritus*, which signifies both breath and wind. Professor of career counselling Mark Savickas has observed that when spirit blows through a person's life and work, it imbues the person with a sense of meaning that moves them in a certain direction and breathes life into situations.[2] A spirited person is full of courage, energy and enthusiasm. These are qualities which should certainly be desirable in any workplace, because spirit contains the sparks of creativity, insight and motivation. Yet organisational and corporate life can readily snuff the spirit out of people.

I recall, for example, attending a leadership retreat for a 100-year-old publishing company where I worked, which had undergone major restructuring following an acquisition. The retreat was viewed as an opportunity to build camaraderie, rekindle enthusiasm for our work and set a vision and strategy to help the organisation flourish in the 21st century. At one stage, the newly appointed Vice-President asked us each to reflect on our 'purpose'. She then drew an enormous $ sign on a whiteboard, before telling us in no uncertain terms that making money was our highest purpose. All else was subordinate to that god, and we had better be worshipping it! Of course, most companies are in business to make a profit, but it turned out I was not the only one who was disturbed by her pronouncement of my *raison d'être*. Depending upon our respective roles, we had envisioned our purpose within the company as being to design and deliver excellent knowledge resources for our clients; or to develop the talent in our employees; or to build collegial and productive relationships with our authors. If we did these things well – with diligence and integrity, innovatively, efficiently – then our company would make money. Tellingly, even those whose positions were more directly measured by financial benchmarks, such as the sales and marketing directors, realised that to be inspired in their work, they needed to believe that their working lives were in service to some larger meaning or purpose beyond just making money. The words that were intended to rally us, flattened us. Our spirits were snuffed.

It is now more widely recognised that the questions about meaning and purpose at work with which I have wrestled since leaving high school are part of a much, much larger web. As Rabbi Michael Lerner put it in 2017:

> On the spiritual level, tens of millions of people are suffering because they desperately want meaningful and purposeful lives and instead are trapped in jobs that do not produce anything of lasting value, and feel that they are wasting their lives yet believe that there is no alternative and no way out. What's worse is that many find their work is not really respected (in fact they have a hard time respecting it themselves because they can't see how it connects to anything with a higher purpose than a paycheck for themselves and massive profits for the super rich).[3]

To add to this, what's now much, *much worse* is that the work which many people do for a paycheck is complicit in hurtling our earth's delicate biosphere towards devastation. Jobs in the fossil fuel industry rather than sustainable energy, for example. Or these jobs are what the anthropologist David Graeber has brazenly called 'bullshit jobs', part of a neo-liberal capitalist system which is keeping people under control. Or what I call 'vampire jobs' – jobs which suck the life and soul from us, and now, from the Earth itself.

So the book *Career as a Journey of Spirit* began as an antidote to the widespread and virulent notion of 'career as a journey of power and money'. However, in the years that I have continued to research and explore this topic, my understanding has been refined, and the emphasis has shifted. Today, I lean towards the word *vocation* rather than *career*, and *soul* (psyche) rather than *spirit*. Influenced particularly by the writings of the archetypal psychologist James Hillman, I have come to appreciate that there is a significant distinction between the notions of spirit and soul. In common parlance, these words are often used synonymously, as both suggest a mystical dimension or sensibility beyond the hard-edged collective 'reality' of daily life. However, as Hillman described in his essay "Peaks and Vales", though spirituality and soul-making are related, they are in fact very different psychic topographies.

Spirit, according to Hillman, resides in the 'peaks', the transcendent experiences. Spirit is always up; spiritual places are always high, spiritual experiences always looking for the light, because there in the more rarefied air one finds clarity, discernment, principles. Spirit is that which beckons us to grow and to transcend our day-to-day lives. From this perspective, my move to leave the perceived security of corporate life and to make a tree-change was initially a spiritual quest. Conversely, *soul* dwells in the 'vales' of life and is encountered through our humbling experiences of love and yearning, loss and grief. Soul resides in the swampland places, the hollows and depressions of the psychic landscape; in our honest wrestling with our lived experience, our troubling symptoms, our complexes, our limitations and our fate. Soul-making happens in the places where things fall apart. As depth psychologist Glen Slater has explained, something that is soulful can be a lot more amorphous than something that is spiritual, and therefore not amenable to the realm of purely rational philosophical thought. That is why, as we shall see throughout this book, navigating one's career as *a journey of soul* calls for imagination and a symbolic way of thinking.

For many people today, who are seeking a connection to something of more enduring meaning and sustenance beyond the empty materialism and fragmentation of contemporary life, a spiritual path is appealing. Witness the popularity and preponderance of various New Age spiritual movements. The spiritual peaks possess a rarefied allure and the promise of transcendent moments of bliss. However, if we are not very conscious, the pursuit of higher, transcendent states may also be a means of denial or escapism from the swampland, soul places of our lives. The embrace of spirituality may be an avoidance of an honest engagement with the wounded places in our psyches which have their origins in childhood, family or cultural traumas. Ultimately, we need to find the right relationship between these principles of spirit and soul. It is not an argument to banish spirit, because spirit contains the sparks of creativity, insight and motivation. However, often people become so enamoured of that upper world of spiritual experience that the lower realm of soul is neglected. To experience the transcendent moments and blissful highs of the peaks, sooner or later we must also do the conscious work of traversing the vales.

On this relationship between spirit and soul, the Romantic poet John Keats wrote a letter of remarkable insight in April 1819, at the age of 23, shortly before his death from tuberculosis:

> Call the world if you Please 'The vale of Soul-making'. Then you will find out the use of the world. . . .
>
> I say 'Soul making' Soul as distinguished from an Intelligence – There may be intelligences or sparks of the divinity in millions – but they are not Souls till they acquire identities, till each one is personally itself. Intelligences are atoms of perception – they know and they see and they are pure, in short they are God – how then are Souls to be made? How then are these sparks which are God to have identity given them – so as ever to possess a bliss peculiar to each one's individual existence? How but by the medium of a world like this? . . .
>
> Do you not see how necessary a World of Pains and Troubles is to school an Intelligence and make it a soul?[4]

Keats understood that while spirit can be imagined as an intelligence or spark of the divine, to 'school' this intelligence and to give it the identity of an embodied soul, a journey through the pains and troubles, the vales of this world, is required. Soul brings us down into the humus of the earth. This is an initiatory journey to which each one of us is beckoned at one or more critical junctures in our lives. Moreover, with the unprecedented world of pains and troubles we are now facing in the Anthropocene, we are now collectively living in soul-making times.

Darkening times are soul-making times

Evidently, we are now in a catastrophic epoch, as any number of indicators show if we are able to acknowledge them. As William Butler Yeats predicted 100 years ago, the centre cannot hold. Things are falling apart. With our growing awareness of climate change and the desecration of the Earth – the melting ice caps, burning forests, warming oceans, the horrific rate of human-caused mass extinction, the pollution and exploitation of natural resources – coupled with the billions spent on military and warfare, the global plight of refugees, exponentially escalating wealth inequity, the spread of disease and depression, the use of information warfare and the global demise of democracy as oligarchs ascend to power . . . on these counts and more, the prognosis for our precious Earth is grave indeed. In the Western world, the horror and realisations around this have been magnified under pluto-cratic administrations and the rise of kakistocracies. Each year the collapse seems to be accelerating, propelled by the ignorance, self-centredness, vanity and hubris of human beings. For many, the darkening times are not only outer, but inner, too, as depression, angst, guilt, grief and despair come to visit.

What do we do in such times? How can we personally make any difference? To what work do we best apply ourselves? In the course of my career, I've worked in projects and movements which had the intention of shifting collective consciousness, mediating differences and effecting systemic change. These included the inaugural National Interfaith Festival in 2007, endeavouring to bring peace to religious schisms, and the inaugural National Children's Summit in 1998, aimed at giving young people a voice in the political and corporate decisions which affect their futures. Yet despite the varying success of these projects, I remain ambivalent about the value of heroic 'grand narrative' endeavours to effect change. In my experience, any real shifts that occurred through these projects were unplanned and less visible. They took place in a smaller way, in the hearts and minds of those individuals who were in some way deeply touched and transformed by virtue of their involvement.

Each of us has our own unique soul's calling to follow, our own contribution to make if we are to weave the broken pieces of our world together into a sustainable new pattern. These callings will manifest in a myriad of ways. For one person, this may be through scientific advancement, for another, through leadership with integrity in business; for others, it may be through carrying the torch of justice, or caring for family, or protecting the natural world, or teaching dance, or playing music, or inspiring healing laughter. All of these things, and many more, matter deeply. Collectively, any one of them might be the straw that tips the scales in favour of a sustainable and enlightened future for our planet. But whatever the outer work to which we are called, the real revolution that needs to happen – and to keep on happening, if we are to find our way through these darkening times – is the revolution within the psyche of humankind. As CG Jung observed towards the end of his life, "The world hangs on a thin thread, and that is the psyche of man".

Living in these times is a final clarion call to the soul-spark within each of us, to wake up and show up, and do what we are each called to do in our precious time on this Earth. As Michael Meade wrote in *The Genius Myth*, "Rather than the need to heroically save the whole world, the real work of humanity at this time may be to awaken the unique spark and inner resiliency of genius within each person"[5] – *genius* meaning both the source of purpose and the seed of destiny within each one of us. As I endeavour to show in this book, navigating our way through darkening times requires the cultivation of a softer, 'lunar' style of consciousness, which is quite different from the sharp 'solar' clarity with which we often engage the workaday world.

Towards this purpose, in my own work, I have been drawn to explore how a depth psychological perspective can illuminate our understanding of the particular and personal vocational calling we are each tasked to answer with our lives. Depth psychology reveals how a 'psychological revolution' entails a process akin to an initiation, or a descent into the *nekyia* or underworld. This may be precipitated through collective events. But it is also something that we must each suffer in the course of our own personal lives, if human consciousness is to come into a relationship of service with a larger sphere and the ecology of the whole. By undergoing this essential psychological work, we collectively creep towards the capacity for an authentic, multivalent consciousness.

In particular, a depth psychological perspective invites a radically different experience of 'vocational education' – a phrase which has become synonymous with skills training, often at a technical college level, for induction into pre-existing occupational categories, organisational positions or purposes. Instead, it invites a return to the true meaning of the word 'vocation', from the Latin *vocātio*, meaning calling, or to be addressed by a voice, and of 'educate', from the Latin *ēdūcere*, which means to lead or bring forth what lies within.

In 2016, with the collaboration and support of significant others, I relaunched the Life Artistry website, which had been 'under reconstruction' for nearly ten years. Since its commencement, the educational programs hosted by the Life Artistry Centre for Archetype, Imagination and Vocation have attracted psychologists, career counsellors, artists, writers, psychiatrists, social workers, molecular biologists, dance teachers, university professors, Jungian analysts, transpersonal counsellors, secondary school teachers, nurses, medical doctors, organisational change managers, learning development consultants, geologists, lawyers, yoga and meditation practitioners, pastoral care workers, sustainability educators, architects, town planners, speech therapists, business coaches, art therapists, musicians and more – aged 24 to 86. Many of these professionals have come from fields in which they have excelled, yet recognise that in their own personal and vocational development, they have reached the limits of their current paradigm.

Cultivating soul in our work and our world

This book originates from my personal lived experiences and struggles with navigating vocation. It has been further honed through teaching the depth psychology of vocation to many enquiring, talented and diverse postgraduate students from around the world. Writing any book is hard graft, but it has seemed to me that what has made writing this book particularly hard has been the necessity to build an ontological bridge across worldviews – from the literal, logical and ego-directed towards the symbolic, metaphoric and psyche-receptive. Many references and a lengthy bibliography have been included to persuade the discerning or sceptical reader that this latter worldview is indeed a legitimate one and that the perspective presented here is one that can be substantiated. In terms of Jungian psychology, the ideas and principles presented here are well established. The work stands on the shoulders of many reputable and insightful scholars and practitioners. What is new, however, is the way these ideas are brought together in conversation with the field of career development and vocational guidance.

This book has been written with the educated layperson and professional in mind. My hope is that it will be accessible and helpful to curious readers and seekers with no formal background in either vocational guidance or Jungian psychology. But I also hope it offers sufficient scholarly substance and fresh insights to be of interest to people experienced in those fields, stimulating new ideas, directions and further interdisciplinary work. Academics may find the style and tone rather personal or subjective in places. Non-academics may find the notes and bibliography rather scholarly. Hopefully that means the balance is about right.

It is my further hope this book will speak to people from various countries and nationalities, and to anyone wrestling with Western ideas of work and careers.

However, it also feels important to disclose upfront that my cultural background has significantly shaped both my own vocation and my approach to this book. In many ways, my calling to this work has been borne out of the difficulties I have experienced as a woman from working/middle-class Anglo-Saxon origins growing up and living in white Australian culture, which, for all its ostensible wealth (mostly derived from the exploitation of natural resources), suffers from a deafening silence about matters of soul and spirit. Though my parents were caring and well-meaning, I was raised in a cultural and educational environment that left me psychologically and spiritually malnourished, and often treated in a dismissive or patronising manner due to my gender and typological disposition, as an intuitive, feeling type.

Conversations with others reveal that I am not alone in this experience. As David Tacey has observed, Australian schools and universities are rationalistic, drawing on the British tradition of philosophers like Locke, Hume, Hobbs and Russell, and usually subscribe to reductive materialism – or, at best, to forms of humanism that exclude the visionary dimension. In academic and professional circles, concepts like spirit and soul are too often regarded as superstitious and unreal, if not downright delusory. Therefore, the introductory yet practical approach taken here towards Jungian psychology, as well as the evidentiary use of supporting references, is a considered response to the exclusory ideological stance so common in my culture towards any perspective which countenances 'fuzzy' matters of soul. Australians pride themselves on being practical people, yet we have been educated out of a symbolic way of understanding. Jungian psychology is currently not taught as a course, let alone a degree, at any university in Australia. Ways of knowing through intuition and the feeling function, associated with women and the feminine, tend to be dismissed and disrespected.

When I wrote this material in the form of a doctoral thesis, I was instructed to remove anything personal to me: any reflection on my own experiences, anything that was not deemed strictly 'objective', any language which had the slightest whiff of metaphor or poetry, or could not be backed up by direct reference to what another scholar (usually male) had written or thought before me. This constricted approach to research assumed that any perspective I had gained from my lived experience was not a valid way of knowing and could not inform my doctoral research, and, furthermore, that I should not give voice to this dynamic inter-relationship between the psyche of the researcher and the research itself. At best, I believe this approach was profoundly misguided; at worst, it was demoralising and soul-destroying. Though my work was an endeavour to re-engage a sense of soul in our understanding and experience of career and vocation, my doctoral thesis had the soul driven out of it. Effectively, the ontological ground of my research was denied. Both I and the work suffered tremendously for that. A work that began as enthused and pioneering became dampened and belaboured.[6] The process of weaving my own voice, insights and experiences back into this book to illustrate why the ideas canvassed herein ring true for me, the author, has been a practice in recovering some of the soulfulness which was banished in the academic process. It is my hope that this book is now a more authentic and engaging read as a result.

As well as synthesising theoretical insights from an extensive range of literature, each chapter includes stories and experiences from men and women from North America, Europe, South Africa and Australia which illustrate how these ideas play out in people's lives. Theory is of little use unless it works in practice. These are real-life stories (pseudonyms are used) from people I have interviewed of varying ages, backgrounds and circumstances, living with inspiration and courage to navigate fulfilling careers that are making a difference. I am deeply grateful to the special people who have been so generous with sharing their stories with me, and who have given me permission to share their stories with you.

From Career to Calling begins by looking at the distinction between work which is perceived as a job, a career or a vocation (calling). In Chapter 2, I consider the benefits and limitations of conventional approaches to vocational guidance and career development. Chapters 3 and 5 shift to take a more symbolic, soulful perspective towards vocation, drawing on Jungian concepts and insights about the psyche, such as the role of dreams in guiding us vocationally. Chapter 4 offers a brief interlude on the relevance of psychological type to understand why some people will naturally comprehend and resonate with this symbolic, depth psychological perspective, while for others, it seems foreign indeed. Chapters 6 and 7 explore how we may find ourselves initiated into our soul's calling, particularly around midlife, through experiences which deeply reconfigure our sense of identity into relationship with a larger whole. Obstacles and setbacks are inevitable; Chapter 8 reconceptualises what we usually term 'career constraints' to reveal how we are paradoxically asked to love our fate so deeply that it transforms into our destiny.

In Chapters 9 and 10, we consider the Jungian concept of complexes, stemming from childhood, ancestral and/or cultural wounds, and how we might work more consciously and transformatively with our complexes as pathways to vocation. Chapter 10 focuses on money as a motivator and a complex which is commonly activated in connection with work. Yet money remains one of the most neglected issues psychologically. In this chapter, we consider money not just as a literal, pragmatic concern, but as an archetypal, psychic reality which can offer psychological growth as an inescapable part of our vocational journey. Lastly, the book concludes with some thoughts on how navigating our careers as a journey of soul and soul-making ultimately requires that we come to engage the world with a kind of 'double vision'. We can view our work not only from the perspective of consensual, material reality, but become mindful too of another ever-present mythic, imaginal or psychic reality which runs alongside this. It is in living on the edge between these worlds that the experience of a meaningful life and of one's work as a soul calling arises.

A glossary of Jungian terms is included at the end of the book. In general, I have used UK-Australian spelling and punctuation throughout this book, except where a quoted source uses American spelling and punctuation, in which case the latter is retained.

At the end of each chapter, there is an invitation to reflection and journaling, or suggestions for further research and reading, if you would like to work further with the ideas presented. People I teach frequently comment that their greatest insights and 'aha!' moments arise through completing these journaling exercises. I encourage you to complete these reflective activities, and to consider sharing your reflections in a small group, book club or class with like-minded others who are interested and engaged in this work too.

May your path be blessed as you heed psyche's calling.

Notes

1 Bolded terms in the text are included in the Glossary.
2 Savickas 1997b, p. 4.
3 Lerner 2017, para. 4.
4 Colvin 1925, pp. 255–256.
5 Meade 2016, loc. 774.
6 A note for the academic researcher: the application of an appropriate research methodology which countenances a more subjective and embodied – a more *soulful* – approach to the research, ought to have been sufficient to circumvent these problems. My doctoral thesis engaged hermeneutic phenomenology as a methodology, although other approaches such as heuristics, alchemical hermeneutics or organic inquiry may have been brought to bear on the research topic. However, the thesis supervisor did not appear to appreciate the significance of methodology for contesting the hegemony of the orthodox disembodied academic voice with its façade of 'objectivity' and was adamant in directing how doctoral research must be approached and represented. Neither did the supervisor appear to appreciate the difference between method (interviews) and methodology (hermeneutic phenomenology). Consequently, I felt profoundly disempowered and alienated in that environment to defend the integrity of my work.
Of course, logic and rational analysis are hallmarks of scholarly argument; however, this does not need to be exclusive of a reflective, feeling, intuitive approach too, particularly where the research is not quantitative. See Yakushko and Nelson (2013). Moreover, the exile of soul and of a soulful sensibility in academic work is, in my opinion, a significant if unacknowledged reason behind why many PhD students in Australia experience alarmingly high rates of depression and even suicidal thoughts. As such, the educational system fails to fulfil its mandate to 'educe', in the true sense of the word, meaning to lead or bring forth what lies within the individual.

Author Note

As this book goes to press, my homeland of Australia burns in the middle of an apocalyptic summer.

Alongside the loss of human lives and homes, over 1.25 billion native animals to date have been incinerated. Surviving creatures suffer from burns and starvation, hundreds of billions of insects have been obliterated, and over 12 million acres of habitat have gone up in smoke (larger than the fires in California and the Amazon combined). The magnitude of this wildlife holocaust is unfathomable. A wondrous and beautiful ecosystem which has evolved since Gondwanaland, and with which our origins and our fates are intricately entwined, turns to ash. Evolutionary biologists foresee more than 700 vulnerable species, including the Greater Glider, the Long-Footed Potaroo, the Sooty Owl, and the Giant Burrowing Frog, may be driven to extinction.

Grief is a proper response. It is the sign of a healthy psyche, activated as part of the Earth's immune system. We are being called to bow to the Earth, and to remember her. With the swelling ocean of grief, grows a nucleus of fiery rage. Properly hosted in the psyche, it transforms us and channels itself into creative responses and strong activism on many fronts, to challenge oppressive systems, obsolete narratives, and the lies and obstructions of those who deny this ecological crisis and its anthropogenic causes. It also calls us to look deep within, and to ask: in what ways, through what small betrayals, am I complicit in this? What is the real work that I am in service to?

Australia's climate-change-driven fires make the ideas and perspectives in this book even more critical and timely. CG Jung, whose psychology I draw upon, knew that the earth has a soul, and that the psyche *is* Nature itself. One of the central themes of this book is how an authentic vocational calling may be awakened through initiatory experiences, of darkness, disruption and trouble. Our collective prognosis is, at present, bleak. Yet my hope for these fires is that they may serve as a collection initiation for Australia – indeed, for the world. One that will awaken us from the stupor of 'business as usual', the economy as god, and into our deeper work. One that may reunite humankind's hard-won consciousness with the very ground of our being: our Mother, the Earth.

Amidst the juggernaut of destruction, images of beautiful, heartfelt, courageous, soul-making work appear. The exhausted, ash-covered volunteer firefighter tenderly cradling a rescued echidna in his hands; the women who claim the ancestral mantle of 'mad witches' to campaign against media misrepresentation of climate change; the lawyer working hard alongside her indigenous colleague to draft a new Earth-jurisprudence. The particular callings to which we find ourselves beckoned arise as a *cri de coeur* from the *anima mundi*, the soul of the world itself. Let us not forget that civilizations' most poignant and stirring art, literature and music have always germinated and borne fruit from such places and times of darkness. Now is the time we most need our writers, our artists, our poets, our musicians and our storytellers to attend, to bear witness, to help us grieve, and to imagine from the ashes a new, sustainable vision for our world.

We live in soul-making times.

20 January 2020

1   Job, career or calling?

The difference between work that is experienced as a job, a career or a calling is an ostensibly simple place to begin this book but a pivotal distinction to make. There is an old parable known as "The Three Stonecutters", made famous in 1954 by Peter Drucker in *The Practice of Management*, which neatly illustrates this difference. The story goes that a traveller comes across some workers who are breaking up rocks. When asked what they are doing, the first one answers miserably, "I have to move these huge stones around to make some money. But it is barely enough to eat". The second worker is engaged industriously and explains, "I'm earning a living by doing the best job of stonecutting in the country". Sweating but happy, the third worker replies, with a visionary light in his eyes: "Why, can't you see? I am building a cathedral!"

The responses of the first and second workers suggest they approach their work as a *job*, focused on specific tasks – "I am breaking up rocks" – or possibly even a *career*, focused on longer term financial rewards – "I am making a living". Yet psychological studies have shown that one of the deepest forms of satisfaction and psychological success occurs when a person experiences work as more than a job or career – when it is a *calling*.[1] There is a larger vision encompassing the discrete tasks, which extends beyond making money. As the third worker enthusiastically explains, "I am building a cathedral".

In everyday life, the words *work, job, career* and *vocation* are frequently used synonymously. Yet an essential step in taking stock of our situation and gaining clarity about work which holds genuine meaning for us is to differentiate between these concepts and to consider the relevance of each in our own life.

In this first chapter, we'll explore the difference between these terms from historical, etymological and phenomenological perspectives. Throughout the chapter, I interweave real-life stories, anecdotes and perspectives from people with whom I have worked, interviewed or taught. I'll also touch on some of the difficulties people experience in the struggle to integrate a calling into the matrix of contemporary life.

Perspectives on work, career and vocation

Throughout Western history, people have held very different perspectives regarding the meaning of *work*. The ancient Greeks considered work to be a necessary evil, with no intrinsic value for the individual. Work caused degeneration of the body and soul, robbing people of the leisure necessary for physical, intellectual and psychological health. Plato spoke of workers "whose souls are bowed and mutilated by their vulgar occupations even as their bodies are mutilated by their mechanical arts".[2] In the Renaissance, philosophers reversed this idea. Work became an opportunity for humanity to exert control over nature and establish itself as sovereign over a world of its own making, thereby likening man to the divine.[3] In the 19th century, Karl Marx argued for work as an act of self-realisation, although, under the aegis of capitalism, work had become so disagreeable that it was "avoided like the plague".[4] By the late 20th century, American positivist psychology was promoting work within the capitalist system as a viable pathway towards self-actualisation and fulfilment.

Over the centuries, the pendulum has swung back and forth between views of work as a form of self-denial or a form of self-fulfilment. In 1927, in *The Future of an Illusion*, and in 1930, in *Civilization and its Discontents*, Sigmund Freud was the first to bring a psychoanalytic lens to investigate the nature of work. Freud observed that the compulsion to work is created by external hardship. Now, many people would hardly argue with that today. We have bills to pay and mouths to feed, and work provides us with money to do that. But the motivation to work, thought Freud, is counter-instinctive. It requires the suppression of libidinal impulses in favour of civilization and communal needs. "Every civilization rests on an obligation to work and a renunciation of instinct", said Freud, "and therefore inevitably provokes opposition from those affected by those demands".[5] In other words, according to Freud, we only work because we have to work. Really, we'd rather not work at all.

On the other hand, perhaps this depends on the nature of our work. Freud's analysis speaks to the coercive nature of individuals' relationships with work in industrial and capitalist societies, but he tends to overlook the sense of meaning and satisfaction which many people derive from work. Freud did concede that a person may be able to heighten his yield of pleasure and happiness in life by sublimating his libidinal instincts into finer or higher creative or intellectual work, and he gave the example of an artist or a scientist. Even ordinary professional work, Freud conceded, may provide happiness, although work as a path to happiness has not been highly prized by men (at least, Freud's implication goes, not as much as sexual activity has been prized as a path to happiness).

Amongst four dozen definitions of the noun 'work', the *Oxford English Dictionary* includes: "Action or activity involving physical or mental effort and undertaken in order to achieve a result, especially as a means of making one's living or earning money; labour; (one's) regular occupation or employment". This is the definition of work towards which most vocational guidance and employment initiatives are directed, focused on supporting people to secure employment from which they can derive an income. Work in this context entails 'getting a job'. The focus is on necessity and remuneration rather than pleasure or fulfilment.

A *job* refers to a piece of work, a place where a person is employed or a particular thing one does to earn money. Samuel Johnson, the author of an

18th century English dictionary, described 'job' as a low or vulgar word, of uncertain etymology. In previous eras, 'job' has referred variously to a task or transaction performed opportunistically for private interest or advantage; as criminal slang for an arranged robbery; and also to a cartload that a horse could pull. I've also heard it said that a job is an old Scottish derivation from 'jobbie' (to defecate) – it was an expression for shovelling a pile of manure from one place to another. I've been unable to verify this, but I like it anyway. For is it not an apt metaphor for what many people do feel about the jobs they do each day?

Occasionally, the term 'work' is used in the loftier sense of *opus*, referring to an individual's life work or major work. Our 'inner work' of personal self-development is also experienced and described as work. But in general, when people think about what the word 'work' means to them, it's usually associated with exertion and an effort of will at a mundane level, propelled by material or economic necessity, as Steve describes here:

> *It's what you do to earn money, without necessarily having any sense of progression, growth or development in a career or vocational sense. It's a cliché that if you are doing what you love, you don't experience this as work.*

> (Steve)

In contrast, the word 'career' refers to where we have begun to think about our skills and aptitudes and translated them into a recognised occupation (such as a marketer, engineer or financier). We have started to manage and direct our professional life in a longitudinal sense, beyond a particular job. With career, there is a focus on advancement, economic return and progression over time.[6]

> *Career for me refers to the progression of a role or skill set that has more of a material orientation, or at least has a dollar value in the market place. I see career primarily as having an economic connotation.*

> (Steve)

Interestingly, the etymology of 'career' refers to "a running, course, or course through life". It is related to the French word *carrière*, which means racecourse, and the Latin *carrus*, meaning cart, and it implies a certain organised, competitive focus. The word career is also associated with the swift movement of a horse,[7] the flight of a bird in falconry and the course of the sun or a star through the heavens. These are all ancient symbolic associations which intimate the possibility of a more transcendent, purposeful flight of spirit in our careers.

Although we may work hard in various jobs throughout our lives, this does not necessarily correlate with the sense of having a career. At age 38, Steve, for example, did not consider himself to have a career:

> *in the sense that I have built momentum and achieved steady progress within an institution or within the market place. This hasn't happened to date. I don't*

think I have a career. I have more of a 'rap sheet' with a long list of positions I've filled to get money.

(Steve)

Annabella was a woman in her sixties who never self-identified as someone with a career, although as a single mother she had worked hard in various jobs – including claims examiner and medical assistant – and she expressed a strong sense of vocation:

Career means having a plan – an aspiration, a goal and a plan to get there. It's a socially acceptable narrative about how a professional work-life should be defined.

(Annabella)

After years of work in the financial services industry, Jim had developed a strong disdain for the notion of career, which he associated with being corralled on a defined course:

A career is a series of moves within a discipline, providing a certain level of satisfaction. A career usually begins as someone else's idea of what you should do to make money.

(Jim)

Jim resisted applying the word 'career' to what he later discovered to be his passion, his vocation, as a filmmaker. So committed was Jim to following this calling that he said he would leave the work if it became a career, pursued only for financial ends.

Jim's resistance to the notion of 'career' is not unusual, particularly amongst millennials. Career is a concept which tends to belong more to a 20th century modernist paradigm of ascent and progression, and many young people are understandably disillusioned with that paradigm. A 2015 report by the Foundation for Young Australians indicated that the average Australian is likely to have up to five career changes and 17 jobs in their lifetime – and, more alarmingly, that up to 60% of jobs for which university students are currently studying are likely to be automated in the future.

To be honest, 'career' for me has always felt like a bit of a dirty word. I think due to the fact that I've never felt very clear about exactly what I'd like to do long-term in life and work, listening to others speak of 'career-mindedness' and 'beginning a career' has always felt somewhat alienating and confining to me, and has always been a source of stress in that it only served to remind me that 'time is running out' (to decide what I want to do) and that I didn't have a 'plan'. As such, I think it's a concept that I've mostly just avoided, even throughout my studies at university. Until now.

(Leo)

When Leo learned about the concept of vocation, a term he had previously associated with the work of tradespeople and professional labourers, he recognised what he was really seeking was not a career, but a *vocation*, a life calling.

Today, the word vocation is commonly associated with skills training for a trade or blue-collar work. However, if we look to history, we discover there is a much deeper spiritual or soulful meaning to *vocation* which dwells in its etymology. Vocation comes from the Latin *vocātio*, meaning a calling, or to be addressed by a voice. Vocation is a fascinating concept and a rather loaded term, which continues to intrigue and puzzle scholars from a variety of disciplines who have looked into it.[8] Over the centuries, the concept of vocation (and its cognate, calling) has undergone a number of significant transformations and even reversals of meaning.

Traditionally, vocation described a calling to a religious occupation. To receive a vocation implied that a person was divinely guided or called towards a religious career, to exercise some special function of a spiritual nature or to perform some special work in life. In medieval times in the Western tradition, to have a vocation meant to receive a call away from the world of productive activity in order to dedicate one's life to prayer and contemplation, or to monastic service.

However, in the 16th century, Protestant reformers such as Martin Luther and John Calvin challenged the assumed superiority of the medieval monastic calling. They proposed that secular occupations – the work of a nurse, a miller or a stone mason, for example – could hold spiritual significance and be viewed as divinely ordained. So the idea of daily work as divine vocation became a central tenet of the Protestant work ethic.[9] However, by the 1930s this Protestant ideal of vocation was being severely critiqued by the German sociologist and political economist Max Weber as a malign force underlying the growing dominance of capitalist economic rationality. Weber observed that the concept of vocation or calling had become separated from its original spiritual context and instead linked with the demands of modern industrial society's occupational structure and economic growth.[10] We see this continuing legacy today, in the appropriation of the term 'vocational education' to describe training for a specific job or industry. Vocation's spiritual or soulful roots have almost been forgotten, a dim relic of times past, as today the term vocation has been conscripted for service in a post-industrial paradigm propelled by a neo-liberal economic agenda.

But there was another aspect of the historical notion of vocation that morphed in a different direction. During the Victorian era, as portrayed in the novels of Thomas Mann and George Eliot, for example, 'calling' moved further from religious or spiritual promptings towards a sense of *inner* conviction in service of society, based on one's passionate commitment to a particular work, of art, for example, or social improvement.[11] The idea of vocation as a form of self-expression, personal authenticity and fulfilment came to the fore – the idea that one could make something beautiful, creative, artful, useful, meaningful through one's work in the world. The idea that one could do work of which one might feel justifiably proud, and in the process, craft *oneself* through one's work.

To summarise, the concept of vocation has undergone a number of significant transformations and reversals over the course of centuries. As vocational researcher Jane Dawson observed, what began as a removal from the productive and economic sphere later became a spiritual ally of that sphere, and later still transformed into a moral critique of this sphere. Today, these different views of vocation still jostle alongside one another.[12] The quest for vocation has become a secular concern for many people, a part of self-actualisation. Although some people may still pursue a calling out of religious beliefs, psychological studies have found that having a set of religious beliefs is neither a necessary nor a sufficient condition for having a calling.[13]

However, while the quest for vocation is now a secular concern for many, Weber's wry comment that "the idea of duty in one's calling prowls about in our lives like the ghost of dead religious beliefs"[14] remains discomfortingly true even in a secular era. There is the sense of one's vocation as having a non-ordinary, transpersonal, spiritual or soulful dimension, of which one's ego or personal will is not entirely in control. For example, when I talked people for my doctoral research about what 'vocation' (as distinct from job or career) meant to them, their responses included the following:

Vocation has always meant to me 'heart work'. It's like the artist can't not do art. This is going to start sounding religious, but it's that whole idea of who we are and what we are here to do, whatever that is.

(Alyce)

For me, vocation is a larger understanding of what it is we are going towards. What is our calling? Only after we get to the second part of life . . . like now I am 47 years old and I start realising – hey, there has been this path, which I have been going on with no awareness. And how great it would have been if there had been some awareness! So I would distinguish vocation as this larger thing that we are basically unaware of, even though we are called by it, we are on it, but we don't know it.

(Jana)

To me, the ability to hear vocation is a manifestation of our relationship to things that are non-ordinary, to a realm of life that has been called spiritual, or soulful. It is something more than personal; it's a transpersonal dimension, which implies that our ego is not 100% in control.

(Claire)

Vocation relates to who I really am – my most intimate self. Vocation relates to the deeper mysteries of my life, to the question, 'What is my purpose here?' Vocation relates to my desire to heal my wounds and to explore the mysteries concealed within those wounds – to know this ghost within me, this presence, this soul, this love, this deeper self. For me, there is no real separation between vocation and the work of ensoulment. The whole process of individuation is hard graft.

(Steve)

Comments like these suggest that the experience of having a vocation is implicit in what Jung called **individuation** – the process of becoming the self you were meant to be. They also suggest that the sense of having a vocation or a calling is entwined with a growing comprehension of one's own place in the universal drama of humanity. However, even if one has this enlarged sense of vocation, the truth is that most people struggle to align their work, career and vocation. Vocation is not necessarily the thing that supports us financially. It can involve a long process of patience, application and perseverance to integrate one's calling into a life matrix.

The quest to accommodate a calling in a life matrix

Claire was an author and teacher who testified to the convergence of work and vocation in her life. Claire loved to work hard writing her books:

> *For me, when I am doing work that I love, it is a vocation. When I am doing work that demands more of me than I even think I have on offer at the moment, it's vocation.*

> (Claire)

Lynn, an eco-psychologist, also felt no demarcation between her experiences of work, career and vocation:

> *I took a number of jobs to get through school, but there was nothing that I didn't love. There is also something that separates out over a period of time, being 'stepping into a calling' – something that your whole life or body is dedicated to – you live and breathe for that. Teaching eco-psychology is a calling for me.*
>
> *When you realise that you have been called to do something, there is an alignment. It's good because your energies are aligned. If career and vocation are separate, you will get split. A calling catalyses and pulls together your energies so that you can channel them into particular areas. Which doesn't mean there isn't diversity.*

> (Lynn)

Claire and Lynn appear to be living the ideal of integrating work, career and vocation – an optimal state if one can accomplish it, through application and good fortune. Empirical studies have shown positive reciprocal relationships between the presence of a vocational calling and career planning, motivation and decisiveness.[15] Experiencing a calling can motivate us to navigate complex career terrain and address challenging career development tasks.

Many people who feel a sense of vocation, such as artists in one medium or another, desire to parlay their vocations into paying work or careers. But the truth is that most people struggle to craft a career which integrates their vocational purpose. One research study indicated that most people see their work as *either* a job (with a focus on financial rewards and necessity and not a major positive part of life), or a career (with a focus on advancement), or a calling (with a focus on fulfilling or socially useful work).[16] As Steve reflected:

I've spent most of my time thus far engaged in 'work' rather than 'career'. I've tried to uncover vocational insight and I've continued to develop my skills as a storyteller, but I am still aiming for a career that germinates from an ongoing exploration of soul and vocation. . . . It has been a bit of a struggle to bring what I would call my 'vocational intent' into the real world: to make career and vocation a unified, singular thing, to realise vocation in the material world, to see vocation as having some kind of material value.

(Steve)

Rose was another who struggled with a sense of dissonance between career and calling. Rose had a very well-paid career in IT. She distinguished this from what she called her vocation as a writer. Even as a child, Rose wrote constantly in her journal, and she realised that writing was all she wanted to do:

My career hasn't really had anything to do with a calling. My career had to do with making money. I work as a database administrator. I think of this as my work – I get dressed, I have to drive there, I'm expected to do certain things, I get paid for it. My vocation is a writer, but because it's difficult to make money as a writer, I don't usually call that my career. But then, with my work of teaching, I have this larger umbrella of an academic vocation, which for me is the teaching, writing and research.

(Rose)

Rose's experience not only shows how an individual may work at more than one occupation but also suggests that one's vocation may find its route through different channels or outlets. Most of us today will work not just in a number of different jobs but also in different occupations and careers during our lifetimes. Studies have recognised that calling is a dynamic phenomenon which changes over time.[17] What may appear on the surface to be a disconnected, peripatetic career path may well be an intuitive allegiance to the mysterious pulse of one's vocation. Vocation goes beyond making a career choice to encompass a lifelong process of courting meaningful work that connects us to a sense of purpose. This is our vocational 'red thread' – the theme unifying seemingly disparate jobs and activities. It can take some reflection to discern one's own particular red thread. Some people identify theirs as 'ways of knowing', 'making things work', 'bringing love and beauty into the world' or 'developing potential'.

Psychological studies have shown that frustration, depression and other negative effects may arise if calling is viewed as a singular pursuit that can only be expressed through a career or paid work.[18] Viewing career as the only site for enactment of a calling may lead us to overlook avenues outside paid work, such as parenting, voluntary work or leisure activities. A lifelong passion and curiosity for learning might find expression not only in the occupation of a scientist or a scholar but also in various hobbies or avocations, such as mastering the art of home-brewing, making stained glass or learning the piano in midlife.

As I mentioned at the beginning of this chapter, although ostensibly simple, making a distinction between the concepts of job, career and vocation can be very useful in practice. One woman told me excitedly of her realisation that, in her years of struggling unsuccessfully to give expression to a creative vocational impulse while she simultaneously managed a high-pressured, time-hungry and unfulfilling career (which was draining the life from her), what she now needed to do was not to apply for other 'career' positions but simply to look for a 'job'. To give her calling towards creative work a chance, she needed to allow it time and space. She recognised that she had become unwittingly trapped over the years by an all-consuming 'career', whereas at this stage what she really required was simply a job which would pay the bills and enable her to attend to the real work of her vocation. Being able to distinguish between the notions of job, career and vocation was an important part of her process of clarifying next steps.

Of course, it is possible to have a job or career *and* a separate creative vocation. The Pulitzer prize-winning poet Wallace Stevens springs to mind, who spent most of his life working as an insurance company executive. However, it can be near impossible to find the time to move into a creative inner space if one is working long hours in a demanding career. In my early twenties, I had a calling to write a film script, which was a creative re-working of a personal coming of age experience. To free up time for this over a few years, I re-negotiated other work arrangements and moved back to live with my parents for a while. This was not ideal, but I could not afford to rent an apartment while I was writing. The script met with some success and received good feedback and funding from film bodies, though ultimately the movie was never made. So while my career fantasies of becoming a filmmaker did not eventuate, nevertheless the calling to write had been heard and served, albeit with some sacrifice. Ultimately, however, heeding the calling seemed to support a larger process of the psyche integrating, healing wounds and becoming more whole – or what Jung called the process of individuation.

Steve shared a similar experience of how the creative filmmaking work of his doctorate was really a means of addressing this deeper call from the psyche:

> *I was trying to use the Australian bush and wilderness and the colonial experience as a setting, an environment, a storyworld where the psyche is broken open and archetypal figures and energies coalesce and mingle with waking reality. . . . I was interested in creating that kind of storyworld where you have an infusion, or intrusion of unconscious contents into a shared reality. . . . In reality, what I was doing with this story and the doctorate, I was using it as a tool of discovery, working through this stuff that is wrapped up in vocation. I was working through my own experience. Maybe ultimately it's not really about filmmaking or storytelling, it was just a device for me to create a fictional world in which I could tease out or wrestle with these things.*
>
> (Steve)

While our job, career and vocation may not always converge as we might wish, *the essential point is that our job or career must not sabotage or cannibalise our vocatio*n. When that happens, as Jung said, the inner voice becomes more and more muffled, more unconscious, so that "in the place of the inner voice there is the voice of the group with its conventions, and vocation is replaced by collective necessities".[19] Joseph Campbell offered some timeless advice for artists (in any field), which speaks directly to this situation:

> The normal situation is that, perhaps for years, you work away at your art, your life vocation, your life-fulfilling field of action, and there's no money in it. You have to live, though, so you get a job, which may be a low-degree activity relative to what you are interested in. You could, for instance, teach people the art you are operating in yourself. So let's say you have a teaching job, and you also have sacred space and time to perform your own work. . . .
>
> Then, you are doing so well in your job that your employer wants to move you into a higher position. You'll have to give more to the job than before, and you will receive a higher salary, but your new commitments will cut down your free time. My advice is: Don't accept the promotion. Don't accept anything that piles more on you than what you must do to earn your base income, because you are developing, not in your job, but in your artistic work. You can see on campuses all the time what happens with promotions: you move up, up, up, until you are in administration, and it uses up everything you've got. The artist must build a structure, not in the way of being of service to society, but in the way of discovering the dynamism of the interior.[20]

This is the Faustian bargain that each of us faces at some point in our career journey. Go too far down that path and sooner or later there is the realisation that we have lost our way, our soul's purpose and that which brings vitality to our life and the possibility of transformation to our world.

However, if we maintain a sense of our calling, a career may also offer a satisfactory medium or channel to fulfil it. A recognised occupation can be a good 'cover story' for a vocation, enabling us to serve our vocation and make a living under a socially credible guise. A woman I know who is a highly intuitive and creative artist (her vocation) and is employed in a casual position as a science teacher confessed that she sees her real role with the high school students as that of an 'undercover shaman'.[21] Approaching her paid job in this way makes it a more meaningful experience for her, and a more transformative one for her students. In Chapter 7, I discuss how the process of initiation into a vocation can indeed lead to work as an 'undercover shaman'.

Aged 72 and still working, Michael described his vocation as being "in service to the psyche". More than forty years ago, that is what drew Michael to a career in psychology. However, with the emerging movement in the United States to locate psychology as a STEM (science, technology, engineering and mathematics) discipline, Michael foresees that in the future his vocation may be better served by the occupation of a poet than the profession of a psychologist.

You may need to let go of a career to serve your vocation. Psychology has been a good cover story for me. But what has always been drawing me out is what the psyche wants – the deep currents in the water.

Again, there is this sense that vocation and career are not necessarily the same thing. A career or occupation may provide a suitable guise or vehicle for fulfilling a vocation, but ultimately it is the service to one's vocation which must be paramount. In successive chapters, we will venture into these deeper currents in the water which Michael described as drawing him onwards and begin an enquiry into the nature of the psyche and how it pulls us in particular directions.

Invitation to reflection and journaling

- What distinction do you make between the concepts of work, career and vocation? Reflect upon and write about your past and current situation in relation to these concepts.
- As we will see in later chapters, depth psychology has been described as a psychology of metaphor and image. Increasingly, vocational guidance practitioners are recognising the value of working with clients' metaphors and images to explore ways of moving forward.
- Is there a metaphor or visual image that describes your current work/career/ vocational situation? (For example, "I am in a fog, blindly feeling my way", or, "It feels like I'm a tree planted in the wrong place, where I'm struggling to grow"). Write about or draw your resonant metaphor.

Notes

1 Hall & Chandler 2005.
2 Volf 1991, p. 126.
3 Hardy 1990, pp. 28–29.
4 cited in Hardy 1990, 33.
5 Freud 1995, p. 10.
6 Wrzesniewski et al. 1997.
7 Jung also interpreted his own dream of a horse's career through the streets to be reflective of his career ambitions (Haule 1993).
8 See, for example, Berkelaar & Buzzanell 2015; Bogart 1992, 1994; Bunderson & Thompson 2009; Dawson 2005; Dik & Duffy 2009.
9 Dawson 2005, pp. 224–225.
10 Bogart 1992, 31.
11 Dawson 2005, p. 226.
12 Dawson 2005, p. 227.
13 Hall & Chandler 2005, p. 161.
14 Weber 1930, p. 124.
15 Hirschi & Herrmann 2013, p. 59.
16 Wrzesniewski et al. 1997, p. 21.

17 Dobrow 2013.
18 Berkelaar & Buzzanell 2015.
19 Jung 1934b, CW17, para. 302.
20 Campbell 1991, p. 267.
21 See also Mayes (2005).

2 A very brief history of approaches to vocational guidance and career development

When I was faced with choosing a career towards the end of high school in 1984, the 'guidance' offered was, quite frankly, abysmal. The social science teacher who was tasked with acting as the school careers advisor possessed a single dog-eared book listing occupations, related college or university courses and their entrance requirements. She would ask a student what she or he wanted to do. If the student had an idea of an occupation, the advisor would look it up in the book, match the requirements against the grades on the student's school report and advise whether this was a valid choice or whether the student was deluded about her capabilities and should set her sights lower. If a student had no idea what he might do, the careers advisor would review his existing subjects and grades and prescribe something from a small range of occupations further narrowed by her assumptions around gender and socio-economics, her own limited experience and lack of imagination. Many a young person's enthusiasm to achieve and his or her sense of possibility for the future was dampened if not quenched by this process.

It would have been helpful at that time to known about the classic 5-stage model of career development outlined in this chapter, and certainly to have paid attention to stages 1 and 2 of this process. Indeed, it was not until I had completed two university degrees and transitioned through two careers that I discovered this model and set about applying it in my own life. In my experience working as a career counsellor, most people have been influenced by parents', teachers' or peers' opinions about what they should do; taken a 'best subjects at school approach'; made their choice based on perceived job availability, pay level or job image; or simply drifted into work according to what was offered to them at the time. When people discover this approach, they find it to be a reassuringly systematic method which can yield very good results. However, as I discuss at the end of this chapter, it has significant limitations too.

The traditional approach to career choice and development

Vocational psychology as we know it today emerged with industrialization in the late 19th century, as a process of matching humans with machines and manufacturing processes. Dr Frank Parsons is regarded as the father of vocational psychology. Parsons was an engineer, law professor, social reformer and the director of the delightfully named Boston Vocation Bureau and Breadwinners Institute. He was primarily concerned with the ability of high-school graduates to choose an occupation.

In 1909, Dr Parsons published a three-step model of career decision-making, called *Choosing a Vocation*. The steps involved:

1   personal investigation, or self-knowledge;
2   the investigation of available occupations; and
3   a decision-making process to match the individual with an occupation.

Parsons was the first to apply a 'scientific method' to vocational counselling, emphasising clear thinking, logical reasoning and a careful, painstaking weighing of all the evidence. "These vital problems", advocated Parsons, "should be solved in a careful, scientific way, with due regard to each person's aptitudes, abilities, ambitions, resources and limitations, and the relations of these elements to the conditions of success in different industries".[1]

Since Parsons' time, the goals and paradigm of career counselling in practice have remained largely unchanged. Most theories and techniques of career choice and development remain rooted in a logical positivist worldview, where career decision-making is portrayed as a rational, cognitive process in which decisions are made on the basis of so-called objective data.[2]

Parsons' work gave rise to what became known as the 'trait and factor' theory of vocation. This holds that each person has a unique combination of traits, and each occupation contains a number of objective factors for its successful perfor-mance, and that it's possible to identify a fit or match between these traits and fac-tors using a straight-forward problem-solving approach. Somewhat like putting the round pegs in the round holes and the square pegs in the square holes. Vari-ations of the trait and factor model continued to dominate the field of vocational guidance throughout its history to the present day.

How does this work in practice? In Figure 2.1, I illustrate a classic 5-Stage Model of Career Choice and Development. The model provides structure and guidance which can be reassuring during a transitional time. Usually people go through this 5-stage process over a period of many months. The circular nature of the model suggests that this is an ongoing cycle that we can expect to revisit at different times in our lives.

Stage 1 – Exploring Inwards – asks: *Who am I?* This stage is about taking a personal inventory or career audit, looking at one's skills, interests, preferred environments, values and personality type. This is a foundational stage of the process. Many career counsellors will use psychometric instruments to help a cli-ent compile an inventory of personal characteristics and match them with known occupations.

Other career counsellors use online tools or card sorts to help clients and stu-dents gather and sort this information about themselves. Card sorts are tools for self-assessment. They involve no scores, and there are no right or wrong answers, but they can stimulate ideas which generate options. Sorting the cards with various

A Classic 5-Stage Model of Career Choice and Development

1. Exploring Inwards
Who am I?

2. Exploring Outwards
What are my options?

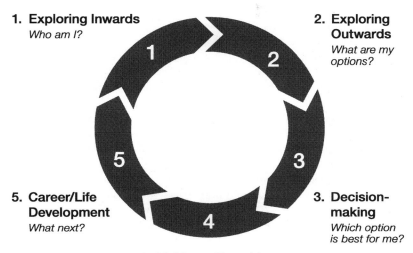

5. Career/Life Development
What next?

3. Decision-making
Which option is best for me?

4. Making a Transition
How do I get where I want to go?

Stage 1 – Exploring Inwards

- Review your career and life journey
- Assemble a comprehensive list of your skills, interests, values, preferred work environments, style
- Identify barriers and constraints to your desired future direction.

Stage 2 – Exploring Outwards

- Research your career options
- Informational interviews and networking
- Reality-test your ideas.

Stage 3 – Decision-making

- Evaluate your career options by matching your results in 1 and 2

- Decide on goals
- Prepare a career action plan or proposal.

Stage 4 – Making a Transition

- Prepare your resume
- Rehearse for interviews and negotiations
- If establishing a business or consultancy: define your product or service, identify your market, write a business and marketing plan, register your company, build your website and social media profile, etc.

Stage 5 – Career/Life Development

- Review and evaluate your situation as a process of life-long career development.

Figure 2.1 A classic 5-stage model of career choice and development.

attributes on them helps a person to build a comprehensive personal database of information which is useful when evaluating potential career directions.

Stage 2 – Exploring Outwards – asks: *What are my options?* Employment options are usually researched via career and occupational websites, speaking to industry associations and education providers, talking to people in one's networks, volunteering or gaining work experience or completing a careers test to generate occupational options.

There are various psychological instruments that match an individual with a range of possible occupations and work environments. One of these is the Myers-Briggs Type Indicator, based on Jung's theory of personality types. There is a wealth of data linking psychological types and careers, documenting the levels of satisfaction and success of different personality types in various occupations. For example, a person with a typological preference for introverted Sensation and extraverted Feeling (an ISFJ) will like careers where they can care for people in a practical way, such as nursing or hospitality; whereas someone with a preference for extraverted Thinking and introverted Intuition (an ENTP) will enjoy work that involves a lot of strategic planning, such as organisational development. I discuss the Myers-Briggs Type Indicator and Jung's theory of personality types further in Chapter 4.

Another well-known instrument is John Holland's theory of occupational codes, which is the basis for most career inventories used today. Holland posited that people can be loosely categorised according to six personality types – Realistic, Investigative, Artistic, Social, Enterprising and Conventional. Occupations and work environments can also be classified according to these same categories. Holland thought that most of us have a combination of all the six types, but that generally three predominate. Once you ascertain your three-letter Holland code (for example, if your preferences are Social-Investigative-Artistic, that would make you SIA), you can look up your code on O*Net, which is the Occupational Information Network published by the US Department of Labor, to help you find the occupations that best match your interests and abilities.[3] The theory suggests that people who choose careers that match their own types are most likely to be satisfied and successful.

The Exploring Outwards stage invites a person to explore alternative workplaces or occupations. Options that emerge might include returning to study, starting a business or practice or crafting a portfolio career, which means that income is generated from a variety of sources. The exploratory process may even lead to a small but significant change, like shifting one's attitude or approach to work or changing something particular about one's work conditions. Often, we have more options than we first think.

Stage 3 – Decision-making – asks: *Which option is best for me?* Once stages 1 and 2 of the process are completed, decision-making (ideally!) becomes easier. Following Dr Parsons' original 'scientific method', once a person has taken time to reflect on his or her personal attributes and to investigate options, the positive and negative aspects of any career choice can be evaluated. Then we can make an informed decision about which option is best and target our energies accordingly.

When we focus on our most interesting and relevant career options, and can articulate how we are suited to that work, the prospects of making a successful career transition increase.

Stage 4 – Making a Transition – asks: *How do I get where I want to go?* This stage focuses on how to present oneself and market one's services. This can include résumé writing, crafting an effective online presence, preparing for interviews and practising salary negotiations. If you're beginning an enterprise, it will include defining the product or service, identifying the market, determining the appropriate legal structure, registering a company or business name, writing a business and marketing plan, building a website and social media profile, and so on.

One of the most important things people learn during this career transitioning process is that applying for advertised positions is one of the least successful ways of obtaining employment. You are competing with many more candidates, and recruiters are looking to eliminate candidates based upon compliance with a narrow set of criteria. This can mean recruiters miss the rough diamonds. Going through the stages of this process, taking the time to research organisations and environments where you would ideally like to work and could make a useful contribution, and then developing an approach to introduce and 'pitch' yourself to the right person in the organisation can even lead to a position being created where none previously existed. Indeed, I have secured most of my employed positions in this way.

Some people hold themselves to account during this transition stage by developing a Career Action Plan, with SMART (Specific, Measurable, Achievable, Relevant and Timebound) goals. A professional career coach may be useful to help a person move through this process and to achieve desired goals.

Stage 5 – Career/Life Development – asks: *What next?* It recognises that this is an ongoing process we will need to revisit periodically throughout our lives. After settling into a new role, eventually we may feel that we have outgrown a particular occupation or workplace and need to move on, even from work which has served us well to date. And so the question arises, 'Who am I *now*?' – and the cycle of career exploration and transition begins once again.

Benefits and limitations of the traditional approach

Now, let me be clear – I think there is value in this traditional approach, although it has significant limitations which I will discuss shortly. Though it can take some time to make a full transition, I have used this approach in the past in my own life and with my career clients, with good results. I still cover this approach when teaching adult postgraduate students about a depth psychological approach to vocation. These are people who have usually achieved a degree of proficiency and success in their field, so they know how to write a persuasive résumé and interview successfully for a position. Some of them are familiar with this classic, structured approach to career choice and transition, but many are not. Even people who have gone through this process in the past, or who have a clear sense of calling and are looking to parlay it into a career, can find the stages in this model helpful to review. Career development is, after all, a lifelong journey. It is likely that we will each make a number of changes during the course of our lives.

So I recommend that people become familiar with this process and revisit it from time to time. At transitional times in life, I particularly encourage people to reflect on their *values* (a Stage 1 activity) and how these have changed as one ages and enters new life stages. While some higher values such as Love, Beauty, Justice or Truth may be enduring through the course of one's life, as if they are 'seeded' in us from birth, others shift over time according to our life stage and circumstance. This kind of fluidity is natural and to be expected. When sorting through a typical list of values, it is not uncommon for a person to realise that values he or she once considered to be highly important, such as 'helping others', 'service', 'structure' and 'reliable income', have given way to other values, such as 'courage', 'integrity', 'time for myself' and 'creative expression'. Often, people discover that a job or career has become unfulfilling because it served values they held when they were younger. Over time and in different life stages, these values often change, and so the occupation or work environment needs to change accordingly to be compatible with the current life values. Being conscious of the values that matter to us can help us to make decisions with clarity and courage, without being unconsciously enlisted in other people's agendas. As Joseph Campbell wryly noted, "It takes courage to do what you want. Other people have a lot of plans for you".[4]

You can go through this model with a career counsellor, who can guide you through the steps and be a sounding board throughout the process. A good career counsellor will also be able to help you work through the fears and conscious *constraints* (such as age, educational qualifications, financial commitments) which inevitably arise during the process. While some constraints will need to be accepted and accommodated as unavoidable limitations, others, such as 'lack of confidence with interview situations', can be overcome given time, support and skills development. It is comforting to know that there are practical steps we can take, including preparation and role-playing, to overcome common fears and hurdles.

A career counsellor or coach will charge hundreds, even thousands of dollars at executive level, to take a client through this process. So instead, you may decide to do it yourself. The most famous guide to job-hunting and career-changing is *What Color is Your Parachute?* by Richard Nelson Bolles, which has been revised and republished annually since 1970. It follows the basic approach to career choice development outlined here and provides activities to help people with each of the stages around this model of career transition. Another practical guide is *Zen and the Art of Making a Living* by Laurence Boldt – which, despite its title and spiritual quotations and affirmations, is still essentially a guidebook to this classic model of career planning.

Having a clear structure and a career action plan can give a person a feeling of direction and purposefulness in an uncertain time. But there are significant limitations to this approach too. It is a highly rational approach which places a great deal of faith in data collection and methodical analysis. It tends towards helping people fit in and adapt to the *status quo* – into which many of us find that we do not readily fit. Responses from the midlife participants in courses I have taught include: "I can see how it might assist someone to identify an appropriate career in which one is meeting the expectations of family of origin, society or high school career counsellor", said Sarah, a psychiatrist, "but in terms of plumbing the depths of self, I'm not sure the rational approach, based on skills and abilities, is the most appropriate method for me now". "There is no consideration of the soul's yearning, the gut-wrenching knowing that one must move in a particular direction", lamented Shaeh, a mother of three who uprooted her family from the city to a country life to follow her calling as a healer. The conventional approach to career development falls short of supporting individuals in the discernment and expression of a *vocation* – a sacred or soul calling – in the sense in which I discussed in Chapter 1. But it can also become an exhaustingly wilful approach, reminiscent of what Parker Palmer describes as "a grim determination that one's life will go this way or that whether it wants to or not".[5]

The traditional model emphasises one's *known* skills, values, interests, preferences and so on. It focuses on what we're conscious of – the **ego**'s view of itself – but it doesn't allow for what we're not yet conscious of – both within ourselves, and what has not yet come into consciousness in our environment. Just as some jobs and occupations are rapidly disappearing, there are also new occupations and positions that haven't yet come into being – and that we may be instrumental in creating, if we notice our symptoms and synchronicities and listen to how the psyche is trying to guide us in a particular direction. For example, Holland's model tends to be weighted historically more towards blue collar jobs and to existing occupations recognised by the US Department of Labor, many of which are rapidly becoming obsolete. It's slow to recognise emerging, pioneering or hybrid fields and occupations, and you certainly won't find any mention of Jungian or archetypal psychologist, or eco-psychologist or urban shaman there, for example. So it doesn't represent the full range of occupational interests or possibilities, and it tells us nothing about how we might find or make our way in those less-clearly defined kinds of occupations which are 'off the beaten track'.

These limitations of this approach are exacerbated if the career counsellor or person administering the vocational assessment has not ventured very far down the path of deep self-reflection and vocational authenticity themselves. Even if they are well-intentioned, career counsellors often have limited education and experience in this respect and may not have ventured far into the unknown waters themselves. So it will be beyond their current knowledge, experience and ideological framework to help others imagine into and traverse more pioneering pathways.

New directions in career development

Recent movements in the field of career development have challenged the dominance of positivist match-making approaches. Innovative career development practitioners and scholars have focused on the role of chance, chaos and complexity in careers;[6] connections between spirituality and work;[7] and applying mythologist Joseph Campbell's model of the hero's journey to the career development process.[8]

Increasingly, career counsellors are being informed by a constructivist worldview.[9] Constructivism favours how people make or *construct meaning* in their careers. A champion of the constructivist approach, Mark Savickas, has emphasised the notion of 'life design'. This recognises the interconnectedness between different life domains (such as work, family, friends, health, leisure, spiritual practice, community) and the impossibility of artificially compartmentalising work from life. The process of life designing involves constructing career through small stories, reconstructing the stories into a life portrait, and co-constructing intentions that advance the individual's career story into a new episode.

Canadian careers professor Norman Amundson has built on the constructivist narrative approach to emphasise the importance of metaphor, creativity, imagination, cultural awareness and positive affirmation as career development strategies. Amundson uses techniques which shift career-seekers into a more symbolic and metaphorical mode of reimagining their careers and work-life. He has emphasised that what lies at the root of most career impasses is a "crisis of imagination":

> Many clients come to counselling because in some way they feel 'stuck'. They are dealing with a 'crisis of imagination'. To create new perspectives counsellors must be prepared to be more imaginative and innovative in their counselling approach.[10]

Amundson suggests that career counsellors listen for metaphoric images in clients' descriptions of their stories and then help the client to manipulate the metaphor to enhance their personal agency and action. For example, a client feels as if they are standing under a heavy raincloud with a deluge of problems showering down upon them. The metaphor is translated into a drawing, which also shows there is some sunshine in the distance, but the client isn't sure how to get there. Shifting the problem to this more externalised form supports the client with imagining ways of altering the metaphor, such as how to get out from under the raincloud or at least how to acquire an umbrella.[11]

Shifting away from the positivist traditions of career guidance, approaches such as Amundson's offer a bridge towards a more symbolic, imaginal mode of consciousness. There is increasing recognition and interest amongst career counsellors concerning how metaphor can provide deeper insight into career situations and facilitate vocational guidance.[12] Metaphor has been envisaged as an "all-terrain vehicle" which carries the therapeutic process "off the paved roads of prior meaning structures out into uncharted territories where new meanings are yet to be created".[13] Social science researchers are now musing on what it means to explore, discover and live out one's calling. Yet their empirical focus still fails to illuminate the mystery of vocation. It is inadequate to make space for a soulful sensibility.

In summary, at this new threshold in career counselling practice, depth psychology offers fascinating and valuable insights for development and refinement of these metaphor-based methods. Throughout this book, we will engage with stories and metaphors to deepen our understanding of aspects of vocation, enabling us to cross boundaries otherwise impossible to traverse through reason only.

Invitation to reflection and action

- In what way(s) does the traditional approach to career development and vocational guidance seem beneficial to you?
- In what way(s) do you consider this approach to be limited, particularly in light of the notion of vocation explored in Chapter 1?
- What aspects of the 5-stage model for career development might it serve you to pay (or re-pay) attention to now?

Notes

1 Parsons 1909, p. 3.
2 Brown & Brooks 2002; Patton & McMahon 2006; Walsh & Savickas 2004. The theoretical models, research methods and statistical techniques that emerged in the middle of the 20th century with the rise of vocational psychology as a behavioural science remain in widespread use today and are still presented as foundational material in the discipline's textbooks and handbooks (Savickas & Baker 2004). A logical positivist worldview remains implicit in documentation such as "Strategies for Vocational Guidance in the Twenty-first Century" (International Association for Educational and Vocational Guidance n.d.).
3 See www.self-directed-search.com and www.onetonline.org/find/descriptor/browse/Interests/
4 Campbell 1991, p. 62.
5 Palmer 2000, p. 4.
6 Bloch 2005; Bright et al. 2009; Bright, Pryor & Harpham 2005; Guindon & Hanna 2002; Pryor & Bright 2014; Pryor & Bright 2007, 2009, 2011.
7 Bloch & Richmond 1997; Duffy 2006; Weiss et al. 2003.
8 Bezanson 2004; Grant 2005; Tocher & Simon 1998.
9 Brown & Brooks 2002; McMahon & Patton 2006; McMahon & Watson 2011; Savickas 1997a, 2002, 2005, 2011, 2013.
10 Amundson 2005a, p. 16.
11 Amundson 2003a, pp. 80–82.
12 Inkson & Amundson 2002; Lyddon, Clay & Sparks 2001; McMahon 2006; Mignot 2000; Mignot 2004.
13 Lyddon, Clay & Sparks 2001, p. 273.

3   Vocation as soul's opus

A symbolic perspective

At the age of 24, I began my first career position, as a lawyer in a prestigious Sydney firm which specialised in entertainment law. After years of arduous university studies, I had successfully competed with over 400 applicants for this coveted position, working in a glittering skyscraper with high-profile clients. A legal career is frequently presented on film and TV as prestigious, exciting and even glamorous. But before long, something about this career did not feel right to me.

Some part of me felt like I was dying in this work, spending long hours engulfed in paperwork and bureaucracy and sorting through clients' claims over money, all in a highly pressured environment. My neck and shoulders became tight and painful under the strain. My skin started to break out in big lumps. I was ill at ease in a culture that seemed to value and reward arrogance, one-upmanship and ruthless competition, and regarded the expression of empathy, emotion and intuition as weakness. I was drained by the long hours in a glass tower that felt cut off from the real world and was self-referencing according to its own rules, conventions and protocols. I hated the time sheets that became the measure of my value. Most of all, I was disheartened by the pointlessness of the work: the hours spent trawling through documents in discovery to compile a paper trail of money moved from this company to that, to defend a wealthy executive living an extravagant lifestyle funded at the expense of his employees, shareholders, environment and community. How was this genuinely helping people or society? – which was, after all, what had attracted me to a career in law in the first place. Somewhere in the distance, the holy grail of law firm partnership lay; the trouble was, those who had risen to those ranks seemed neither happy nor admirable role models to me. It felt like something inside me, my spirit, would die if I kept on doing this job.

Two things happened around that time which brought a consciousness of soul to the forefront and ultimately prompted me to leave an unfulfilling career in search of a vocation. The first was my discovery, one lunch break when I wandered into a bookstore looking vaguely for some kind of help, of Thomas Moore's just-published *Care of the Soul: A Guide for Cultivating Depth and Sacredness in Everyday Life*. Thomas Moore is an archetypal psychotherapist, musician and former monk. Through this book, he became a kind of mentor to me, speaking about the nature and needs of the *soul* – a word rarely mentioned in the world around me, and certainly not in the legal profession. From his therapeutic practice, Moore observed that the conditions of work, dominated by function and efficiency, have at least as much to do with disturbances of the soul as do marriage and family. Moore enriched my imagination of work by comparing it with alchemy. He suggested that we could imagine our everyday work as an alchemical opus, the stuff of soul-making:

> Work is an attempt to find an adequate alchemy that both wakens and satisfies the very root of being. Most of us put a great deal of time into work, not only because we have to work so many hours to make a living, but because work is central to the soul's *opus*. We are crafting ourselves – individuating, to use the Jungian term. Work is fundamental to the *opus* because the whole point of life is the fabrication of soul.[1]

It was through Moore's book that I was first introduced to a thoughtful discussion of soul and to the field of Jungian and archetypal psychology. Drawing on insights from philosophy, religion and mythology, Moore suggested that work also has a symbolic and reflective meaning and is far more than the secular enterprise the modern world assumes it to be. From a positivist, mainstream careers perspective – certainly among the lawyers with whom I worked – Moore's ideas could be critiqued as idealistic or fanciful. Yet he does not shy away from engaging with the gritty and shadowy aspects of work, such as the complications of money, the role of failure as a surprising source of potential soul and how a soulful kind of creativity may emerge from wrestling with our fate.

The second thing that happened around this time which radically corrected my vocational course was an encounter with a tree. I was walking home after another long and uninspiring day in the office, wondering how I might escape from the gloomy psychic prison of my work. Yet after years of study to gain my professional qualification, I was in a financially fragile position. I had no idea what else I might do. Feeling bereft, I stopped by a tree growing alongside the footpath.

I couldn't tell you what type of tree it was, but I touched its leaves and placed my palm on its bark. I noticed the ants that crawled upon its trunk, an insect that hovered around the tiny blossoms that were coming into bloom and the birds that rested in its branches. I felt the life that coursed through that tree, from its roots sunk deep into the earth to its branches reaching up to the sky at dusk.

In a strange moment of clarity, I thought, "This tree is more real than anything I do in that office any day". For the tree had life in it, and the environment in which I operated each day, for all its busy-ness, its manmade rules and procedures, and its artificial constructs, was but a pale imitation of that.

Without ever saying a word, it was this tree which gently and eloquently counselled me to leave a job that was sapping the life out of me. It gave me the courage to step into the unknown and to head in a vocational direction that was ultimately more life-affirming and true to my soul. As Jung wrote in a letter to a colleague in 1947, "Sometimes a tree tells you more than can be read in books". Jung also commented that the tree acquires this quality of wisdom through its symbolism of the life opus, as a mystery of life, death and rebirth. My experience with the tree was emotionally powerful and numinous, suggesting that in that moment I was in the presence of something archetypal. The tree embodied and channelled what Joseph Campbell described as a "transcendent energy . . . an energy that comes from a realm beyond our powers of knowledge. And that energy becomes bound in each of us – in this body – to a certain commitment".[2]

The humble tree is one of humankind's most universal symbols, appearing in myth, ritual, legend, shamanic initiation, sacred literature, art and poetry, as well as in the dreams and visions of ancient and contemporary seekers and seers.[3] As Ralph Metzner has observed, the tree has served as a preeminent symbol of growth, renewal and transformation. Jung noticed that in his patients' drawings of trees, which were most frequently done by women, the tree was a guiding symbol of the soul and a projection of the individuation process.[4] Throughout history, the tree has offered a metaphor for the unfolding and growth of an individual. My encounter with this particular tree that day precipitated my departure from a path worn by others and the beginning of a quest to follow my bliss and find my authentic vocation, my own unique path, my own myth.

In this chapter, I will begin to explore how bringing a symbolic perspective to our lived experiences of work can awaken our imagination and insight to a deeper understanding that our vocational journeys are also an opus of the soul. I will explain how terms which are difficult to define, such as 'vocation' and 'soul', are more fruitfully understood and approached as **symbols**, applying the Jungian technique of **amplification** rather than semiotic or allegoric interpretation.

The meaning of soul

What do we mean by the word 'soul'? Freud described the soul as "the fragile insubstantial essence of the self which needs to be approached gently and with love".[5] Though difficult to put into words, soul has something to do with genuineness, depth, love, longing, beauty, the poignant ephemeral nature of life and the capacity for imagination. We move towards a sense of soul when we reflect on what moves us or what we value deeply; when we feel the need to know the meaning of life or of our own life; when we feel a connection with a vast living universe or yearn to connect with something greater than ourselves; or when we contemplate our own mortality. Life has felt soulful to me when I have sat by the bedside of a dying person; when I have listened to a timeless piece of music such as Mozart's Piano Concerto No. 21; and when I have talked intimately and laughed easily with a friend or lover, especially one I may not see again. Life has felt soulful when I have stroked the soft ears of my faithful old arthritic dog and watched a radiant sunset on a deserted beach, and even when I have waved my placard participating in a march for climate change action with tens of thousands of other people from all walks of life. This sensibility of soul is aligned with a long intellectual and artistic tradition in Western civilization. It stretches back to Heraclitus and Plato, and includes Romantic poets such as John Keats and William Blake and archetypal psychologists such as James Hillman and Robert Sardello.

Perhaps due to my temperament, and also to the circumstances of my childhood and youth in which an unusually high number of relatives and friends passed away, a sense of soul has always felt close and intuitively self-evident to me. My sense of allegiance to the soul, even – especially – through dark and difficult times, is reminiscent of a fidelity to what the ancient Greeks understood as one's *daimon*, or the Romans as one's *genius*, the ancient Platonic notion of a mythical companion that accompanies us from before birth and nudges us towards our vocation. However, even for those who feel a sense of soul, it is impossible to define precisely what the soul is. When the founder of archetypal psychology, James Hillman, was asked what he meant by the word soul, he replied that while you can't make a nice clean idea of it, in rational or conceptual terms: "it has something to do with the depth of you. It has to do with something that matters. It has something to do with love, with connection; something to do with risk, and death. . . . Also tragedy. Think of soul music. There's a deep sense of beauty and tragedy together, that's all to do with soul".[6]

Let's not forget that *psyché* is the Greek word for soul. Psychology literally

> *You could not discover the limits of soul, even if you travelled every road to do so, such is the depth of its meaning.*
>
> – Heraclitus (500 BCE)

means the study of the soul. *Psyché* was often depicted in ancient Greco-Roman art as a butterfly-winged woman. When we reflect on the difficult metamorphosis a caterpillar undergoes to become a butterfly, it is a perfect metaphor for the painful life transitions we too experience. With the dissolution of an old identity, it is time to embody a new way of being, a new perspective and to spread our wings towards our new calling in the world.

Jungian and archetypal psychology is sometimes called a psychology of the soul. But archetypal psychologist James Hillman thought that mainstream psychology was afraid of soul and does not even use the word anymore; that it "invents boxes, diagnoses, tests, statistics, graphs, rules, and laws, to keep it away".[7] Because of the mysterious, indefinable nature of soul, and its religious connotations, psychologists as well as academics tend to be suspicious and wary of it. When I was writing my doctoral thesis, my supervisor warned me strongly against mentioning soul, concerned it would take me into academically precarious territory. Yet at the heart of my thesis was this idea that soul is an essential yet neglected consideration in vocation. It required all my advocacy skills as a lawyer to build a case for the word *soul* in an academic context. Paradoxically, I was compelled to take a very literal, rational and detached (supposedly 'objective') approach and tone to justify an ineffable concept which is best approached and understood through metaphor and poetic language, through story and through deep subjective experiences of love and of loss.

For the poet Mary Oliver, the soul arises through an attitude of noticing, coupled with an ability to "love the world". Parker Palmer imagined the soul as an exceedingly shy, wild animal that retreats from attempts to invoke it through logical analysis and linear thought processes.[8] Jung too criticised psychology for this tendency, to stalk the psyche or soul from within, "like a slain creature of the wild which can no longer run away".[9] By holding this sensitivity towards the wild and shy nature of the soul, we can perceive something of the problem with seductively logical, linear, practical approaches, including those towards securing the 'right job' or the ostensibly 'perfect career'.

As I endeavour to show in this book, awareness of *soul* and of *soul-making* (as John Keats coined that term) is fundamental to an experience of meaningful work. In my experience and conversations with people over several decades about work, including in my practice as a careers counsellor, I have noticed that *soul* is a word for which people grasp when trying to articulate something vital, profound yet nebulous that is missing from their work, the absence of which goes to the core of their suffering. Consider, for example, phrases such as "this work is soul-destroying", "I'm selling my soul here" or "this is a soulless workplace". Conversely, Thomas Moore encapsulated the vital relationship between work and caring for the soul when he observed that "finding the right work is like discovering your own soul in the world".[10]

Beyond literalism: seeing through metaphor and symbol

Bringing a sensibility of soul into our experiences and conversations about work and career requires that we make a radical pivot from a literal to a metaphoric perspective. The essential point I wish to emphasise here is that the notion of soul is best understood not as a scientific term or even as a theological concept but as a **symbol**. This means that we approach and appreciate soul not as a thing but as a quality of knowing, a *perspective*. According to Hillman, soul is that unknown component which makes meaning possible, deepens events into experiences, is communicated in love and which also has a religious concern, derived from its special relationship with death.[11] Importantly, soul also refers to "the imaginative possibility in our natures, the experiencing through reflective speculation, dream, image and *fantasy* – that mode which recognises all realities as primarily symbolic or metaphorical".[12] So to awaken a sense of soul in life and work requires firstly that we cultivate a symbolic perspective.

To entertain a metaphoric or symbolic perspective, one must not fall into the trap of interpreting and concretising a *symbol* as a *sign*. Although these words are often used synonymously, in Jungian psychology, they have different meanings. A *sign* points to a known or knowable thing, and therefore the meaning of a sign can be defined. Typically, a sign has a meaning given by culture. A *symbol*, on the other hand, resists definition. Instead, a symbol has qualities of the numinous, the unknown or the unknowable.

To present a simplified example: if an image in a dream, such as a sickle-shaped sword, is read using a semiotic approach, as a *sign*, it is interpreted in a literal or reductive manner as standing for something else that is already known (such as, if you're a Freudian psychoanalyst, a phallus). This is the approach that popular dream interpretation books tend to take – purporting to state conclusively that X means Y. If, however, the image is read as a *symbol*, an approach that Jung favoured, then rather than attempting to *define* what it means, the symbol becomes "the best possible expression of a relatively unknown, highly potent power".[13] Taking a symbolic attitude does not mean that we completely ignore conventional usage or associations but that we also try to remain aware that symbolic words and images are doorways and openings into *mysteries*.[14]

So how do we begin to comprehend the meaning of a symbol, like the word 'soul'? The term *hermeneutics* is familiar to scholars of literature, the humanities and the arts. It refers to a methodological approach used to interpret a symbolic expression or ambiguous text or speech. Hermeneutics is essentially the art of interpretation, beyond mere logical analysis. Jungian film studies scholar Don Fredericksen argued that a *hermeneutic of amplification* is the appropriate posture of inquiry to adopt towards a symbol, as it expands and opens possibilities by revolving around the word or idea. This is in contrast to a *hermeneutic of suspicion*, which seeks to limit and define.[15] Definitions state what something is and where it is separated from what it is not. While definitions are appropriate in the sciences, the best way to perceive the meaning of a symbol is by adopting a hermeneutic of amplification.

Amplification means that we seek parallel uses or images for the symbol, often looking to the repository of the world's mythic and ancient traditions, which can include religion and fairy tales. Amplification is a technique more familiar in the humanities and the arts than the sciences, and it allows for a different kind of understanding and meaning-making to emerge. A hermeneutic of amplification uses metaphor, image and story to revolve around the symbol in question, stimulating psychological animation and revelation. So if we return to the example of the sickle-shaped sword, this might also be related to mythological imagery of the crescent moon, such as the moon goddesses, and the rising power of the archetypal feminine.[16] It is the nature of a true symbol to be both universal and to be perceived anew by each person, according to resonances within the individual psyche. Amplification allows ideas and themes to associate with each other to illuminate hidden psychological connections.

One way to imagine the difference between definition and amplification is that it is akin to the difference between pinning a butterfly to a board in order to dissect and define it or observing it in different environments in a more open-ended way. Jungian psychology endeavours to work with symbols and images as living expressions of the psyche. In doing so, the butterfly, the psyche, the soul, is kept alive. By adopting a hermeneutic of amplification, we are consciously nurturing an ongoing receptive relationship with the whole living psyche, including the unconscious.

Words which may be used to amplify the meaning of soul include 'heart', 'life', 'warmth', 'humanness', 'personality', 'purpose' and 'emotion' as well as 'troubled', 'lost', 'innocent' and 'inspired'.[17] But to appreciate the fullness and dimensions of a word like soul, we must each bring a symbolic perspective rather than a semiotic or allegoric interpretation to the task. When I teach this symbolic approach in my introductory courses on vocation, I invite students to share a resonant image which symbolizes 'soul' for them. These symbols are frequently drawn from the natural world, and less often from the world's religious or mythological traditions, such as a goddess figure, the Black Madonna, a mandala, the yin-yang symbol or the Buddhist unalome. Usually, the symbol has come to the attention of the person through a dream, a childhood memory or a synchronistic encounter. Often, they are connected with flight, such as feathers or wings, or of a particular bird with which the person feels a connection, such as an owl, dove, crow or kookaburra. Other times they are images of water, such as the ocean, a familiar river or a beach that a person has walked along. Or the image which holds soul may be connected to the earth, such a special tree that a person loved to sit beneath or the enduring presence of certain rocks and stones. One young man, Leo, offered the image of a focused flame as symbolizing the soul: "I have always felt, when gazing into a fire, a deep sense of peace and an indescribable feeling of reverence and awe, as if there were some kind of profound wisdom being communicated through the movement of the flames". Witnessing each other's symbols of soul, everyone present feels a sense of sacredness, deepened connection and reverence. These soul symbols drawn from nature also variously embrace the four elements of earth, air, fire and water, which are the quarters of a sacred circle of life in many indigenous and pagan traditions.

Vocation from a symbolic perspective

Just as the word 'soul' is best approached from a symbolic perspective, so I suggest is the word 'vocation'. I found it interesting when I researched the career and management literature that scholars who have tried to define the words 'vocation' and 'calling' have been unable to reach any consensus on their meaning. One scholar described her disorienting experience researching the history of the term 'vocation', whose meanings "pitch and sway and steadily retreat from easy grasp", as like "a woozy stagger through a hall of mirrors"![18] The fact that the words 'vocation' and 'calling' are so difficult to define suggest that here we are dealing with a *symbol*, an ambiguous concept resisting conclusive definition, or a known thing which stands for something which is relatively unknown or ultimately unknowable.

Approaching vocation from a symbolic perspective allows us to respect and appreciate something of its mystery, as far more than the secular enterprise the modern world assumes it to be. Perhaps an intuitive appreciation of the aptness of a symbolic approach towards understanding vocation is why *metaphor* is now advocated as one of the most powerful tools in vocational guidance.[19] If we allow ourselves to draw upon the metaphors and images that arise when reflecting on our lived experiences of vocation, we will find that this naturally opens the door to seeing the world with a symbolic perspective.

For example, Annabella was a 65-year-old woman whose story we will hear more of later:

> *Vocation means to me . . . that I have landed where I was always meant to be. I've stepped into the deepest rivers of my life. And I've made whatever adjustments along the way – almost wholly intuitively, but with a lot of effort and commitment – I've made adjustments like a sail, to align myself with this deep current. And now I'm living it, in a way that . . . I feel like my whole life has prepared me for this, where I am now with my work.*

(Annabella)

It is interesting that Annabella naturally gravitates to images of water (river, currents, adjusting her sails) to describe her felt experiences of vocation and response to life calling(s). Water is a pre-eminent symbol of the unconscious. A central theme of this book is the idea that our vocational callings arise through our attendance to the watery depths of the unconscious. Metaphors of water often appear in connection with the vocational journey. Consider for example the title of poet David Whyte's book *Crossing the Unknown Sea: Work as a Pilgrimage of Identity*. In the introductory courses I teach on the depth psychology of vocation, people frequently share dreams and images of the sea, suggesting a readiness to engage with the oceanic realm of the psyche.

When I was poised to leave my job as a lawyer, the image that came to mind was that I was on the edge of an ocean swimming pool, of the type found along Sydney's beaches. I needed to let go of the edge of the pool, which also seemed to represent the security of my position. The ocean was rough and where I was heading unknown. In real life I am a poor swimmer. I wasn't at all sure that I could swim, but I needed to start paddling fast if I didn't want to drown!

For about ten years after letting go of the edge of that ocean pool, it seemed as if I was 'at sea'. The various occupations and organisations in which I worked felt like different ships and boats on the ocean – some large, some small, one no more than me and a few others adrift in a dinghy. The challenge was to stay afloat and survive, not least financially, and to keep my spirits buoyed until one day I might plant my feet on *terra firma* again. Sometimes it was apparent that a transnational corporate ship, while grand and luxurious, was travelling in the wrong direction, so I was obliged to seek passage on a humbler craft. Once or twice, ambushed by the pirates and politics of corporate life, I was forced to walk the plank. There were lonely and scary periods when I was without work, treading water way out of my depth and knowing I couldn't wait too long for the next ship (or life raft) to come along. Yet, through passage on these various vessels of employment, I eventually made my way to land on a new and distant shore – a life closer to nature, away from the city and independent of corporate values and collective mores. In this place, I became reacquainted with the rhythms of nature and with my own indigenous psyche and began to imagine into and slowly create a different kind of life and work.

Seeing my career journey in metaphoric terms – letting go of the edge, being at sea, landing on a new shore, building a small sanctuary and later a 'lighthouse' to help guide others through the rocky passage – gave me an imaginative, intuitive sense of where I was situated in the psychic landscape and how I could best direct my energies at each stage. Such guiding symbols and images may arise through our faculty of imagination or visit us in our dreams.

Some career counselling approaches are now realising the potential of engaging symbol and metaphor to shift stuckness and awaken new possibilities. However, the move beyond formulas and certainties, towards a more imaginative and metaphoric mode of perception, remains largely neglected in career development. The conventional approach to career choice and development remains squarely focused upon tasks pertaining to ego-development (a paycheck, a good job). Rarely does career development support individuals in the expression of a vocation – a sacred or soul calling.[20] A sacred calling, I suggest, is one that arises from a deeper place in the psyche than the ego. The ego may be the captain of the boat, but it is a tiny vessel indeed compared to the immensity of the psyche, that great ocean of mystery upon which the ego sails.

There are certain dimensions of life which can only really be understood symbolically and which will not be resolved through reliance on rational, logical thought. Trying to do so will keep us going around in circles or caught in an ever-tightening net from which we cannot extract ourselves by will or by thinking without becoming further hopelessly ensnared. Whitmont observes:

> As we progress from the world of simple external facts into the more intimate dynamisms of life, into the intimate functioning of the unconscious psyche, we find ourselves reaching domains in which our logical understanding no longer suffices; it can help us no further.[21]

This is where the insights of depth psychology can help release the trap. Depth psychology doesn't abandon rational, logical thought, but it is equally inclusive of a symbolic approach. It has been described as a psychology of metaphor and imagination, in which the most important words are "it is as if". We can liberate ourselves intellectually and psychologically, away from a reductive, literal mode of analysis and into a symbolic mode of perception which may gift us with a new understanding of our situation and how to navigate it by using the words "as if". So, for example, in narrating the previous story of leaving my legal career, I wrote that it seemed "as if" I was at sea for ten years, after letting go of the edge of an ocean pool. The words "as if" signpost a symbolic perspective and simultaneously re-locate my account of my career experiences in the symbolic realm.

In Chapter 5, we will engage a Jungian model of the psyche as a guide to navigating these symbolic waters. As we will see in the next chapter on psychological type, taking a symbolic approach requires a shift away from the dominance of purely rational, *logos-* or fact-based approaches to life and towards a re-valuing of the faculties of feeling and intuition.

Invitation to reflection and journaling

* What do you consider to be the relationship between the loss of symbolic perspective and a loss of meaning or loss of soul in life today? Deepen your reflections by writing about an example from your personal experience or from the collective level of experience.
* Is there a symbol or image which holds a quality of mystery or soulfulness for you? Take or find a photograph; or paint, sculpt or draw the image. Or write a poem which gives expression to the image. Meditate upon the symbol or image. Write about what it means to you and any associations that arise.

Notes

1 Moore 1992, p. 185.
2 Campbell 2004, p. xvii.
3 Metzner 1998, p. 198.
4 Jung 1945.
5 cited in Bettelheim 1992, p. 15.
6 Hillman 2010.
7 Hillman 1975, p. 2.
8 Palmer 2004, p. 58.
9 Jung 1954a CW8, para. 356.
10 Moore 1992, p. 186.
11 Hillman 1975, p. xvi.
12 Hillman 1975, p. xvi. See also Kalsched's discussion of soul (2013, pp. 14–22). It is also worth noting Jung's understanding and use of the word 'soul' in a psychological sense, as a functional complex in the psyche that could best be described as a personality, typically the *anima* in a man (Jung 1921 CW6, paras. 797–811).
13 Whitmont 1991, p. 21.
14 "A critic with a semiotic attitude would work within the assumption that the word 'soul' is a known thing standing for another known thing, perhaps by appealing to traditional usage or stipulative definition. At a certain point the questions about soul stop. A critic with a symbolic attitude would appeal to traditional usage as well, but . . . tries to remain aware that symbolic words, images . . . are doorways, openings, into mysteries. Because of this fact the [symbolic] critic knows the questions will go on and on" (Fredericksen 2012, p. 13).
15 Fredericksen 2005, p. 33.
16 See Whitmont (1991, p. 22).
17 Avens 1980, p. 31.
18 Dawson 2005, pp. 226–227.
19 Amundson 2005b, 2010, 2011; Inkson 2004; Inkson & Amundson 2002.
20 Gallos 2005, p. 12.
21 Whitmont 1991, p. 31.

4 A short interlude on the relevance of psychological type

Just like swimming in water, a symbolic perspective will seem completely refreshing and natural for some and yet be unfamiliar and disorienting for others. This difference between people's proclivity for a symbolic approach is, I believe, best understood through Carl Jung's theory of psychological types. Jung's theory forms the basis of the Myers-Briggs Type Indicator, which is one of the most widely used personality instruments in the world today.

Many people have an aversion to typology because they don't like the idea of being pigeon-holed into one of sixteen types. I was one of those people. I'd seen psychological instruments like the Myers-Briggs Type Indicator (commonly known as the MBTI) used and abused in corporate environments, employed in a reductive, heavy-handed way to stereotype people according to other people's agendas. When I established my career guidance practice, I thought it would be useful to become qualified as an MBTI practitioner. I was fortunate to have an excellent instructor who taught me the deeper dynamics and nuances of the instrument and how to use it sensitively, appropriately and ethically. Later, in my postgraduate studies, I was taught by the Jungian analyst and medical doctor John Beebe, who is internationally renowned for his expertise in psychological type and for his extensions of Jung's early theories. Over the years, I have found the theory of psychological type and the MBTI to be extremely useful in a number of ways.

Psychological type has immense implications for learning, for cultural and environmental fit, in marriage and at work. In particular, our typology plays a huge part in our sense of appropriateness of employment and our satisfaction, or lack thereof, in our experiences of work. Typology can deepen our insight into our strengths and our stressors. Knowing something about the shifting dynamics of our psychological type across the lifespan gives us a framework for understanding our attitudinal changes in midlife and beyond. In addition, an informed understanding of typology helps us to appreciate individual differences and perspectives, including why some people quickly resonate with depth psychology and perceive life readily with a symbolic perspective, while others baulk at what appears to be impractical or unrealistic.

The basics and evolution of Jung's theory of psychological type

Jung's theories have deeply influenced the world of vocational guidance and career development. However, many people are unaware of this influence in the history and theoretical origins of the MBTI.

Jung first published his theory of psychological type in his book called *Psychological Types* in 1921. He also published an essay called "A psychological theory of types" in 1931, which appears in his book *Modern Man in Search of a Soul*. This essay gives an interesting background into Jung's development and thoughts about this theory – a background which usually disappears from contemporary manuals about psychological type, with their focus on applications of the theory. For example, Jung drew historical analogies between classifying people according to psychological type and with the ancient cosmological scheme, represented by the astrological elements of earth, air, fire and water; and also with the Greek classification of four physiological dispositions corresponding to four humours of the body, which were termed phlegmatic, sanguine, choleric and melancholic.

Jung identified differences in how people 1) draw energy, 2) gather information and 3) evaluate that information. He categorised those differences as opposite poles of three dimensions – 1) Energy, 2) Perception and 3) Judgment (see Figure 4.1). Jung developed the modern-day theory of psychological types based on years of clinical observation and work with patients. It was also his attempt to understand the roots of his own differences with the man who had initially been his mentor, Sigmund Freud, as I discuss later.

Psychological type is an extensive and complex topic. I encourage readers who are unfamiliar with but interested in understanding this topic to follow up with the books and resources listed at the end of this chapter. In this section, I will briefly sketch the basics of Jung's theory.

In a nutshell, Jung identified four basic psychological functions which each person possesses, which he called Sensation, Intuition, Thinking and Feeling. It is interesting that the word 'function' comes from a Sanskrit root, meaning 'to enjoy'. Jung considered that every person enjoys or prefers using certain of these functions, related to how they perceive things and then how they make judgments about what is perceived.

Perceiving refers to the process of gathering information. This can be either by Sensation, where one gathers information in a concrete way using the five senses and focussing on facts; or by Intuition, which is a more abstract manner of gathering information, focusing on patterns, connections, possibilities and meaning. (Note that in typology, Intuition is designated by the letter N to distinguish it from Introversion, which is designated by the letter I.)

Judging refers to how we process information in order to make decisions. According to Jung, people make decisions by either using their heads, which Jung referred to as the Thinking function, or their hearts, referred to as the Feeling function. When we make decisions with our heads (the Thinking function),

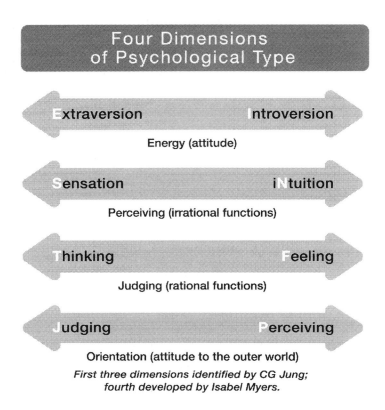

Figure 4.1 Four dimensions of psychological type

we engage logic and analytical reasoning. When we decide with our hearts (the Feeling function), we rely on values and use a relationship-centred approach to decision-making.

Jung also called the Perceiving functions (Sensation and Intuition) the 'irrational' functions because perception is a somewhat involuntary process. By this he meant that we do not categorise or consider the information we absorb, we merely encounter it and absorb it as a reflex action. It is the Judging function (Thinking or Feeling) that takes the perceived information and evaluates it. Therefore, Jung considered that the Judging functions, even the Feeling function, were 'rational' functions because individuals must use a purposeful and reflective process to evaluate information.

In addition to these four functions, Jung identified two *attitudes*, Extraversion and Introversion. Most people don't know that it was Jung who coined the terms 'extraversion' and 'introversion'. In common parlance, 'extraverted' has come to mean sociable, while 'introverted' connotes shyness. However, Jung used these

> *Sensation establishes what is actually present, thinking enables us to recognize its meaning, feeling tells us its value, and intuition points to possibilities as to whence it came and whither it is going in a given situation.*
>
> CG Jung (1931a para. 958)

terms in a particular fashion to refer to the different ways in which we draw and direct our energy. Extraversion refers to a tendency to draw energy from external sources and through engaging with others. Introversion is the tendency to draw energy from inner sources, such as reflecting on events, and to consider information and decisions subjectively before presenting the outcome of one's thoughts. Rather than considering that individuals themselves are introverted or extraverted, Jung found that each of the four functions (Sensation, Intuition, Thinking, Feeling) may be variously introverted or extraverted, leading to eight variants (introverted Sensation, extraverted Sensation and so on).

Jung's ideas regarding psychological type were later taken up and developed by a mother and daughter team, Katherine Briggs and Isabel Myers. Around the time of World War I, Katherine Briggs became interested in the similarities and differences in human personality. She began to develop her own typology, largely through the study of biography. Then she discovered that Jung had developed a similar system, which she quickly adopted and began to explore and elaborate.

During World War II, many women were entering the workforce to replace the men who were called up for service. Myers and Briggs wanted to aid the war effort by assisting women entering the workforce. They believed a Jungian-based instrument could help people to easily identify their typology and point them towards work tasks which they might enjoy. This led to the development of the Myers-Briggs Type Indicator (MBTI), a personality instrument designed to make Jung's theory of psychological types understandable and useful in people's lives.

So the MBTI instrument was originally conceived as a way of using Jung's personality theory to match women with jobs during the war. But because Myers and Briggs were neither formally trained psychologists nor statisticians (and probably moreover because they were women), their work met with much opposition within the academic community. As a result, their instrument was repeatedly challenged and tested for validity, reliability and statistical significance, so that today, ironically, it has become the most verified personality instrument in the world. Today the MBTI is one of the most widely used personality instruments, particularly in career guidance and counselling.[1]

In addition to the three dichotomies which Jung identified – of Extraversion and Introversion, Sensation and Intuition, Thinking and Feeling – when developing the MBTI, Isabel Myers added a fourth dimension, called the Orientation (or attitude) to the outer world. This considers whether a person prefers to interact with the outer world using a Perceiving process, to gather information, or using a Judging Process, to make decisions. In this context, it is important to understand that Judging does not equate with being judgmental, just as a Perceiving orientation does not mean that a person is particularly perceptive or discerning!

Together, a letter from each of these four dichotomies makes up one's MBTI code (such as ENFP or ISTJ). It is, however, important to be aware that this four-letter code is merely a shorthand formula for a much more complex and nuanced underlying psychological dynamic. We each have access to *all* the psychological functions, even the ones that don't appear in our particular four-letter code. According to our psychological makeup, our various functions are ordered as dominant, auxiliary, tertiary and inferior. As we progress through the different stages of life, in the process that Jung called individuation, we are psychologically tasked with developing and integrating each of the functions to varying degrees.[2]

This begins to take us into complicated territory, and the novice who wishes to understand the theory and practice of psychological type further is referred to resources at the end of the chapter. A rough chronological progression is that during childhood, our dominant function develops according to our preferred attitude of Extraversion or Introversion and takes the lead. (In this paragraph, I will give specific examples for an INFP, for whom the dominant function is introverted Feeling.) In adolescence, the auxiliary function (extraverted Intuition) develops in the opposite world to the dominant function and begins to support it. This means that if the dominant function is extraverted, the auxiliary function will be introverted. In early adulthood, the tertiary function (introverted Sensation) develops in the same world as the dominant function. Then in midlife, the fourth or inferior function develops (extraverted Thinking) in our less-preferred world.

The inferior function is that which we are most likely to lose control over when we are stressed or drained. Conventional wisdom suggests for good reason that we minimise or avoid work which places excessive demands on our inferior functions. Yet from a depth psychological perspective, the inferior function can also be a seed for significant psycho-spiritual vocational development, especially from midlife onwards.[3]

There's a wealth of data linking psychological types with various careers, identifying which types tend to be most successful, or most stressed, in different occupations.[4] For example, I identify as an INFJ. My first career as a lawyer seemed like a reasonably good idea at the time. I possessed the intellectual ability and an interest in justice, advocacy and human rights. However, with my dominant and secondary functions of introverted Intuition and extraverted Feeling, I became very depressed and stressed with what to me was the tedious, profoundly unimaginative nature of the work in a competitive, conflict-ridden environment. Years later, I came across the Myers-Briggs data and discovered that people of my type didn't particularly flourish in that profession or environment at all. If only I had known about that earlier!

To be sure of your type, it is recommended to take the full MBTI instrument (not just a free online personality test). Even then, the instrument has a margin of error, perhaps as high as 20%. It can be easy to mis-identify one's psychological type, for a variety of reasons. These include behaviours to which we've been conditioned, as well as our particular stage in life where we may find ourselves drawn to expressing less conscious aspects of our type, such as our inferior function. To be confident of the accuracy of your type diagnosis, it is recommended to verify your results in conversation with a qualified MBTI practitioner.

How we perceive and process the world in different ways

Typology can help with understanding workplace dynamics, how people get on and work together, and why we sometimes don't see eye-to-eye. Jung developed the theory of psychological types in an endeavour to understand his own significant differences with Freud, which eventually caused them to part ways. In a nutshell, this came to centre around what Jung decried as Freud's reductive and narrow thinking, and what Freud called Jung's "charming delusions", such as his interest in occult phenomena. One particular point of difference was their understanding of the concept of *libido*. Freud equated the libido wholly with sexuality, and Freud's psychology looked specifically to the roots of an individual's behaviour in their past and in their childhood experiences. Jung, however, understood libido in a much broader sense – as a more generalised creative energy or life force, which can include sexuality but is not limited to this. For Jung, there was a spiritual aspect or nature to libido. Jung's psychology assumes that there is not just a past wound but a purposive or teleological nature to the symptoms of the psyche, which are pushing one to realise one's own potential.

So Jung became frustrated with what he called Freud's "materialist prejudice" and "shallow positivism", just as Freud became suspicious of Jung's mysticism. But typologically, their differences can in a very large part be attributed to the difference between their dominant perceiving functions. Freud perceived the world predominantly through the Sensation function, which is about taking things in through the five senses and trusting concrete experience. Jung, however, gathered information through the faculty of Intuition, which is more about perceiving patterns and connections and trusting hunches and the imagination. In particular, Jung preferred introverted Intuition, which is the function most closely associated with the perception of the archetypal level of experience.

So typologically, these two men were always going to perceive and process the world and their experiences in fundamentally different ways. Jung expresses his view of their differences and the relevance of typology in Chapter 4 of *Modern Man in Search of a Soul*. Jung also makes the point that Freud's psychology is not wrong but is true to his type, and it is the truest expression of Freud's own psychic makeup. As such, it will resonate most with others who share Freud's typology.

> *The shoe that fits one person pinches another; there is no universal recipe for living.*
>
> – CG Jung (1954b CW16, para. 81)

How readily a person identifies with the depth psychological perspectives presented in this book will also be influenced by their psychological type and their stage of psychological development. Jung knew how subjective psychology is, admitting that "Every psychological theory which is the work of one man is subjectively coloured".[5] It has been shown that the various psychological theories tend to duplicate the internal psychodynamics of their founding theorists.[6] Jung observed that his own following consisted "presumably of people who have my psychology"[7] and commented that "most of my patients are socially well-adapted individuals, often of outstanding ability, to whom normalisation means nothing".[8] In a similar vein, post-Jungian James Hillman has been described as "the artist's psychologist".[9] The approach to vocation presented in this book draws on the psychological theories of both Jung and Hillman, and as such is well suited not to those who desire to adapt to or maintain the *status quo* in their careers but to those who feel called in some way to creatively transform their world.

A vocational approach that appeals to intuition

This leads us to the significance of the Sensation/Intuition dichotomy for an appreciation of or affinity with the field of depth psychology. Depending upon which source one consults, it is estimated that between 65–73% of the general population prefer Sensation. This means a preference for realism, detail, practicality and what exists according to the five senses. For a person with a Sensation preference, the symbolic mode of consciousness and the more abstract and imaginal ideas of depth psychology can seem strange and confusing. Only 27–35% of the general population prefer Intuition as a mode of perception. However, among my students and clients interested in depth psychology, the overwhelming majority prefer Intuition (and to a lesser extent, for Introversion). They are much more readily attuned to metaphor, abstraction, archetypal patterns and other ways of knowing beyond logical analysis.

In particular, individuals with dominant *introverted* Intuition (INTJ and INFJ), like Jung, who comprise a tiny 2.4–4.6% of the population, will always perceive meaning and symbolism through the world of the senses. According to the renowned Jungian analyst Ed Whitmont, "People of the introverted intuitive type experience and realize life in terms of the unconscious; to them the world of the archetypes is a concrete reality. They perceive ideas, images and inner possibilities; they are attuned to the psychic atmosphere".[10] No wonder that Jung, with his typological preferences, was a pioneer in a psychology of symbol, imagination and the unconscious.

So typology can be a good way of understanding why some people instinctively 'get' depth psychology and take to it like a duck to water, while for others it is a complete enigma. This does not mean, however, that if you are not a dominant Intuitive type, you won't understand or benefit from depth psychology. In fact, whatever your type, if you are engaged in the process of individuation and growing into the fullness of yourself, you will find that at some point in life you'll be psychologically tasked with coming to terms more consciously with the Intuitive function. So a person with a dominant Sensing preference may find that in the second half of life they suddenly become more interested in this aspect of themselves – for example, through exploring dreamwork, meditation, innovation and symbolic meaning – as they do the psychological work of developing their inferior function.

In a nutshell, I have observed that individuals with a preference for Intuition (as opposed to Sensation) in their typological makeup are more likely to find a depth psychological approach to careers and vocation to be resonant and relevant. This is because Intuition is the process of "indirect perception by way of the unconscious, incorporating ideas or associations that the unconscious tacks on to perceptions coming from outside",[11] whereas Sensation is a process of perception directly through the five senses, which emphasises realism, concrete detail and practicality. *In other words, a person with a psychological predisposition towards Intuition will more readily feel validated by a vocational guidance approach which values the unconscious and imaginative potential.*

Having said this, I do not suggest that a depth psychological approach to vocation is only relevant for intuitive types. It will also be valuable for those with a Sensing preference,[12] particularly in the second half of life when they are tasked with psychologically coming to terms with their neglected inferior function of Intuition. As Jung observed, "You can see how they [Sensing types] get into a hole that is just nothing but reality and they need intuition very badly in order to crawl out of it, to have the feeling that life is really lived".[13] Individuation necessitates a developing clarity and relationship with the whole of the psyche, including coming to terms with one's inferior and undeveloped functions. Sooner or later, we are each tasked with coming to terms with all of the functions and the particular hierarchy which they assume within us.

A person whose typology does not conform to the general style of his or her family, or profession, or culture, will likely conclude that he or she is wrong, or inadequate, or not fitting in. This is how I felt working in the legal profession, where I tried to adapt to an environment which placed heavy demands on my functions of Thinking and Sensation, when my innate typological preferences were Intuition and Feeling. Many people inadvertently do this, working exhaustively against their innate typological preferences to try to fit into cultures which simply value and reward different preferences – the preference for extraversion, for example, over introversion. Or vice versa. It is healing to accept our innate typological makeup and to find an environment which recognises and values the particular gifts we have to bring.

The collective devaluation and deprecation of certain psychological functions is a major reason why I have considered it important to write this book articulating an approach to careers and vocation from a depth psychological perspective. Mainstream assumptions and approaches to career development have tended to reflect the bias of Western culture towards extraversion, thinking and sensation over introversion, feeling and intuition. As Whitmont observed:

> Western development has overstressed abstract, rational thought. It has concerned itself predominantly with the practical utilization of external things and external needs and has . . . largely disregarded – or at least relegated to a position of lesser importance – the emotional and intuitive sides of man. . . .
>
> The types most likely to be injured in this respect – victims of our current Western cultural bias – are those of introverted feeling and intuition. While still children they may find themselves misunderstood and may easily be deflected into an attempt at functional adaptation which is not genuinely their own.[14]

More often than not, such types who have been victims of this current Western cultural bias are girls and women – as well as those boys and men who are in touch with what have been regarded as the feminine aspects of the psyche.[15] There is a good proportion of the population – and of our own psyches – that is not sufficiently served by traditional approaches to vocational and career guidance, with their emphasis on methodical reasoning and analysis based on known data. Yet we know from quantitative research, for example, that Intuitive types consistently obtain higher average IQ scores than Sensing types.[16] So as a society, why are we not offering an approach to education and vocation that acknowledges and engages this mode of intelligence too?

It is now time that the Sensation-Thinking dominant approaches to work and vocational guidance which were developed in the modernist paradigm of the early 20th century evolve to re-value and encompass the faculties of Feeling and Intuition as ways of knowing too. In the next chapter, we consider a Jungian model of the psyche, which makes a move in this direction.

Suggestions for reflection and exploration

- What role has Intuition played in receiving your vocational call and enacting that calling in and for the world? What are the roles of Feeling, Sensation and Thinking in the dynamics of your vocation?
- Take the online MBTI instrument at www.mbtionline.com or self-assess your MBTI type using one of the following books. Identify the associated functions and their order of your type. You may wish to have a follow-up discussion with an MBTI professional to gain a better understanding of your best-fit type.
- What insights does your typology offer into your career choices? In what ways might a knowledge of psychological type be useful for you going forward?
- For more on psychological type, occupations and the MBTI:

  - Haas, L & Hunziker, M 2011, *Building blocks of personality type: A guide to using the eight-process model of personality type*, TypeLabs, Temecula, CA.
  - Jung, CG 1933, 'A psychological theory of types', in *Modern man in search of a soul*, Harcourt, New York (ch. 4).

- Martin, CR 2009, *Looking at type: Your career: Using psychological type to find your best-fit career*, Center for Applications of Psychological Type, Gainesville, FL.
- Myers, IB & Myers, PB 1995, *Gifts differing: Understanding personality type*, Davies-Black, Palo Alto, CA.

Notes

1 Myers et al. 1998.
2 Whitmont 1991, pp. 146–147.
3 Spoto 1995.
4 For a discussion of type and occupation, see Myers and Myers (1995, ch. 14) or Martin (2009).
5 Jung 1933, p. 118.
6 Atwood & Stolorow 2004; Ellenberger 1970, p. 288.
7 Jung 1935 CW18, para. 275.
8 Jung 1954b CW16, para. 83.
9 cited in Tacey 2014, p. 468.
10 Whitmont 1991, p. 152.
11 Myers & Myers 1995, p. 2.
12 See, for example, my comments regarding Peter, who identified with a Sensation preference, in Chapter 6, note 4.
13 Jung 1960a, p. 148.
14 Whitmont 1991, pp. 16–17, 155.
15 See Chapter 6 and note 27 for discussion of feminine aspects of the psyche.
16 Myers et al. 1998, p. 269.

5   A Jungian understanding of the psyche and vocation

After I resigned from my job as a lawyer and made my sea/tree change, I eventually requalified as a careers practitioner and established a holistic private practice working with adults in midlife. However, I remained troubled by the feeling that there was a deeper calling that I was just not heeding; that somehow I was not yet fully *in* the current of my own life. My dreams troubled me too. For about ten years, I had been visited by recurring dreams. Dreams repeatedly presenting similar motifs indicate that a vital message is endeavouring to reach consciousness.[1] My recurring dreams were of frustrated journeying – on a train, bus, elevator, boat, airport terminal – trying to arrive at some unknown but vitally important destination. The etymology of the word 'career' means "a running or course through life", and it became obvious that these dreams signified some acute career frustration. Caught up in other people's journeys, I was being frustrated from going on my own. Yet even with my professional repertoire of career counselling approaches, I could find no outward solution to my dilemma.

One day, I decided to try working with the dream images instead. I had yet to learn about the various depth psychological techniques of dream tending, but I let myself drop into a relaxed reverie, allowing myself to re-enter the dream state and reimagine its ending. For example, what if, instead of being stuck in traffic, in the dream I could *fly*?

This imaginative work with my dream images (similar to the Jungian technique of **active imagination**) seemed to expand my horizons, not only psychologically but physically. Inspired by the idea of flight, I imagined escaping from my dreamscape logjams in Wonder Woman's personal glass plane. I began to look further afield and abroad for my next vocational steps. Over the internet, I discovered the Pacifica Graduate Institute in California, offering graduate degrees in the tradition of depth psychology. It was a long way from my home in Australia, but I was gripped with a sense of excitement about studying there.

On my first trip to California for an admissions interview, I had the uncanny experience of all my frustrated travel dreams actually playing out in real life. The weather was bad and the bus to the airport was delayed, I went to the wrong terminal, officials were difficult and obstructive and the lines were so long that I almost missed flight connections . . . it seemed I wound never arrive at my destination. Eventually I did arrive at Pacifica, and this synchronistic convergence between my dreams and waking life, heightened by further synchronicities on campus and a profound sense of coming home as I walked the land and sensed the *genius loci* (spirit of the place), all affirmed to me that this was indeed the important place that my dreams were telling me I needed to be.

This experience vividly illustrated to me what Jung described as "the prospective function" of the dream which, he said, "is sometimes greatly superior to the combinations we can consciously foresee".[2] Indeed, the dreaming psyche knew much better than I did what my next career steps should be! After I began my postgraduate education in depth psychology, those travel dreams I'd had for ten years abruptly stopped and never recurred. Other persistent physical symptoms I'd suffered which spoke symbolically of stuckness, such as a fungal nail condition in my big toe which had been doggedly resistant to all medical treatment, suddenly cleared up too.

Years later, after I had completed two Master's degrees in the United States and was wondering about my next direction, I had another simple but significant dream:

> *An Australian cattle dog, known as a blue heeler, is waiting for me in the back garden. It looks like the dog which belonged to my great-Grandmother [who was born and lived in country New South Wales]. The dog wants to go south.*

The Jungian analyst Marie-Louise von Franz observed that if there was one single rule which had no exception, whether in dreams, in fairy tales or in real life, it was always to follow the helpful animal.[3] This dream counselled me that my path at that juncture was to 'go south', to return to Australia and to complete my PhD thesis in my home country. Upon waking from this dream, I experienced a synchronistic amplification of its message. I wandered to the particular place in my garden where the dog had been waiting for me in the dream and unexpectedly found a dark purple plum on the ground. Upon investigation, I discovered that the plum came from a nearby native rainforest tree, *Davidsonia jerseyana*, commonly known as Davidson's plum. Davidson is my married name, by which I was known at the time – so this fruit literally had my name on it! Davidson's plums grow on the trunk of the tree, completely hidden under the leaves, but are quite inedible in their natural state. They are highly nutritious and earthy but also sour and quite bitter, requiring a cooking process to be palatable. Over time I came to see this fruit as a metaphor for my PhD thesis: it too was to require a lengthy alchemical cooking process for its fruits to become palatable. It has seemed to me that writing this book has been part of the final cooking process. The dreaming psyche is fond of puns, and the pun of the "blue heeler/healer" in the dream was not lost on me either. Blue is the colour of the throat chakra, and like many women, I have discovered that following my vocation is related to healing my voice and power of expression. I discuss this further in Chapter 10.

So I discovered that paying attention to dreams could be a method of vocational guidance. It is as if our dreams are a call from the psyche beckoning us more deeply towards individuation and our unique vocations. Dreams are one way by which the psyche provides guidance for the soul's opus through symbols and images. Jung considered that dreams are spontaneous expressions from the unconscious or the objective psyche, which is the source of wisdom and insight beyond what is known to the ego.

A Jungian model of the psyche

In this chapter, I want to introduce and clarify some key ideas in Jungian psychology, as they pertain to vocation – concepts such as the **psyche**, the **unconscious**, **archetypes**, **individuation** and the **Self**. I offer suggestions for further introductory reading at the end of the chapter.

Figure 5.1 illustrates a basic Jungian model of the psyche. However, Jung's theory of the psyche is indeed difficult to convey in a two-dimensional diagram, as it is not a two-dimensional, nor even a three-dimensional, thing. Nevertheless, this diagram may be helpful to visualise the relationships between the concepts I will discuss.

The Jungian model of the psyche is of course one of many psychological theories. In fact, Jung himself said he didn't have a theory of the psyche so much as a 'working hypothesis'. Nevertheless, Jung's structural fantasy of the psyche is the best conceptual framework I have found to begin to comprehend and work with lived experience from a psycho-spiritual perspective. Jung developed a valuable vocabulary to describe different psychological dynamics, although it is important to remember that all the terms used here are simply commonly agreed upon "code words . . . to denote certain areas of symbolic experience".[4] A Jungian framework

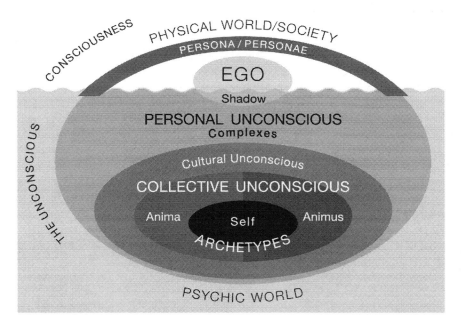

Figure 5.1 A Jungian model of the psyche.

provides an intellectually rigorous yet flexible and creative way of understanding the mysterious and compelling nature of vocational callings. It also offers us insights into how we might receive and collaborate with our callings more mindfully, by paying attention to symptoms, synchronicities and our dreams. I will return to discuss the role of dreams in providing vocational guidance at the end of this chapter.

The unconscious and the archetypes[5]

From a depth psychological perspective, our movement towards wholeness – and vocational authenticity – emerges through the relationship between the conscious mind and the unconscious or imaginal worlds. For Freud, the unconscious was of an exclusively personal nature. It was the gathering place of forgotten and repressed thoughts, emotions and memories. For Jung, the term *unconscious* had a more expansive meaning. It included both contents repressed or inaccessible to the ego (the **personal unconscious** or subjective psyche) *and* a psychic arena with its own properties and functions (the **collective unconscious** or objective psyche).

Jung believed that the collective unconscious does not derive from personal experience but is universal to all people. It is a field of fundamental possibilities inherited from the long history of experiences of the human species which finds expression through various cultural and personal filters, such as myths and dreams. The Jungian unconscious is both vast and inexhaustible, including not only thoughts and emotions that have been repressed but also contents that may or will become conscious:

> The unconscious depicts an extremely fluid state of affairs: everything of which I know, but of which I am not at the moment thinking; everything of which I was once conscious but have now forgotten; everything perceived by my senses, but not noted by my conscious mind; everything which, involuntarily and without paying attention to it, I feel, think, remember, want, and do; all the future things that are taking shape in me and will sometime come to consciousness: all this is the content of the unconscious.[6]

Jung theorised that the collective unconscious is populated by **archetypes** as inherent structuring principles. Archetypes might be described most simply as universal patterns of the psyche. Related to instincts, Jung considered archetypes to be pre-existing psychic formations which inform experience and being.[7] The etymology of *archetype*, from the Greek *arkhetupon*, refers to the original pattern or stamp from which copies are made.

The archetypes . . . are the ruling powers, the gods, images of the dominant laws and principles, and of typical, regularly occurring events in the soul's cycle of experience.

~ CG Jung (1960b CW7, para. 151)

Yet, in truth the term 'archetype' defies simple definition. There is a great deal of misunderstanding about archetypes which misses the nuance and specificity of Jung's understanding. In popular and new age parlance, the notion of an archetype is frequently treated in a simplistic, reductive fashion, becoming synonymous with a stereotype. Jung's theory of archetypes is one of the most misunderstood aspects of his work. In part, this difficulty relates to the different ways in which Jung described these patterns.

Jung spoke of the "indefiniteness of the archetype, with its multiple meanings"[8] and offered numerous thoughts about the nature of archetypes throughout his life. Among these was his description of archetypes as "active – living dispositions, ideas in the Platonic sense that preform and continually influence our thoughts and feelings and actions".[9] One of the metaphors Jung used to describe the relationship between archetypes and instincts was the infrared-ultraviolet light spectrum, where at the infrared end, the archetype pertains to the world of instincts, such as mothering and nurturing, and the patterned way in which a bird builds its nest; whereas at the ultraviolet end of the spectrum, there is the realm of imagery, symbols and spiritual principles.[10] Jung also likened archetypes to riverbeds, in which the water of life has flowed for centuries, digging deep channels,[11] and to a crystalline structure which contains the propensity for certain types of formation and experiences. Archetypes are often envisaged as gods and goddesses or by names such as Hero, Lover, Sage, Trickster, Child, Mother and Healer. They have been described as 'partial personalities' appearing in myth, art, cinema and literature, as well as in dreams, family roles, emotions and pathologies. Archetypes appear in the artefacts of culture, the motifs of nature and the patterns of humanity. We encounter archetypes as well in the perspectives that rule our ideas and feelings about the world and about ourselves.

There is a tendency in popular writing and on occasion by Jung himself to personify the archetypes of the collective unconscious. This can make the concept of archetypes appealing and accessible; however, it can also lead to reductive literalism where the images that gather around an archetype collapse into something closer to a stereotype. Technically, it is incorrect to suggest that the archetype itself can be known: it can only be perceived by its effect, or through an **archetypal image**, which is the form or representation which the archetype takes in consciousness. Jung considered that archetypes are "the imperishable elements of the unconscious, but they change their shape constantly".[12] In other words, the archetype itself is unrepresentable, but it manifests and takes shape in consciousness as an archetypal image, which is always coloured by the individual and the cultural and historical context in which the archetype appears. So when a person speaks of this or that archetype, he or she is more accurately referring to an archetypal image.

Most importantly, archetypes connect us with the power of imagination. James Hillman observed that archetypes throw us into an imaginative style of discourse, leading us to envisage the nature of the soul and approach questions of psychology in an imaginative way. This creative imagination, which some have called 'the divine power in men', is not only the source of art and ingenuity but also a means of discovering deeper truths about our world.

Perhaps Jung's most significant accomplishment was to reveal the unconscious and the archetypes as the creative source of all that we eventually become as individuals:

> The unconscious also contains the dark springs of instinct and intuition, it contains all those forces which mere reasonableness, propriety, and the orderly course of bourgeois existence could never call awake, all those creative forces which lead man onwards to new developments, new forms, and new goals. . . . The influence of the unconscious . . . adds to consciousness everything that has been excluded by the drying up of the springs of intuition and by the fixed pursuit of a single goal.[13]

So if we want to experience creative, revitalising breakthroughs in our lives and work, then appreciating the magnitude and the role of the unconscious and the archetypes is essential.[14]

Individuation and the Self

Jung considered the **Self** to be the central archetype, or the archetype of wholeness, which unifies the various archetypal contents of the psyche. Among other images of wholeness and totality which could be seen to represent the Self, Jung demonstrated that the Self was expressed by symbolic images called mandalas. During the period of Jung's own midlife "confrontation with the unconscious", to bring to consciousness and develop his relationship with the Self, he painted a series of mandalas which are reproduced in *Liber Novus (The Red Book)*. Some of these were representations of images Jung received in dreams.

Jung described the Self as the inner empirical deity, or the God within,[15] the central source of life energy, the fountain of our being. It comprises all the possibilities of our life; everything that we are capable of becoming. Jung went as far as to write that the Self might as well be called "God in us".[16] In this sense, the ego-Self relationship mirrors the human-divine relationship. The **ego** is the centre of the conscious personality, while the Self is the ordering and unifying centre of the total psyche. Jungians have taken to capitalising the term *Self* to distinguish it from the commonplace use of the word *self*, which is equivalent to the personal ego or 'I' (though Jung himself did not capitalise the term in his writing, which has led to some confusion).

In his classic book *Ego and Archetype*, the Jungian analyst Edward Edinger observed that the relationship between the ego and the Self can be imagined as that creative point where God and man meet, where transpersonal energies flow into personal life. However, since the ego and the Self are two autonomous centres of psychic being, the ego's relationship with the Self is not only important but also highly problematic. It can be likened to man's relation to his Creator as depicted in religious myth, particularly the Christian myth, which can be seen as a mythic expression of the ego-Self relationship. "Many of the vicissitudes of psychological development", observed Edinger, "can be understood in terms of the changing relation between ego and Self at various stages of psychic growth".[17] The relationship between the ego and Self is one which develops over a lifetime. A healthy ego is one that recognises and maintains this connection (or axis) to the Self. When we talk about following our inner guidance, or higher Self, or being on our path, in Jungian terms, what we're referring to is the axis between ego and Self.

Jung coined the term **individuation** to describe this cultivation of an ongoing dialogue between the ego and the unconscious, and particularly with the archetype of the Self. Jung's approach to individuation entails working with dreams, wrestling with complexes, engaging with fantasy life and withdrawing projections.[18] Jung described individuation as:

> a process informed by the archetypal ideal of wholeness, which in turn depends on a vital relationship between ego and unconscious. The aim is not to overcome one's personal psychology, to become perfect, but to become familiar with it. Thus individuation involves an increasing awareness of one's unique psychological reality, including personal strengths and limitations, and at the same time a deeper appreciation of humanity in general.[19]

According to Jung, the goal of individuation is the development of the individual personality, or becoming one's own self, as distinct from the general, collective psychology. As we shall see in the next chapter, Jung considered that individuation was properly triggered around midlife, although it is indeed the work of a lifetime.[20] Jung described the goal of individuation as being reached (if indeed it is ever reached) when a person experiences the Self "as something irrational, as an indefinable being to which the I is neither opposed nor subjugated, but in a relation of dependence, and around which it revolves, very much as the earth revolves around the sun".[21] So individuation involves the dethronement or displacement of the ego as the centre of the individual's sphere. Let's not underestimate the magnitude of this shift! This is an ontological shift of profound magnitude, a revolution in the worldview of each and every individual. This is indeed no small thing in our comprehension of the universe and our place in it.

Although individuation is on the one hand a solitary process, Jung believed that ultimately it must "lead to more intense and broader collective relationships and not to isolation".[22] This suggests that, far from being a 'selfish', egocentric removal of oneself from the collective, individuation (like vocation) is a *call from* and a *response to* the psyche, with the ultimate potential of bestowing some benefit on the community or the collective. This is the real meaning of Joseph Campbell's reference to returning with the 'boon' or the treasure from the epic hero's journey.

Jung's concept of the Self remains relevant today. His ego-Self relationship model has profound implications for how we can understand the nature and source of our callings. As we've seen, Jung likened the Self to an approximation of the God-image, where the ego-Self relationship mirrors the human-divine relationship. So an analogy may be drawn between traditional religious notions of vocation as entailing a call from God (often indicated through dreams, 'signs', meaningful coincidences, etc.) and a Jungian notion of vocation as involving a call from the Self, or the unconscious.

> *We cannot tell whether God and the unconscious are two different entities.*
> *Both are borderline concepts for transcendental contents.*
>
> ~ CG Jung (1952a CW11, para. 757)

However, the Jungian archetype of the Self has also been critiqued as a monotheistic concept reflecting Jung's Christian heritage, problematically defined and possibly redundant given its interchangeability with Jung's use of the word *psyche*.[23] Glen Slater has suggested that the Self is best considered as a concept bridging traditional religious thought and the emerging depth psychology and new sciences of the 21st century.[24] I prefer to use the term *psyche* rather than Self to describe the source from which vocation springs; in part because I feel that *psyche*, a term favoured in post-Jungian and archetypal psychology, is more encompassing of a postmodern pluralistic perspective which accords with people's experiences of work and careers today. Jung also paradoxically defined the Self as both the centre and the whole of the psyche.[25] So for the purposes of this book, I will largely leave the notion of the Self behind and talk about the psyche instead. However, the Self remains a useful psychological concept and a significant archetype in the pantheon of the psyche, particularly when envisaged as "an entity which draws the ego out of its central controlling position and into dialogue with the psyche as a whole".[26]

The psyche and vocation

As the word **psyche** is a central concept in this book, it is important to understand the depth psychological meaning of this term. As I've previously mentioned, *psyché i*s the Greek word for soul. For traditional cultures such as the ancient Greeks and the Navajo, *psyché* was also associated with the breath and with the air, that enveloping invisible medium in which we are always immersed and which gives us life.[27] Similarly, the Jungian concept of the psyche is radically different from and not a synonym for the personal mind. Unlike the Cartesian notion of the personal mind, which is interior and separate from the outer world,[28] the Jungian psyche is not 'in' each of us. Instead, Jung described the psyche as something that surrounds the human being, inside and out, and is antecedent to him or her.[29] According to Jung, the psyche is no more 'inside us' than the sea is inside the fish.

Roger Brooke undertook a very comprehensive study of Jung's use of the word psyche across Jung's *Collected Works*. He arrived at the conclusion that "In contrast to psychoanalysis, for Jung *the psyche is not in each of us, we are in the psyche*. This point is crucial but is often forgotten. It is forgotten that the psyche is the person's world of work, interpersonal relations, and so on".[30] Citing examples from Jung's work as well as case studies from his own analysands, Brooke describes the psyche as "not mind but a landscape within which things are alive with meaning and mystery".[31] The psyche encompasses our world of work and is the "matrix within which our loves, hopes, fears, prayers, and meaningful relationships are embedded – but this matrix is largely unconscious".[32]

Joe Coppin and Elizabeth Nelson, in their beautifully written book *The Art of Inquiry*, summarise this depth view of the psyche as "the great repository of ideas, images, emotions, urges, and desires that appear in the world, whether its source is personal or collective, conscious or unconscious".[33] So just as we are in language, cultural history and the human imagination that surrounds and contains us, we are in the psyche.[34] In this sense, the psyche is similar to what phenomenology situates as the life-world (Husserl's *Lebenswelt*).[35]

In terms of vocation, some scholars have quibbled over the difference between callings considered to stem from an *internal* source – an individual's sense of self and meaningfulness, sometimes classified a secular calling – and an *external* source – which may range from God or a higher being to societal needs or serendipitous fate.[36] Concluding that a calling may arise from either source, one study found that "as long as workers feel they are living out their calling, the source of their calling matters little in terms of how calling links to job and life satisfaction".[37]

However, if we consider vocation as *a calling from the psyche*, the distinction these scholars have debated between 'inner' and 'outer' sources of vocation, or modern and neoclassical approaches to calling,[38] becomes a moot point. "To be more precise, the psyche reveals 'inside' and 'outside' to be powerful cultural metaphors".[39] When a calling arises from the psyche, it will embrace a combination of both 'internal' and 'external' factors – if indeed, we can ever really distinguish between 'internal' and 'external' sources where calling is concerned.[40]

In this book, I explore how we can intuit and navigate our vocations as a process of collaboration and co-authorship with the psyche, or soul. Jung considered that the psyche has a teleological imperative towards individuation, a propensity towards maturation, which means each individual becoming more fully himself or herself. So there is a symbiotic relationship between vocation and individuation, both of which turn on a vital relationship between the ego and the whole of the psyche, including the unconscious. Jung emphasised the psycho-spiritual nature of work that is based on vocation. Work that is based on vocation is also an act of individuation.

What is it that inexorably tips the scales in favour of the extraordinary? It is commonly called vocation: an irrational factor that destines a man to emancipate himself from the herd and its well-worn paths.

~ CG Jung (1934b CW17, paras 299–300)

In contrast to the dominance of positivist, rational approaches to vocational guidance, Jung considered that a defining feature of vocation, beyond heredity or environment, was an "irrational factor", which he likened to a daemon or inner voice.[41] However, Jung believed that to hear this inner voice entails separating oneself from normative paths and assumptions. The history and practice of depth psychology suggests that vocation is not something that we choose but that we experience as a calling from the psyche, which speaks through non-rational means, such as symptoms, complexes, synchronicities, images . . . and through our dreams.

The role of dreams in vocational guidance

Attending to dreams is an integral method of Jungian and archetypal psychology and a prime example of the symbolic approach. There are many ways of working with dreams.[42] In this chapter, I offer only a brief introduction to this fascinating topic to highlight how dreams are one way by which the psyche may guide us vocationally. Psychologist and dream specialist Steven Aizenstat advocated that listening to dreams is integral to a vital workplace and fulfilling work-life, yet he "knows of no career counselling methods or organizational development approaches that include dreamwork".[43] The only example I have found is a research article published in 2002 by Mary Guindon and Fred Hanna, who discussed the dreams of two clients in career counselling as examples of synchronicity (meaningful coincidence) which affirmed their decisions to accept job offers. Yet the authors fall short of advocating dreamwork as a method of vocational guidance. Ironically, professor of career counselling Norman Amundson described a stunning predictive dream he had which foretold a major Lotto win. He lamented that he did not act upon the dream and confessed trying to repeat the dream without success.[44] Perhaps the real golden opportunity waiting to be discovered is how listening to dreams may offer unexpected riches for the field of vocational guidance and career counselling.

In Jungian literature and the practice of analytical psychology, there are often instances of people receiving vocational clarification or insight through dreams. In his autobiography *Memories, Dreams, Reflections*, Jung described how, when facing a career-choice dilemma as a young man, two dreams directing him to seek knowledge of nature convinced him to favour science. It was clear to Jung that he was "living in a time and place where a person had to earn his living",[45] and yet "the spirit of the depths" taught him to consider his action and decision as dependent on dreams.[46]

I began this chapter with a personal account of how attending to recurring dreams led me through a career impasse to engage with my work as a career counsellor at a much deeper level. History provides many examples of writers, artists, designers, architects, scientists and inventors for whom dreams have been a source of inspiration and problem-solving in their work. Novelist Robert Louis Stevenson and surrealist artist Salvador Dali are two obvious examples from the humanities and the arts, but perhaps the most famous instance from science is the German chemist Friedrich August Kekulé, who told of two dreams that he had at key moments of his work. In his first dream, in 1865, Kekulé saw atoms dance around and link to one another. When he awoke, he immediately began to sketch what he saw in his dream. Later, Kekulé had a second dream, in which he saw atoms dance around and form themselves into strings, moving in a snake-like fashion. This vision continued until the snake of atoms formed itself into an image of a snake eating its own tail, which the Greeks called the *ouroboros*, one of the oldest mystical symbols in the world. Kekulé credited the dream with giving him the idea of the cyclic structure of benzene, a discovery which revolutionised modern chemistry.

Unlike Freud, who considered dreams the products of wishes repressed from consciousness and the images in dreams signs pointing to repressed libidinous conflict or trauma (usually sexual), or others who disregard dreams as no more than waste products of consciousness and the residue of daily experience (though dream researchers in general agree that dreaming *per se* is beneficial), Jung considered that dreams have a teleological function. Dreams can provide guidance or prognosis for a situation by working with their symbols. From this perspective, as the Jungian analyst Ed Whitmont wrote, the unconscious is not merely "the cesspool of rejected conscious material but is also the clear spring of future development and growth".[47]

> *The dream is a little hidden door in the innermost and most secret recesses of the soul, opening into that cosmic night which was psyche long before there was any ego-consciousness, and which will remain psyche no matter how far our ego-consciousness may extend.*
> ~ CG Jung (1964 CW10, paras 304–305)

Dreams and vocation, I suggest, come from the same place, the autonomous psyche. Paying attention to the images in one's dreams may help illuminate the unconscious impulse which is guiding us vocationally. Michael Meade beautifully portrays this mysterious relationship between the dream and an authentic calling:

> It is a dream that first calls the soul to life and one's 'calling' in life can come from a dream or seem like a dream. Those who awaken to a genuine calling stand at the junction of the dream and the waking world.[48]

We can follow our dream images like breadcrumbs through a forest, as subtle signs from the psyche to keep us on our vocational trail. For example, Alyce recalled a powerful dream she had when deciding whether to attend graduate school:

> *I am on a boat on a canal looking at this lovely setting [the imaginary graduate school]. . . .*

There is something incredibly soothing about the whole scene. . . . Look-
ing at this beautiful building that has glass on the front of it . . . reflecting the
glassiness of the waterway. For me, after such a tumultuous time . . . this was
such a beautiful juxtaposition of contrasts to all that tumultuousness . . . that's
what mattered . . . the sensation, the calmness of the scene. But I'm moving. I'm
on the boat. . . .

I looked at the scene with longing. This was very much a soul call. How do
I want to live my life now?

I woke up with a strong knowing that this was the right choice.

Alyce experienced a "great longing" as she gazed on this scene of a beautiful place of learning that offered a calming reflection of a waterway (which could be read as a symbol of the unconscious). This affirmed her vocational decision to enrol in a graduate degree in depth psychology. The dream also involved movement on a boat. As I have previously mentioned, dreams relating to movement and travel may be particularly suggestive of one's 'career' through life.

Such accounts suggest that attending to the images that surface in our dreams can help us to intuitively discern our next steps and chart our vocational course. Of course, many Jungian analysts, though not necessarily focused on resolving clients' problems with work, have long been aware of the potential of dreams to offer guidance in this area. Whitmont wrote about a patient whose dream-consciousness operated in anticipation of events. At the time when she dreamed of being given roses by a boss in a new job, she had not even fully realised her frustration in her current position. Subsequently she became aware of it, and with some hesitation and misgivings decided to change employment, a move that ulti-mately gave her a great sense of joy and fulfilment.[49] This example supports the observation that "if one is in touch with the unconscious, one will usually have a glimmer of precognition before a major movement in one's life, whether this movement is created by oneself or happens to one".[50]

Jung considered that dream images appear in symbolic form as compensatory to consciousness, particularly where our conscious position requires balance or redress. In other words, dream images can function to correct a one-sided per-spective that we may hold. Steve, for example, was visited by "really archetypal dreams" just before he started his doctorate. Fish, water, crocodiles and serpents were recurring dream images. As his dreaming became "more articulate", Steve described a "feeling of an intelligence that isn't my ego speaking to me":

I have had many dreams . . . which allude to a direction which must be taken –
not necessarily to do with a career in the material world, but a general trajec-
tory of where I need to be moving. . . .

In one dream, I am in an art gallery, with an acquaintance who in real
life is becoming successful with his filmmaking projects. We are staring at
a massive painting, of a crow in a gum tree. He says, "Look down there" –
and as I look into the shadow, it starts moving, and it is a snake. . . . I fol-
low the snake and . . . enter into that world within the picture. . . . So I'm
there with this guy who possibly represents success, or burgeoning success,

in the material world of filmmaking. It's almost like before, that this is what I should be looking at, but my friend says no, look here, this is what you need to focus on.

There's a specific constellation in this dream that has occurred quite a bit: that what I think I should be doing is interrupted by something else that I need to follow. I feel this has been a recurring element in a lot of my dreams. They are telling me, "you need to pay attention to this".

Whereas Steve might be tempted to jump into pursuing preconceived career avenues, his dreams constantly remind him there is something else important he needs to focus upon. "Look down there", the dream says, "pay attention to these creatures of the underworld". Steve has found his dreams to be instructive regarding how his conscious ideas about his career direction may be different from where the unconscious or the psyche would lead him, illustrating what Jung called the compensatory function of the dream.

Michael told of two significant dreams which helped prepare him to enter and, years later, to leave his occupation as a psychologist. He described a significant dream he had in his junior year of college, when he was enrolled in pre-med:

I decided I had to study the mind. In my dream, I am walking down a long hallway. There is a door with frosted glass, and I see my name on the door, as "Dr Michael X . . ., proctologist". Well, I didn't know what to do, but I knew I couldn't stay in med school. I graduated with an undergraduate degree in psychology. The dream told me: you really want to know the mind? You have to work through the shit.

Michael did not read this dream literally, as a sign that he was to become a proctologist, but symbolically. The dream told him that as a psychologist he needed to be prepared to look hard at the unappealing, "shitty" aspects of life. Decades later, Michael has been working with another dream which he understands as intimating his next vocational stage, to take leave of his work as an academic psychologist. The following is from a written description Michael offered of that dream:

A few years ago I had a dream in which 'I' find myself in an ill lit and stuffy Victorian type parlor where a group of academics, many of whom seem familiar, are gathered in a circle around a discussion. Two details that stand out are how well suited and tied they are and how invisible I seem to be to them. . . .

I begin to wander through the house and find myself in a room where a poet figure, whose guise and dress is vastly different than that of the academic colleagues, is speaking with a woman about the poet Rilke. The poet figure is dressed in shabby clothes, seemingly indifferent to how he might appear to others, and his fingers and teeth are tobacco stained. It is clear in the dream that he has lived life fully and on the edges and margins of convention. The scene is erotic and I am jealous that the poet is with the woman because Rilke has been an important companion in my work as a psychologist. A mood of abandonment comes over me and as I continue my wanderings I find myself with the poet beside me in a kitchen area where ordinary folk are preparing food and drink for the well suited and tied academics. They are talking with each other in loud friendly voices, and even at times breaking into song. The room is airy and light and filled with the nourishing aromas of the food being prepared and the fresh smells of early spring mornings. The poet takes me to a screen door that opens onto a sunlit park where many people are eating, playing ball and with animation and energy living and enjoying life. Standing beside me on the threshold, the poet opens the screen door and points in the direction of that scene. The dream ends there on the threshold.

Like many dreams, this dream is not conclusive for Michael. He is left "on the threshold", on the verge of taking leave of one environment but not yet stepping into another. This illustrates one of the difficulties of relying on dreams for vocational guidance. Dreams are often elusive and always mysterious. Seldom do they expressly announce or dictate a vocational direction. Instead, a dream may leave us "on the threshold". Rather than interpretation, a creative act of imagination may be called for, as I worked with my own dream images of stuckness to find a way through my career impasses, imagining that I could fly.

Michael also described feeling "absolutely released" by this dream and being on this "pivot of the threshold":

That is the perfect myth of my life, and my vocation to be psychological – to be on the threshold.

Michael went on to explain that the dream image of the threshold symbolizes the metaphoric character of psychological life, that place between matter and mind, the domain of soul whose elusive images are neither matters of fact nor ideas of mind.

The examples I have offered here show how dreams may indicate that something (external or internal) needs changing in our career situation, or they may beckon us to our next step. It's been said that dreams "depict the difference between vocation and obligatory employment. They offer ideas about unrealized aptitude and point to inherent gifts".[51] Dreams supply those permutations of our individual 'myths', the stories or perspectives we are living, which consciousness excludes or ignores. "Write down your dreams", counselled Joseph Campbell, "they are your myths".[52] We can think of our dreams, and our vocations, as both coming from the same place, the deep psyche or soul. As an expression of the psyche bypassing the conscious ego, dreams may direct our attention towards aspects which need tending in the process of our individuation and vocational fulfilment. Paying attention to the images in our dreams can point the way to the authentic impulse at the root of our calling.

Suggestions for research and reflection

- For a more detailed introductory overview to Jungian psychology, I recommend:

  - Dunne, C 2000, *Carl Jung: Wounded healer of the soul – an illustrated biography*, Parabola Books, London.
  - Stevens, A 2001, *Jung: A very short introduction*, Oxford University Press, Oxford, UK.
  - Tacey, D 2006, *How to read Jung*, Granta Books, London.
  - Tacey, D (ed.) 2012, *The Jung reader*, Routledge, Hove, UK.

- Keep a dream journal by your bed. Be particularly sure to record any dreams you have on the threshold of this work and as you read this book, as well as any 'big' or recurring dreams.
- For further guidance on working with your dreams, consult with a Jungian analyst or Jungian oriented psychotherapist and/or read:

  - Aizenstat, S 2009, *Dream tending: Techniques for uncovering the hidden intelligence of your dreams*, Spring Journal, New Orleans, LA.
  - Bosnak, R 1986, *A little course in dreams*, Shambala, Boston.
  - Johnson, RA 1986, *Inner work: Using dreams and active imagination for personal growth*, Harper Collins, New York.
  - Jung, CG 1974, *Dreams*, trans. RFC Hull, Princeton University Press, Princeton, NJ.

Notes

1 Whitmont 1991, p. 43.
2 Jung 1974, p. 41.
3 von Franz 1995, pp. 145–146.
4 Whitmont 1991, p. 35.
5 Several paragraphs in this section are reproduced from my article published in the *International Journal for Educational and Vocational Guidance* (Cremen 2019).
6 Jung 1969 CW8, para. 382.
7 Jung (1911–12 CW5, para. 224). In recent times, the notion of whether the archetype is pre-existing or emergent has been contested in some Jungian circles; see for example Colman (2015) and Hill (2015).
8 Jung 1946 CW16, para. 497.
9 Jung 1938 CW9, para. 154.
10 Jung 1954a CW8, para. 414.
11 Jung 1989a, p. 20.
12 Jung 1940 CW9:1, para. 301.
13 Jung 1918 CW10, para. 25.
14 It is worth noting in passing that archetypal psychologist James Hillman (1972) advocated for the renunciation of the term *unconscious*, which he argued perpetuates a fantasy of opposites. He favoured the idea of an *imaginal ego*, in the lineage of Henri Corbin and Jung's more developed ideas, which builds awareness of the deep psyche into its field of consciousness. This idea becomes significant as the reader advances in an understanding of Jungian and archetypal psychology.

15 Jung 1952a CW11, para. 757.
16 Jung 2009, p. 218.
17 Edinger 1972, p. 4.
18 For practical guides on these techniques, see, for example, Johnson (1986), Aizenstat (2009) and Bosnak (1986).
19 Jung 1921 CW6, para. 758.
20 Jung 1970 CW18, para. 1099.
21 Jung 1928b CW7, para. 405.
22 Jung 1921 CW6, para. 758.
23 Brooke 2009, p. 604.
24 Slater 1996, p. 171.
25 Jung 1974, p. 115.
26 Slater 1996, p. 173. Drawing on Hillman's (1975) work, perhaps there is room in the psyche for both monotheistic and polytheistic "styles of consciousness" such that the (monotheistic) Self leads the ego into dialogue with a (polytheistic) psyche. In this way, individuation may be imagined as an ongoing dialogue with an array of inner figures and forces in the psyche, for "the ego is not the whole psyche, only one member of a commune" (Hillman 1975, p. 31), and "the ego's submission is to the many archetypes that comprise the self and call that particular individual" (Brooke 2015, p. 20).
27 Abrams 2017, pp. 237–238.
28 Bordo 1986, p. 451.
29 Jung 1967 CW13, para. 75.
30 Brooke 2015, p. 80. However, even for Jung, whose intuitive understanding of psychological life arguably surpassed many of his theoretical formulations, there are many reasons for 'forgetting' this understanding of psyche. Brooke identifies the historical drag of Cartesian thought as well as analytical psychology's relationship with psychoanalysis (see also Slater 2012, p. 28). Jung introduced the term *objective psyche* to stress that the psyche is not to be confused with or limited to the boundaries of the individual person, whose personal psychology or *subjective psyche* is organised around the ego (Jung 1960b CW7, para. 103). The ego is the centre of the conscious personality and the seat of one's subjective identity. However, in my opinion, Brooke makes a convincing argument that the terms *objective* and *subjective* psyche are essentially redundant, as "the 'subjective psyche' refers essentially to the ego complex, and the 'objective psyche' refers to no more than what Jung had called psyche all along" (2015, p. 80). Therefore, unless otherwise qualified, I use the term psyche in the all-encompassing sense described in this section.
31 Brooke 2009, p. 609.
32 Brooke 2015, p. 90.
33 Coppin & Nelson 2005, p. 5.
34 This perspective is echoed by Hillman, who states that, "Man exists in the midst of psyche . . . it is not the other way around . . . and there is much of psyche that extends beyond the nature of man" (1975, p. 173). Organisational theorist Gareth Morgan describes Jung's "holistic view of the psyche as a universal phenomenon that is ultimately part of a transcendental reality linking mind to mind and mind to nature" (2006, p. 230). See also Sabini (2002) for how psyche and nature are inextricably woven.
35 Brooke 2015, p. 82.
36 Dik & Duffy 2009; Hall & Chandler 2005.
37 Duffy et al. 2013, p. 562.
38 Duffy & Dik 2013, p. 429.
39 Rowland 2012, p. 38.
40 Metcalfe (2013) also argues that vocation suspends notions of 'inner' and 'outer', subjectivity and objectivity.
41 Jung 1934b CW17, para. 299.

42 To briefly summarise four of the main approaches to working with dreams: Sigmund Freud (1952) considered the dream's primary purpose was wish-fulfilment, to be approached by free association leading to analysis and interpretation of the dream images as signs pointing to repressed libidinous conflict or trauma. Carl Jung considered that the dream is compensatory to consciousness, particularly where the conscious position requires balance or redress. He endorsed the prospective function of the dream, by which he meant that a dream may foretell a scenario and "is sometimes greatly superior to the combinations we can consciously foresee" (Jung 1974, p. 41). Jung's principal methods of working with dreams were amplification – a method of association based on the comparative study of mythology, religion and fairytales – and active imagination – a method of voluntary involvement with the dream or fantasy image to assimilate it into consciousness using some form of self-expression such as drawing, painting, writing, sculpture, dance or music. James Hillman believed that the dream is not compensatory but initiatory, as "each dream is practice in entering the underworld, a preparation of the psyche for death" (1979, p. 133), and warned against modes of dream interpretation which surreptitiously inflate the ego. Robert Bosnak's (1986, 2007) "embodied dreamwork" trains an individual to simultaneously hold a variety of feelings and sensations in the body by working with a dream image, with the aim of therapeutic healing on many levels including the psychological and the physical.

43 Aizenstat 2009, p. 129.

44 Amundson 2003c, pp. 162–163.

45 Jung 1989b, p. 85.

46 Jung 2009, p. 233.

47 Whitmont 1991, p. 50.

48 Meade 2010, p. 141.

49 Whitmont 1991, p. 216.

50 Kaufmann 2009, p. 63.

51 Aizenstat 2009, p. 129.

52 Campbell 1991, p. 124.

6 The abduction from career to calling

My experience of the belly of the whale is that it's not a choice and you see where it takes you, but it's almost as if you are abducted or forced into the belly of the whale. And many times we are abducted into our vocations.

(Lynn)

Dreams are one way by which the psyche may guide us in life and work. In this chapter, I discuss some other ways by which we are beckoned, sometimes even abducted, by the psyche beyond existing career paths into a deeper sense of vocation. For many people, this occurs around midlife, as we encounter the shadow parts of ourselves that have been repressed. Symptoms such as depression may arrive, as well as discomfort with the mask or persona that has developed to fulfil occupational and societal expectations.

We do not work in isolation but always in some kind of cultural, occupational or professional context. In Chapter 3, I spoke of the feelings of discomfort and depression I experienced in my early career as a lawyer. In this chapter, I bring a depth psychological perspective to consider the shadow side of occupations and workplaces, with a particular focus on the high incidence of depression throughout the legal profession. The chapter concludes with some compelling stories and discussion of the descent into the *nekyia* (night sea journey), a psychological experience by which one may find oneself 'abducted' into a vocation.

Encountering the shadow

As we have seen, the **ego** is the centre of our personal identity and consciousness. It is the originator of our value judgements and our personal will, which translates our decisions into actions towards specific goals. The development of a strong ego is necessary for a sense of agency in the world, which requires firstly learning collective moral standards and taboos. Approaches to career development focus upon helping individuals to develop ego strength and negotiate the job market. But along with the brightening light of the ego grows the individual's concomitant shadow.

The concept of the **shadow** corresponds with Freud's understanding of that which is repressed, including unrecognised desires and repressed portions of the personality. It flows from discoveries and analyses made by Freud and Jung of the split between the light and dark sides of the human psyche. Jung described this personal shadow as the *other* in us: "the 'negative' side of the personality, the sum of all those unpleasant qualities we like to hide, together with the insufficiently developed functions and the content of the personal unconscious".[1] Most simply, while the ego is what we are and know about consciously, the shadow is that part of ourselves that we fail to see or know.

Although the shadow will generally consist of what the ego considers to be inferiorities or negative qualities (due to shame, social pressure and/or family and societal attitudes), the shadow may also contain positive elements. There can be 'gold' in the shadow, which occurs for example in the phenomenon of hero-worshipping, where we project qualities onto another that we fail to recognise in ourselves. Our shadow contains much psychic energy and unlived life potential.

In every occupation, certain skills and aptitudes are encouraged and developed while others are relegated to the shadow. For example, Peter was in his mid-fifties and had a successful career as a specialised engineer. Although he enjoyed his occupation, Peter expressed deep disappointment and frustration that as a child he wasn't allowed or encouraged to focus more on the humanities, as were his siblings. It is not unusual for a sibling to carry another's shadow;[2] Jung observed that a man's shadow is often represented in myth, literature and dreams as a brother.[3] The only one in the family demonstrating mechanical or scientific aptitude, Peter felt that he was tasked in that role of scientist and that it became his task to hold that part for the family as a whole.

> *I did not have any apparent talents that I thought I could bring to bear that would earn me a living in the humanities. I justified some of it [my engineering career] by the fact if you're working in a scientific field . . . you can find yourself doing very innovative work.*

As well as carrying the vocational scientific shadow of his artistically inclined siblings, Peter's work as an engineer repressed parts of his own psyche into the shadow: in particular, his conflicted feelings about the ethics and consequences of his assigned work.

> *I had to take those feelings and pretty much put them away. As an engineer you really don't use feelings to evaluate things. You want to approach things very scientifically, on a rational, logical basis. There is room for intuition, but not a whole lot of room for feelings. So I found myself having to take on a certain role in order to be a good engineer. And it didn't feel entirely comfortable at all. It didn't fit me as well as it fit many of the other engineers I was working with.*

After the trauma of a divorce in midlife, what Peter considered to be his vocation in the humanities and psychology began to flourish. He started making stained glass, creating pieces that were "quite alchemical in nature", although he didn't know this at the time.

> *I came to realise that I had an ability that was clearly not nurtured as a child. . . . I took what I was trying to express and expressed it through my artwork. That was very helpful, although I didn't understand what I was creating. . . . There were aspects that I didn't understand at the time but which were expressions of what I was going through and the kind of things I needed to work out. I could never have got there through my regular career work.*
>
> *My vocation for me is where I really address the things that are interior to myself. They are not external aptitudes.*

On the one hand, Peter considers it was right to use the scientific aptitudes he had in a career. On the other hand, he thinks he was only listening to part of himself too.

> *That career was a good move. It was a part of myself that I really needed to feed. But it is just as important, I've come to realise, to feed that other part of myself that I was really suppressing in order to do that work. What I've come to find is that I have to shift between them. And it's quite a shift.*
>
> *Later in life, having achieved a career and a means of support, I could accept and allow those aspects of my psyche that maybe I should have listened to all along. I listened to the [other inner] voice and was able to go in that direction. . . .*
>
> *My career wasn't imaginal; it was much more what I considered to be what was right in front of me. Now I've given myself license to explore those possibilities, and I find it's very important, because we're talking about the imaginal part of the psyche, which is at least half of you. It's a significant part of yourself, and if you ignore it, I think it's going to come back and bring itself to your attention, one way or another.*

Peter's awareness and attention to owning his shadow and developing the previously neglected, "imaginal part" of his psyche accords with Jung's recommendation to confront the opposites within ourselves, the *sine qua non* of the individuation process.[4] It is also a move towards the development of what James Hillman called an "imaginal ego",[5] one which builds an awareness of the deep psyche into its field of consciousness.

Not only in engineering but also in many other occupations and workplaces, qualities traditionally regarded as '**masculine**',[6] such as logical thought, planning, assertiveness, professional detachment and a focus on goals, are regarded as desirable. For many men and women, their countervailing qualities, traditionally associated with the '**feminine**', such as feeling, intuition, vulnerability, empathy and a process-orientation, have been discounted and repressed in the pursuit of a career. It is these latter qualities to which I refer in association with the expression 'feminine consciousness', although I acknowledge that the use of terms such as masculine and feminine can be problematic in wider social discourse. Although depth psychology has long held both men and women to be "psychologically bisexual",[7] the masculine (yang) aspect of consciousness is considered to pertain to "law, order, differentiation, separation, and aggression",[8] whereas the feminine (yin) aspect of consciousness pertains to qualities such as eros, relatedness, contemplation and spiritual wisdom. Feminine consciousness "is a less differentiated, less aggressively defensive and more reflective aspect of consciousness".[9] Symbolically, the feminine mode of consciousness has been associated with the moon, which shines in the darkness of night only after the bright solar light (associated with masculine consciousness) has disappeared and the activities of the workaday world are laid aside.[10]

Now in her early forties, Nikki recounted how in her previous work as a marketer, what she describes as a "lunar, feminine consciousness" was in her shadow. Nikki described this feminine consciousness as "an instinctual knowing that is willing to be very moment to moment, and responsive to the present moment"; prior to this, she was very singular in masculine consciousness.

> *With the feminine consciousness, there is a leap of faith that is present; with the masculine consciousness, there is a bit of a plan laid out. When the plan falls apart, it feels like your world falls apart. The feminine consciousness was very much in my shadow, and it would kind of burst out and I would be able to work very well with symbols, but not very consciously. It was only when I started to become conscious of what I was doing, which was very near the end of my marketing career, that I felt like I couldn't do it with integrity anymore.*

Ultimately, Nikki's need for psychological integrity meant that she could not deny the resurgence of this feminine consciousness in her psyche. As Christina Becker writes, "We are challenged to move to a more sophisticated morality when we see that we have been using denial or self-deception to push the Shadow away".[11] Nikki attributed much of her professional success as a marketer to the ability of the feminine consciousness to work with symbols and archetypes. However, as she became more conscious of how she was using this ability (even apparently benignly) to manipulate the consumption of products and services, it raised nuanced ethical questions about the ends to which those talents were applied.

Nikki described how that lunar feminine consciousness which was emergent in her was also in the shadow of her occupation and the workplace itself.

> *Working in that world of business planning, and marketing strategy, and budgets – that is all very masculine. Very linear, and very cause and effect, and this amount of money goes to this amount of project and it will have this amount of return. . . . It is very wilful. It also felt a bit arrogant, because*

I think we also believed we were individually responsible for the success, and in fact that's rarely the case. Especially in marketing where so much of it relies on creative marketing, and creativity comes from a deeper place. Anybody who is creative can tell you they need to find a space to let that come forward, because it is not coming from them. So there is an awareness of it, for sure, but it is still in a very masculine environment.

Peter's and Nikki's experiences of the shadow aspects of their working lives give phenomenological support to Jung's observation that what is repressed or suppressed, deliberately ignored or devalued, gradually accumulates and over time begins to influence consciousness.[12] As Jung wrote and as Nikki's experiences testify, the unconscious realm is also the space from which genuine creativity and innovation emerge – qualities frequently so elusive to harness in organisational and corporate life and yet so prized by those able to make leaps in their fields. Such creativity will be blocked and stagnate if a linear, logos, 'masculine' consciousness is hegemonic and quells other ways of knowing.[13]

Nikki's account of the shadow aspects of her occupation and workplace also show how Jung's ideas about individual psychology can translate to organisations and workplace systems. An organisation's shadow comprises those aspects incommensurate with its branding, or ideal image of itself. John Corlett and Carol Pearson have shown that repression, denial (hypocrisy), projection and scapegoating are common mechanisms when an organisation's "centre of consciousness" is confronted with its shadow.[14]

Listening to the symptomatic psyche

Jung considered that the over-development of any single aspect of the psyche was dangerously one-sided, often resulting in physical illness, neurosis or even psychosis. His compensation theory postulated that the role of the unconscious is to act in a compensatory manner to the conscious contents of the moment. "Whenever life proceeds one-sidedly in any given direction", observed Jung, "the self-regulation of the organism produces in the unconscious an accumulation of those factors which play too small a part in the individual's conscious existence".[15] This means that when unconscious contents accumulate as a result of being consistently ignored, they are bound to exert a pathological influence. The ignored, unconscious factors can manifest as symptoms, whether physical, psychological or psychosomatic.

For Alyce, a self-described wilful and driven Type A personality (competitive, organised, ambitious, impatient), the shadow spoke somatically. Suppressed figures of the psyche had their voice in other ways, speaking through her anxiety-induced asthma attacks:

I'm sure that is a result of the perfectionist, the one who always wants more. . . . The asthma comes out more when I am stressed . . . my breathing becomes more difficult. If I put an image on that, it's a very dark figure, and it resides in my chest. It is one that is smothering, and comes out very much in a somatic sensation.

Through studying depth psychology, Alyce came to understand how the psyche attracts attention through symptoms. Indeed, the origins of the modern discipline of depth psychology lie in the symptomatic psyche. Freud's starting point in psychoanalysis was the symptom: "the contents of the mind most foreign to the ego . . . they are, as it were, its representatives before the ego – internal foreign territory".[16] He suspected that symptoms such as parapraxes (slips of the tongue or pen) and hysteria were meaningful and could be worked through with a patient in analysis to gain psychological insight. This led directly to his theories about the unconscious and the modern techniques to explore it. Coppin and Nelson have traced the origins of depth psychology to emphasise that the symptomatic psyche is a fundamental assumption of depth psychology:

> Without the symptom, the notion of psyche would be limited to consciousness, uprooting the soul from the dark and fertile ground of its being. . . . For the unconscious or partly unconscious individual, which is all people most of the time, the symptom is psyche's herald.[17]

Our work-related symptoms may also point to a more systemic occupational malaise. James Hillman argued years ago that our societies, cities, workplaces and buildings are making us sick. Mainstream thinking is just beginning to catch up with this idea, with the recognition that society and culture, not just serotonin, contributes towards depression.[18] In my first profession as a lawyer, I suffered from severe back and shoulder pain and mysterious skin conditions for which a medical cure was elusive.[19] I also struggled with depression. Although I held a coveted position in a prestigious firm, these symptoms were the canary that something was amiss in that particular coalmine. As a young female lawyer, the systemic problems in the profession (in which a masculine consciousness is institutionalised[20]) that were at the root of my symptoms were beyond my vocabulary or power to articulate, let alone to withstand or change. Knowing that if I stayed in that environment then something – what I called my spirit or soul – would die, I left. In an age of pervasive disassociation and numbing, our inconvenient and neurotic symptoms may in fact be one of the last indications of a healthy psyche trying to communicate its discomfort.[21] As Hillman put it, "The symptom is the first herald of an awakening psyche that will not tolerate any more abuse".[22]

Depression in the legal profession

Since my departure, research studies and mounting anecdotal evidence have established a link between the study and practice of law and alarmingly higher-than-average incidences of depression, drug and alcohol abuse, and other mental illnesses.[23] Causes of depression amongst lawyers have been posited as a culture of competitiveness and combat, long work hours, pessimism, learned helplessness, disillusionment and perfectionism.[24] In an effort to combat the epidemic, five white male Chief Executive Officers of the nation's biggest law firms spearheaded a working group to de-stigmatize and fight depression, modelling strategies for how to cope with professional stress.[25] Their strategies focused on cultivating resilience and confidence to 'overcome' depression. However, the suicide in 2015 of a successful Sydney lawyer who was the "poster boy for mental wellness in the legal profession" led his widow (also a lawyer) to conclude that "the character traits that make a good lawyer [and that are rewarded and amplified in the profession] are also the traits that contribute to mental illness".[26] Despite the gradual de-stigmatizing, the conventional view persists that symptoms like depression are inconvenient disorders that disrupt a rational, orderly life and career.

It is insightful, I suggest, to reconsider the profession-wide symptoms of depression from a depth psychological perspective. Depression, writes Hillman, remains the "Great Enemy", and much personal energy is expended in manic defences against, diversions from and denials of it.[27] In attempts to eradicate the symptoms of depression, Hillman sees the heroic ego at work, the same figure eager to wage wars on poverty, disease, drugs and any other kind of trouble.[28] Instead, Hillman argues for the *value* of the symptom. What is the psyche saying through the symptom of depression? What is the meaning in the symptom? Extending this idea further, Hillman argues for the need to read symptoms as belonging to the body politic and not just the individual patient. "Maybe the system has to be brought into line with the symptoms so that the system no longer functions as a repression of soul, forcing the soul to rebel in order to be noticed".[29]

Following Hillman's lead, is it so difficult to contemplate that the depressive malaise afflicting those working in the legal profession is a soul-sickness deeply rooted not only in the profession's historic marginalization of women but also in the '**feminine principle**'?[30]

With its focus on logic, rationality, detachment, rules, perfection and measuring worth in billable units, the practice of law has systemically devalued and repressed qualities associated with the feminine principle, such as feeling and intuition, even the claims of the body for movement and rest.[31] Is this the deeper reason behind why so many lawyers experience depression? Could it be that the symptom of depression is psyche's rejoinder to the profession's systemic marginalization of the feminine principle?

From a depth psychological perspective, I believe this is so. The compensatory function of the unconscious steps in to regulate the psychic ecosystem. Jungian and archetypal scholars have written about the re-emergence and rebalancing of the archetypal feminine principle in psyche and culture to restructure the conscious collective value system.[32] The symptoms of depression amongst lawyers can be viewed as the psyche's effort to rebalance itself – individually and on a collective scale – towards inclusion of a more feminine, yin consciousness, encompassing the body, connectedness, feeling, intuition, imagination[33] and the unconscious itself. From a depth psychological perspective, "symptoms are the imaginings of the psyche seeking a better form".[34]

In an occupation such as law, which many people chose for reasons of prestige, wealth, power and family and social approval, and yet where so many suffer from depression, it may be insightful to consider the depressive symptoms as a reaction to unconscious **complexes** which have driven the individual in a certain career direction. James Hollis cites cases of professional men suffering midlife depression, which he attributes to feeling trapped in their careers by family and social expectations.[35] Hollis describes depression as the pressing down of the soul's purpose and the psyche's withdrawal of support from the place where the ego, from the position of complexes, would wish to invest it. I discuss complexes and their relationship with careers and vocation in Chapters 9 and 10.

In this brief excursion and example of the legal profession, I have endeavoured to show how the psyche speaks through symptoms, which we may experience personally, but which may also be cultural and collective. Instead of heroically trying to conquer a symptom such as depression, a depth psychological approach invites us to befriend it. There may be an unexpected therapeutic value in the depression itself, not least the acquaintance with one's own shadow. Our symptoms may compel us to reassess our choice of occupation or the way we engage with it. At a collective level, the symptoms of our communities and environment may be received as a summons to leadership and to work which heals and reconnects on a larger scale. The work and life of a person such as the Indian physicist and eco-activist Vandana Shiva is testament to this.

Midlife's assault on the monarchical ego

Individuation, as we know, is the term Jung coined to describe the process of developing a vital relationship between the ego and the unconscious, informed by the archetypal ideal of wholeness. Jung considered that this process was usually catalysed in the second half of life. In his essay entitled *The Stages of Life*, Jung discussed the changes that happen in the human psyche at midlife. He locates midlife at about the age of 35 to 40. According to Jung's developmental theory, the ego's task in the first part of adulthood is to build one's outer life, adapt to the social world and focus on external work, including building a career. Then at midlife, the focus shifts to the inner life, which is the beginning of the call to individuation. In the second half of life, the value of external work fades, and the focus shifts to inner work.

Jung illustrates this notion of the stages of life using the metaphor of the rising and setting sun. He talks about one's values, and even one's body, starting to change into their opposites at midlife, as with the sun crossing its zenith. He describes the reversals in occupation and catastrophes in marriage that can happen at this time – what people commonly call the 'midlife crisis'. The term 'midlife crisis' was actually coined by a Canadian analyst, Elliot Jaques, in an article entitled "Death and the midlife crisis", published in 1965. But it was Jung who first focused attention on the midlife transition in 1930.

Although an encounter with the unconscious aspects of the psyche can happen at any age, midlife is typically when we find ourselves, via symptoms or external events, encountering our shadow. According to Jungian developmental theory, the ego's task in the first part of adulthood is to adapt to external 'reality', to people and things, and to satisfy the needs of the power drive for survival, competitive control and the avoidance of displeasure. Come midlife, for many people, the ego is now ruling the psyche like a monarch. Rationality, separateness, conscious will and purpose now reign supreme, and any sense of the archetypal or numinous dimensions of experience, which one may dimly recall experiencing at moments in childhood, has faded.

> *The nearer we approach to the middle of life, and the better we have suc-ceeded in entrenching ourselves in our personal attitudes and social posi-tions, the more it appears as if we had discovered the right course and the right ideals and principles of behaviour. . . . We overlook the essential fact that the social goal is attained only at the cost of a diminution of person-ality. Many – far too many – aspects of life which should also have been experienced lie in the lumber-room among dusty memories; but sometimes, too, they are glowing coals under grey ashes.*
> ~ CG Jung (1931b CW8, para. 722)

Midlife is typically the time for those aspects of the personality which have been repressed by the ego – what Jung called "the glowing coals under grey ashes" – to come to light. According to Jung's theory, "at midlife the ego is cut across by a greater will, and the individual is made to realise that life is about larger forces that course through the personality and demand expression".[36] So, whether via symptoms or external events, midlife is typically the time when the shadow comes to find us.

The stories related here are of midlife experiences. However, today, more than eighty years after Jung articulated his stages of life theory, it's clear that a crisis of identity, meaning and purpose is not the sole province of the second half of life. Now it is increasingly an experience of youth.[37] A young person may find himself or herself faced with an existential crisis in the first half of life, even on the very cusp of adulthood. So we can also understand this type of crisis as an archetypal experience, rather than necessarily correlated to a developmental stage or chrono-logical age.

Nevertheless, midlife is the time when the psycho-spiritual crisis most typically hits, in an unavoidable fashion. The midlife crisis still is still a common phenom-enon and the subject of many studies and books. Here I will focus upon stories of individuals at midlife to show how events at this time may disrupt planned careers and established identities, ultimately opening them into a deeper understanding of themselves and their vocation.

Jim was a Wall Street executive who made sure he got the best business education he could. In his thirties, Jim found himself riding the pinnacle of an extraordinarily successful career. He described himself as having a "razor sharp ego", suggesting that he was highly goal-focused in a way that could be cutting. Jim confessed he was very mercenary and that he approached life as all about "getting ahead", even if it was at the expense of someone else. The self-confessed stereotypical patriarchal white male, Jim (now in his fifties) reflected on how relinquishing egoic control had been one of the most difficult things for him.

> *Today, I believe that – while necessary – the ego is the dumbest and most destructive part of the psyche. It's not the guy you want calling the shots. You have to listen to the heart, to the psyche.*

Jim's ego had been so much in command of his life there was no "democracy of the psyche" at all. I asked him if the other aspects of his psyche were held prisoner to the ego.

> *No, I'd say the other aspects of my psyche were more like stowaways. The ego didn't know they were on the ship at all. . . . But then my door got broken down by four deaths. This was a frontal assault, not a simple burglary.*

Jim had started his own financial services company, and his "net worth had sky-rocketed". But the assault on his worldview began the day his second wife rang to say she was not feeling well:

> *That was the worst year of my life. As it turned out, she had cancer. And in three months, four of my closest people developed cancer. Including my first wife . . . they were all in their forties.*
>
> *This was acute damage control. . . . The battleship was stuck in the water . . . at the time it was all very reactive. . . . When I came out of it I didn't have a taste for business. None of the dying people spoke about wealth.*
>
> *After the funerals and everything were over, I thought: Wow, where am I going with this? Both my wives had passed away, and I was a single parent to three young daughters. I wound up thinking money was not so important and started trying to figure things out.*

Whitmont wrote that:

> In middle life the only psychic reality seems to be the ego's subjective experience of itself; we can barely take notice of any other, inner world. This means that in this stage further actualization and confrontation of archetypal energy must occur through one's interpersonal relationship problems.[38]

That is precisely what happened with Jim. He was around the age of 40 when these catastrophic deaths occurred which forced him to "start trying to figure things out", although he notes that "the work thing had stopped being a thrill before then. My persona was already starting to wear thin". Nevertheless, there was no immediate answer to Jim's questioning. It was followed by a ten-year period when he "did nothing", although throughout this time he felt a great sense of resting and re-tooling for the next thing. Today, Jim has engaged in further study and skill development and is crafting a new occupation as a filmmaker. Upset with the way things are going in the world and asking himself what he is doing about it, he wants to make movies that offer a countervailing perspective to balance predominant cultural messages.

Alyce was another whose life was abruptly altered in her forties by an auto-accident. Prior to that, Alyce loved her work as a mediator in the peace-making community. Pushed to the back of her mind had been a lifelong dream to study depth psychology, which she couldn't quite figure out how to do, in terms of time or finance. But then the accident instigated a total shift in her identity.

> *One day I'm working as a mediator, as a program manager, and the next day I can't track conversations and what people are saying. I'm not remembering things.*

Alyce suffered a traumatic brain injury, which affected her ability to continue with the mediation work she loved, work she considered to be both a vocation and a career. After the accident, it took her hours to perform the simplest task. She couldn't follow clients' stories anymore, which was what had made her an excellent mediator, weaving stories and bringing aspects of them forward.

> *As a typical Type A, I was saying: well I'll be done with this brain injury in four months. When life made that major change with the accident, then I really had to slow things down, to pause. . . . I made some really hard decisions. It was too difficult to continue in that work, it was wearing too much on me. So I needed to not do that anymore.*

Before the accident, Alyce had been receiving "seductive" brochures to study depth psychology. Four months after the accident, a brochure arrived for a weekend course on dream tending, a depth psychological practice for gaining insight through dreams. Alyce decided to treat herself to the course, and she enjoyed it. As her cognitive abilities slowly began to return, she applied to a graduate studies program. Initially, her research interest lay in the nexus between depth psychology and traumatic brain injury. While acknowledging the good work with Cognitive Behavioural Therapy and other allopathic modalities, Alyce felt there had been much lacking in her own recovery process. Then a seminar on the impact of working with one's reflection in the mirror caused her to focus upon how this particular practice could be applied to traumatic brain injury recovery. Her autographic methodology involved working with reflections of her face over time that were drawn in the mirror.

> *The faces may have helped me connect in with who I was. Because there are parts of me that have changed. . . . So there is this question of then: who am I in the world?*

So I'm imagining that when these different faces come up, with different aspects and personalities, that something in me gets stirred and says, "Oh, I know that figure! . . . That's the curmudgeon, or that's the ne'er do well. Or that's happy one". For me, this really fed something, real deeply. We all have multiple parts. But some of mine got knocked out of me.

But it's also about fragmentation. And the whole concept of soul-retrieval. I believe something got knocked out of me with the accident. . . . What I feel is that these faces echo something that might be hidden.

From a depth psychological perspective, Alyce's work with the faces speaks to the pantheon of archetypes or personalities, the "multiple parts" at play within and through each of us. Through this artistic practice, Alyce attempts to connect with and reclaim those faces or aspects of herself that have been knocked into the shadow. Now that I no longer do the work I used to do, *who am I in the world?* Individuals who lose their employment – whether through accident, disability, restructuring, retrenchment or retirement – confront similar questions of identity.

Jung described the ego as the complex of identity.[39] It involves a sense of continuity of body and mind in relation to space, time and causality, giving rise to the individual's sense of unity based on the functions of memory and logic. But the ego complex is also a fluctuating composition, subject to fragmentation and changeability.[40] Or as Jung suggests, the ego,

> ostensibly the thing we know most about, is in fact a highly complex affair full of unfathomable obscurities. Indeed, one could even define it as a *relatively constant personification of the unconscious itself*, or as the Schopenhauerian mirror in which the unconscious becomes aware of its own face.[41]

Although they are usually dichotomised, Jung alludes to a more complex osmosis between ego and unconscious. Alyce is still exploring the unfolding meaning and implications of her practice. But her posture of receptiveness and curiosity towards the mysterious and familiar aspects of the faces reflected in the mirror suggests something to do with Jung's description of the ego as "a *relatively constant personification of the unconscious itself*". Alyce's unified sense of professional competence and identity was disrupted, shattered, by the accident. Now, through her artistic and scholarly practice, which she hopes may eventually give birth to a new career in the healing modalities, Alyce is actively inviting and participating in a mosaic-making process with ego as mirror in which the unconscious is becoming aware of its own face – or faces.

Wearing masks, playing roles

Alyce's account of working with her various faces also illustrates the interplay between ego – the 'I' who is conscious – and *persona* – the face (or faces) we show to the world.

The **persona** is the sense of the role we play in the world and how well we play it. This may include our occupation or profession and social position. Jung coined the psychological term *persona* from the Latin word referring to the ancient actor's mask worn in solemn ritual plays. He described the persona as a complicated system of relations between individual consciousness and society, "designed on the one hand to make a definite impression upon others, and, on the other, to conceal the true nature of the individual".[42] He emphasised that the persona is a mask of the *collective psyche*: "One is simply acting a role through which the collective psyche speaks".[43]

The persona is an essential part of being able to function psychologically in the world. Having a decent persona allows a person to navigate through the world and especially through the world of work. Jung wrote that the persona "feigns individuality" and is "usually rewarded in cash",[44] meaning a wage or salary. Most career development activity is focused upon the cultivation of a professional persona – how to wear not only the physical but also the psychological clothing of the manager, the administrator, the negotiator or whatever role is required. Learning how to market and present oneself at job interviews is all about crafting one's professional persona.

There is a delightful portrayal of the masking and unmasking of persona in Charles Dickens' description of the law clerk Mr Wemmick in *Great Expectations*. Every morning when Mr Wemmick walks to the law office, his personality as well as his physical appearance undergo a remarkable transformation. His humanity recedes as he becomes dryer and harder, his mouth tightening into a thin-lipped 'post-office'. Then, as he walks home, the post-office mouth gradually relaxes into a smile again, and Wemmick returns to himself. Although the novel was set during the industrial revolution, I was reminded how alive the image of Mr Wemmick still was when I started work in the legal profession in the early 1990s. Until recently, the dominant belief was that it was only natural for people to display very different personalities at work from those in their private, out-of-work hours. But in the 21st century, observed business ethicists Attracta Lagan and Brian Moran:

> the notion of behaving one way at work and subscribing to a different set of values in social life is no longer tenable. . . . Today, we assess people of sound character to have authenticity at all levels and in every sphere in which they operate. . . . The stress of being two different people no longer appears to be worth the personal anguish.[45]

A healthy persona will be a healthy interplay of outer expectations and who we are in our essential character, conveying a natural sense of authority in our roles. It is vital, however, to develop and distinguish between an adequate persona mask and one's ego. If we become too confused with our persona and do not develop a sense of our own authentic identity, this can lead to rigidity, lack of responsiveness and a state of inflation through identification with our persona. Picture, for example, the bureaucrat or official who is dogmatically blind to the extenuating circumstances of the person in front of her because she is simply 'doing her job'. It is also a great recipe for burnout. A persona psychologically orchestrated by collective expectations makes one vulnerable to running with the herd. When our sense of self is solely dependent upon the role we play in society, we may become too susceptible to the beck and call of social structures and mechanisms.

In the belly of the whale

A midlife crisis can be triggered by an unexpected external event such as a death, relationship breakdown, job loss or accident, derailing the planned trajectory of an individual's life and career. Sometimes, however, it may simply erupt from within, as we feel we can no longer tolerate being clothed in an existing persona. Jim, for example, expressed the feeling that his persona was already starting to wear thin, even before the onslaught of the four deaths. We may have a disturbing sense of something not right in the way we are living our life, heightened by an awareness of ageing and mortality, as Jana describes:

> *Working at [a United Nations organisation] and running important programs there, I reached the age of 38, when I experienced a huge, huge midlife crisis. . . . I have a very good well-paid job and I am in a respected position, and at the same time I am in a crisis. . . . You can't really explain why that happens. . . .*
>
> *It's a sense of not really bringing something into the world that I could bring. It's as if there is some kind of a wall that doesn't allow my contribution to be as big as I have imagined it to be, or as significant, as important. I am working in an institution that helps developing countries, and I sense that what I do does not really benefit the poor people. That's one aspect of it. And the other aspect is of course personal life as well, the sense of not being fully understood for who I really am.*

Jana's midlife crisis was accompanied by a metaphorical death:

> *It's death in the sense of realising that I don't have the time forever, and I need to do something now. . . . The sense that if I continue doing what I'm doing I'll never get where I'm supposed to be. . . . This sense that life is finite, and there is something that I know I have to do, and I'm just not doing it. And at the same time not quite yet knowing what it is. It's the sense that knowing this is the wrong thing that I'm doing, that I'm not getting where I need to go, but at the same time being lost about what it is.*

Who am I apart from my history, my roles? What wants to enter the world through me? These are the questions Jana found herself facing at a major transition in her life.[46]

Jana has entered a *liminal* (from the Latin word *limen*, meaning threshold) phase in her life. The liminal stage has been identified by anthropologists and psychologists as the second phase in a rite of passage or major life transition, after separation from a previous world and before reincorporation into the social body.[47] In the liminal period, we are no longer what we were but not yet what we will become. Crossing a threshold into the unknown involves a symbolic self-annihilation – one enters 'the belly of the whale'. Tracing this womb-like image of the whale's belly throughout the world's mythic traditions, Joseph Campbell wrote, "the hero, instead of conquering or conciliating the power of the threshold, would appear to have died".[48] Metaphorically, the liminal stage has been likened to death, being in the womb, invisibility, darkness, the wilderness and an eclipse of the sun or moon.[49] This experience is also known as the *nekyia*, the night sea journey or descent into the underworld.[50]

In Jana's story, the dark night sea journey in the belly of the whale was a "psychotic break experience". At a time when she was facing a difficult decision about whether to leave her job, Jana had a repeated vision of an S-shaped cut, like a snake, on the floor, which she saw clearly over a week but which no one else around her saw. She described how she was incredibly shaken by this episode:

The psychotic break experience was really dark, dark, dark . . . as in some sort of dismemberment, completely being chopped apart, thrown apart, torn apart, where everything is being taken apart. Everything is being taken apart, and then you somehow, slowly, have to gather it up and put it into some kind of a wholeness, which might not look like before at all. . . . The interesting thing is that the physical body doesn't seemingly fall apart, so that for the people around you, you look like you are the same, whereas in reality you are not the same at all. And then, how do you live in the world with the people around you who are so completely different? That is a huge, huge question, and I think that's what also puts a lot of stress on the most immediate people around you. Maybe leaving the job is one way of getting away from the people who just don't see the enormous change in you. . . . It feels like I just want to leave everybody, because I'm so different that nothing fits anymore.

Joseph Campbell described the passage of "the hero-dive through the jaws of the whale" as a "life-centering, life-renewing act".[51] Sometimes, this passage may be experienced as a break from consensual reality; a disorienting, dismembering experience. However, even through this dark night, we can have faith that a more radical, ontological transformation may be taking place when we consider that the etymology of the word *psychosis* means the "fact of giving soul or life to something, the principle of animation, of life".[52] Such experiences initiate a person into a chthonic underworld of chaos, but from which there is the potential for new forms to emerge, *if* the ego is strong enough to recover itself and integrate the experience. "The only way something like that can be done with a little bit of ease is if there is an understanding of the larger psyche", reflected Jana. "Knowing there is something greater that one can trust".

We need to recover this symbolic dimension so the psyche can go through its mysteries of death and rebirth. In Jana's case, being able to read her experience in a symbolic way allowed her to understand her vision of the snake as a sign of connecting the unconscious with the conscious. What eventually emerged from this for Jana was an unexpected vocational direction. The career Jana left was focused on money in a very literal way, but Jana's vision tipped her towards a more symbolic mode of consciousness. Jana has since brought this symbolic perspective to some very innovative PhD research, looking at what the traditional legends of her Latvian culture may reveal symbolically about cultural complexes related to money. I discuss this further in Chapters 10 and 11.

Lynn was another interviewee who recounted a "belly of the whale" experience, which ultimately birthed her new vocation. With a background in environmental work and degrees in science and education, Lynn had taught mythology and depth psychology, in which she held Master's and Doctoral degrees. At the time of this experience she related, the field of eco-psychology (which was to become Lynn's vocation) had not yet come into the culture in such a way that there was any theory or praxis around it.

Lynn had been living on a boat for several months, working to stop shark finning (the commercial practice of hacking off shark fins and discarding the remainder of the living shark into the ocean to die slowly). Events in Lynn's personal life at that time also made for a "belly of the whale experience". She took her depth psychology books with her on the boat as she tried to read through her personal crisis.

The metaphor of working on the ocean was interesting, observed Lynn, because there are so many layers to it, including the environmental destruction she was seeing. The boat was a vessel – and she was on this vessel trying to understand her own vessel. The ocean is a symbol of the unconscious, and at the same time Lynn was being plunged into her own unconscious and trying to deal with the symbolism of it. She was aware of some of these connections at the time, but not all of them: "If you were conscious of it, you wouldn't be working with the unconscious".

Lynn slept at the bottom of the three-tiered boat, which was very dark and filled with fumes. She remembers thinking, "Oh, this must be what it feels like to be in the belly of the whale".

> *One night I heard this thumping against the boat. I thought, what's the deal with that? It was the middle of the night, and I was on the boat alone. I wasn't scared, but at the same time: you are a woman, out in the middle of the ocean, on a boat, by yourself. . . . I didn't want to be naïve about that.*
>
> *They had thrown a finned shark onto the deck of the boat. Now, sharks are one of my big symbols for fear. Working on the ocean has been great but I've always had a fear of sharks because when I was little I saw a guy get bit by one. . . . The fishermen threw the shark onto the boat. I knew it was a direct threat to me about doing what I was doing.*

I got disoriented on the boat in the middle of the ocean, hit my head on a winch, and knocked myself out. When I woke up I was lying face-to-face with this dead, finned shark. For me – I've written about this and given it so much thought – it was a coming face-to-face with my greatest fears. And my greatest fears of course being not so much the shark, but what I was going to do with the rest of my life.

It was extremely emotional. First of all, the shark is dead and finned. And yet you're lying there and this thing is looking at you and it's what you've always been most afraid of. I didn't know what to do. I know that I got really nauseated. I was afraid I had brain damage. My eyes swelled up. . . . I think I had a concussion. Looking back, it was probably stupid, I should have gone in and had someone check me out. But you don't think about that kind of thing, especially when you're in that heroic mode. . . .

It was so sobering, and so instantly maturing to me, that it just put my life into perspective. It doesn't mean I figured everything out in that moment, because I didn't. It's a process. But it changed my life in that moment. We read about this in mythology, where the hero comes up against the dragon or the monster or whatever. You can kill it, or you can be killed by it. Or – you can find a different way to be in relationship with it so that everything survives. And that's what I think is working with the unconscious. You don't have to control, kill it, annihilate it. Even more than it necessarily has to do that to you. Dismember? – absolutely. Break you apart, tear you apart – absolutely. But it doesn't have to completely annihilate the psyche. It educates the psyche.

This episode was a turning point in Lynn's life and her vocation, when she realised she needed to put together a theory and practice of eco-psychology. She saw that she had the education to put together "a really interesting and psychologically valid approach towards solving many of the world's problems", which has led her to pioneer education in the field of eco-psychology. The *nekyia* birthed a sense of clarity around her vocational call.

For me, figuring out what I was going to do with my vocation, and figuring out what was going on with my personal life, were absolutely connected. Of course I was going to get sucked into this underworld in a big way. I was trying to figure out my ecosystem.

Lynn emphasised her belief that vocation is not something one chooses but something to which we are directed, through an 'abduction' or fall into the unconscious. Her story illustrates the key point of this chapter: that our callings can come through darkness, disruption and trouble. Contrary to reliance on wilful and skilful career strategies, surprising yet meaningful vocational directions may arise when our usual occupational identity is suspended[53] or by attendance to what was formerly relegated to our shadow. In the next chapter, we further explore individuals' experiences of 'initiation' into vocation.

Invitation to reflection and journaling

Imagine that – whatever your age and situation – you are at this time in your life stepping into the afternoon of life by virtue of reading this book.

- What insights or questions does Jung's model of the psyche, the process of individuation (see also Chapter 5) and the stages of life offer for your own career and vocational journey?
- What things (ideas, attitudes, values, behaviours, relationships or jobs) may have served you in the 'morning' of life that you need to leave behind or surrender to step into the 'afternoon' of life?
- What aspects of the psyche have perhaps been relegated to your shadow which you now need to reclaim and own as parts of yourself? Do you have any "glowing coals under grey ashes"? What could fan them alight again?

Notes

1 Jung 1960b CW 7, para. 103.
2 Downing 2007, pp. 126–129.
3 See for example Jung (1960b CW7, paras 51, 279).
4 For readers familiar with Jung's theory of psychological types, discussed in Chapter 4, it is also interesting to consider Peter's career and vocational development in the second half of life from the perspective of psychological type development. According to the Myers-Briggs Type Indicator, Peter identified as ISFJ. I suggest that by engaging more consciously with the "imaginal part of the psyche" in his second half of life, Peter is appropriately engaged in the important work of integrating his demonic/daimonic function (Beebe 2004, 2007), which manifests through the shadow.
5 Hillman 1972, pp. 183–190; 1975, p. 37.
6 Gilligan 2003; Kostera 2012.
7 Neumann 1994, p. 65, note 3.
8 Shalit 2002, p. 55.
9 Shalit 2002, p. 56. See Chapter 6, note 30 for further discussion of the 'feminine principle'.
10 Harding 1971, p. 65.
11 Becker 2004, p. 98.
12 Jung 1918, CW10, para. 25.
13 Hillman (1972) considered that archetypally, this type of masculine consciousness is more correctly termed Apollonic, a structure of consciousness traceable to the masculine scientific mytheme of the Greek God Apollo. It is at odds with what he called a bisexual Dionysian consciousness, which is comfortable with ambivalence.
14 Corlett & Pearson 2003. For more on the organisational psyche and its shadow, see Bowles (1991), Kostera (2012) and Morgan (2006).
15 Jung 1918, CW10, para. 20.
16 Freud 1973, p. 71.
17 Coppin & Nelson 2005, p. 61.
18 Hari 2018.
19 Maguire (2004) provides a Jungian analysis of psychosomatic dermatology and the unconscious psychic background of many skin diseases.
20 It has long been recognised in feminist studies that the profession of law and the legal system involves a hidden gender bias, a male "point-of-viewlessness" (Graycar & Morgan 1990).

21 Slater 2008.
22 Hillman 1989, p. 18.
23 Black Dog Institute n.d.; Medlow, Kelk & Hickie 2011. A 2007 Australian study found that 15% of legal professionals experienced moderate or severe depressive symptoms, a rate two and a half times that of the general population (Beaton Consulting 2007; Black Dog Institute n.d.). This echoed similar findings in the United States (Benjamin, Darling & Sales 1990; Eaton et al. 1990).
24 Kelk et al. 2009.
25 Susskind 2010.
26 Rusiti 2015, p. 38.
27 Hillman 1975, p. 98.
28 Hillman 1989, p. 142.
29 Hillman & Ventura 1992, p. 154.
30 The 'feminine principle' is a term Jung gave to the qualities of eros, feeling, relationship and connectedness (Rowland 2002, p. 176). Historian Richard Tarnas has described the feminine principle or archetypal feminine as all that the Western masculine mind has projectively identified and repressed as 'Other', including imagination, emotion, instinct, body, nature, mystery, ambiguity and woman (1991, p. 442). It is important, however, not to conflate women and the feminine. Jung (1934a CW9:1, para. 653) recognised the androgynous nature of the Self (the central archetype of wholeness); that we each have within us both feminine and masculine qualities. Despite the theoretical severing of sex and gender from the archetypal principles, Susan Rowland has observed that most Jungian writers see women as more likely to be attuned to the feminine principle, men to the masculine (2002, p. 55). The danger in that approach is that women continue to be depreciated in a patriarchal society which devalues the feminine, and that men feel denied to embrace the feminine principle within themselves. "A healthy ego (in both sexes) requires strengthening individual women and their cultural valuation" (Rowland 2010, p. 134). I suggest that it also requires acceptance and inclusion of those qualities rejected and devalued as associated with the feminine: the unconscious, the unknowable, connectedness, intuition, the body, sexuality and nature itself.
31 Of course, law is not the only occupation where the feminine is marginalized. Monika Kostera observed that "Organizations tend to exclude the female element much more forcefully than they exclude women as such. 'Success people' in organizations tend to be the epitomes of the Animus [archetypal masculine principle], regardless of their gender: they are assertive, aggressive, often forceful, with sharp views, holding their positions by virtue of their will. To change the situation, it is not enough 'to let women in the organization' – instead, organizations should open to diversity, both masculine and feminine [and] show more openness to the traits associated with the Anima [archetypal feminine principle]" (2012, p. 87).
32 Tarnas 1991, p. 443; Whitmont 1991, p. 320. Hillman anticipated that the ultimate purpose of therapeutic psychology is the integration of "feminine inferiority" into a more "bisexual consciousness" for men and women: "We are cured when we are no longer masculine in psyche, no matter whether we are male or female in biology" (1972, p. 292). Susan Rowland argued that the Jungian unconscious is constantly compensatory and rebalancing to the structures of ego-consciousness, including the patriarchal ego's bias towards a masculine, *logos* consciousness. "The challenge to the ego's gender bias is ultimately a challenge to cultural gender bias. . . . A society may therefore inherit patriarchal structures, but because the individual unconscious is endowed with archetypal androgyny, it will naturally find itself combating patriarchal dominance. Individuation, which has now come to encompass gender fluidity, thus inherently challenges patriarchy" (Rowland 2010, pp. 134, 141).
33 Benjamin Sells (1994) argues that the law has developed a highly specialised language that seeks to excise metaphor, simile and image. Therefore, the way back to soul for lawyers he suggests is through a radical appreciation of the *imaginative* dimensions of legal practice.

34 Hillman & Ventura 1992, p. 155.
35 Hollis 1996, p. 72.
36 Tacey 2012, p. 39.
37 As early as 1967, Hillman was arguing against the traditional Jungian separation into first and second halves of life, that it dangerously divides the archetypes of *puer* and *senex* (2005c, p. 36). A young person today, Hillman wrote, is increasingly pressed to take up the problems of the second-half of life in the first half, being issues of meaning, of religion, of self-hood. Andrew Samuels also found Jung's split into the first and second halves of life puzzling. Samuels observes that social or career achievement in the first half of life is not always a problem of one-sided development. Social achievement may be an unreflective reaction against, or compliance with, societal or family pressure. But then again, it may not. What is crucial is the person's attitude to their career, their marriage and so on (Samuels 2004, p. 170).
38 Whitmont 1991, p. 279.
39 Jung 1921 CW6, para. 706.
40 Whitmont 1991, pp. 231–236.
41 Jung 1956 CW14, para. 129.
42 Jung 1928b CW7, para. 305.
43 Jung 1928b CW7, para. 245.
44 Jung 1934a CW9:1, para. 221.
45 Lagan & Moran 2006, p. 123.
46 Preceding paragraphs in this section are reproduced from the author's article published in the *International Journal for Educational and Vocational Guidance* (Cremen 2019).
47 Turner 1969; Van Gennep 1960.
48 Campbell 2008, p. 74.
49 Turner 1969, p. 95.
50 The ancient Greek word *nekyia* (ή νέκυια = corpse), the title of the eleventh book of the Odyssey, was suggested by Jung as an apt designation for the descent to the underworld (Jung 1944 CW12, para. 61, note 2) and used by Edward Edinger (1978) in his analysis of the night sea journey in the belly of the whale in Melville's *Moby Dick*.
51 Campbell 2008, p. 77.
52 psychosis (n) *Oxford English Dictionary*.
53 Metcalfe 2013.

7   Undercover shamans at work

I don't think the uninitiated person can clearly hear the call of vocation. I think the first initiatory ordeal, which is probably an expression of the call, prepares one to enter into a relationship with the non-ordinary.

Unless you have died to your small self, and gone through the nekyia in some way, I don't think it's possible to be re-born, if you will, into this much larger work.

(Claire)

Vocation – the sense of having a larger calling in life, which extends beyond a job or career – emerges through the psychological experience of initiation. If we are to respond to the call of our soul's vocation, the ego must surrender into an ongoing relationship of service and dialogue with the larger psyche. To reiterate the words of Claire, a depth psychological educator I interviewed in the course of this research, unless we have died to our "small self", been swallowed into the belly of the whale and gone through the *nekyia* in some way, it is not possible to be born into this "much larger work".

By the "uninitiated person", Claire means someone who has not relinquished the idea of being in control of his or her world, and for whom rationality, wilfulness and purpose still reign supreme. Which, admittedly, sounds like the majority of managers, executives, bureaucrats and professionals in business and government today! However, for the individual whose ego has hardened into a controlling place in the psyche, entering a liminal phase of 'unknowing' is a crucial stage of initiation. This thinking is central to many indigenous traditions and initiation rites. Furthermore, as we shall see, an initiatory experience of some kind is a precondition to hearing and honouring a vocational calling from the deep psyche.

The initiation into vocation

Initiation prepares a person to enter into a relationship with the unconscious and the non-ordinary and to receive a vocational calling. To understand how this occurs, it can be insightful to draw an analogy with the stages of shamanic initiation in traditional cultures, where the novice or initiate is faced with ego death and transformation. I will provide a brief overview of the general process of initiation, though its practice in vocation is nuanced and complex. What I wish to illustrate here is the process of initiation which must be undergone for the individual to align his or her will with the greater will, whereby one's self-interest becomes enlightened.

First, the initiate is separated physically and/or psychically from the community and his or her normal life and thrust into an unknown situation. The initiate is forced to surrender to the situation as his or her usual resources fail. The middle of the initiatory experience is marked by the activation of the initiate's imagination and emotions, making everything feel extreme. In this stage, the initiate fully realises his or her weaknesses, wounds and limitations and that the only option is to give up control – that is, either the ego dies or the whole person dies. According to Christina Pratt in *The Encyclopedia of Shamanism*, "From this place of revelation and surrender the initiate is guided to something within himself that was hidden. If initiates can merge with that hidden aspect, they become greater than they were before".[1] The middle of the initiation is the crucial point, during which a fundamental shift in consciousness must occur. If this transformation occurs, the completion of the initiation begins with the death of the initiate's ego self, or the "little self":

> With the death of the little self the shaman gains the freedom to align consciously with the will of his soul and the soul of the Kosmos. The individual is transformed at this fundamental stage, and the shaman becomes 'the person he or she came here to be'. This necessary loss of the little self is why shamanic initiation is often called the 'little death'.[2]

The essential element in rites of initiation in traditional cultures is the irreversible transformation of the initiate. Without this, it is not an effective or valid initiation, even if it is traditional. The Native American vision quest, where an individual goes into the wilderness to temporarily step beyond the bounds of culture and confront the elements of nature, the spirits and his or her own essential nature, is a pre-eminent example of an initiation ritual to awaken vocation, *dharma* or life task. Paradoxically, the experience of other dimensions of existence will frequently renew the initiate's ultimate participation in community and culture.

In the contemporary Western world, people who yearn for connection with a deeper purpose may actively seek out initiatory experiences to awaken their relationship with the unconscious or the non-ordinary. For Michael, a psychologist, a form of initiation occurred in the therapy room with an analyst who held a great fidelity to the unconscious and took him into the depths where Michael said he "needed to go". Nikki was a marketer who had been actively involved with shamanic journeying. She went to Peru to undergo a ceremony to solicit guidance for her vocational path.

> *It was very succinct and very clear in the first ceremony. The call was simply to work with "symbolic language". This came through as a disembodied*

*voice, as words. I was so thrilled and delighted about this, but then – "what
the hell does that mean?"*

Nikki's fidelity to this disembodied voice irrevocably changed the course of
her life. She embarked on postgraduate studies to align herself with its guidance
and learn about "symbolic language". Today, this has led her to work as a depth
psychotherapist and author specialising in love and sexuality from an archetypal
and symbolic perspective.

It is important to emphasise – particularly for individuals in Western cultures
today, where there has been a breakdown of rituals of initiation that bestow an
experience of inner guidance – that initiations may also arise spontaneously.[3] Psychiatrist and Jungian analyst Lionel Corbett observed that the archetype of initiation may spontaneously manifest (particularly among adolescents) even when it
is neglected in the culture:

> Any numinous experience, any contact with the sacred, is potentially power-
> ful enough to perform the function of initiating the individual into a new level
> of consciousness and moving him or her into a new status. In a sense, then, all
> contact with the numinosum produces an initiation.[4]

In the absence of initiation by the culture, the psyche or the Self may take the
lead to initiate a person by means of a numinous experience, either positive or
negative.[5] Furthermore, the numinous or sacred experience carries its own authority to the individual who experiences it because of its emotional power.

Of course, 'shaman' is not a recognised occupation in modern Western culture.
But that is not to say that there are not people who receive what in other cultures
would be recognised as an initiatory shamanic calling but who, unsupported by
wise elders and cultural rituals, are pathologized and medicated.[6] Greg Bogart
described receiving a "modern form of self-initiation" into his life's calling, which
resulted from a combination of significant events, including a dream, an inner
voice experience, a synchronicity and "a visitation of a mysterious, seemingly
intelligent energetic presence".[7] Education professor Clifford Mayes tells the
story of a woman whose discovery of her husband's infidelity with prostitutes and
her own subsequent diagnosis as HIV-positive were akin to the psycho-spiritual
intensity of a shamanic initiation. At the same time as this ordeal, a stream of
events occurred which pointed her without doubt towards her calling as a teacher.[8]
If the ego container is strong enough to integrate these experiences, the task is
to find some vehicle or means – for example, a career or occupation as an artist, teacher, therapist, writer, poet or healer – to serve out the calling to mediate
between the worlds and between modes of consciousness.

I have experienced two spontaneous initiations by the psyche in the course of
my life. Both rocked the foundations of my being in such a way that for a brief
time I lost my connection with consensual reality and suffered what was whis-
pered in hushed tones as a nervous breakdown, or in medical parlance, a psychotic
break. These experiences occurred unexpectedly at key threshold life stages: the

first, two months after my 18th birthday, and the second, two months after my 40th birthday. What happened was compelling, confusing and shameful to me, not least because there was no one around me, including medical professionals and church ministers, who seemed to empathically comprehend the psycho-spiritual nature of what I was experiencing. The best I could do was to struggle to reconstruct my psychological integrity, re-learn my sense of material reality and merge as soon as I could back into work and community life. Few people were even aware of what I had been through. Today, there is greater awareness and less shame and stigma around mental health conditions. Yet I am still reticent to speak about these experiences. This is partly due to the propensity for misunderstanding and judgment by others, but more so due to the mysterious nature of these experiences of the psychic underworld. In ways that are difficult to put language around, I was irreversibly transformed by them. They were instrumental in catalysing my calling to advocate and educate for attention to the soul.

In hindsight, it was as if love itself, coupled with an unusual constellation of psychologically and emotionally highly stressful events, transpired to set me up for each initiatory wounding. The final blow to my psyche in each case was effected through a profound betrayal in a relationship in which I'd placed my absolute trust: at age 18, in God (as presented to me by the Christian Church), and at age 40, in my husband. The experience of betrayal has an archetypal quality to it; James Hollis observed that it "stings us toward individuation".[9] In each case, the betrayal was felt so deeply that I literally did not know what was 'real' anymore.[10] In any true initiation that invites us to make the painful shift to an enlarged mode of consciousness, I suggest we will experience a feeling of betrayal. Any real initiation of the modern ego into another state comes with a degree of betrayal and shock or wounding, and then being able to incorporate that wound as part of oneself. Otherwise, it will fail to initiate. As Sam Gill writes, "Being forced to abandon one's ingrained notion of reality is to experience a true death of the former self".[11]

The death which an individual undergoes in an initiatory experience will always be a death of identity, a death of the former self. Jungian analyst David Rosen has called this 'ego-cide'.[12] But as well as instigating an ego-death, an initiatory experience may also be instigated through the death or loss of a loved one or the loss of a relationship which has been integral to one's sense of self. For Jim, the deaths of his loved ones were the initiatory wounds which caused the seed of his vocation to germinate:

> *It was the "why am I here?" question that was the companion to death. That is the acorn from which vocation springs. The time when you ask yourself: "Why am I here? What is the purpose?" So vocation is like the pretty sister of death.*

Although death is shunned in our society while vocation is more often courted, Jim's words speak to the close nature of death and vocation as soul-siblings. A confrontation with mortality brings an awareness of what matters most to the forefront. The proximity of death may spark a clarity or remembrance of our soul's purpose, initiating a deeply authentic sense of vocation. "Dying, which can include the death of identity, is the soul's way of education", reflected Michael.

This is not to say, however, that all experiences of vocation will be instigated by a dramatic, traumatic, transformative or lightning bolt event. For some, a vocational calling will be felt clearly at a very young age. Musicians often hear the call first, observed James Hillman.[13] For others, arriving at a sense of vocation will be a longer process of maturation. Indeed, some people – those whom Jung disparagingly called 'midget personalities'[14] – never do arrive at a sense of vocation.

Dying into life, into vocation, takes many different forms. Ultimately, the ego will undergo many little deaths along the path of vocation as it relinquishes its grasp on certainty and steps into unknowing. For Michael, this involved leaving a beloved profession, "leaving the discipline of psychology for the sake of becoming psychological". For Claire, it necessitated leaving the home and city she knew and loved, her friends and family, work and clients, to respond to an emerging calling. For Lynn, it required letting go of a certain heroic mode in her work with the environment. For Peter, it entails letting go of certainty and trusting in the process and where he is at now, doing the work that is required, putting himself in service to the psyche at an age where for many men this would be too big a task. The climate and extinction crisis may also be viewed as a collective initiatory experience for the post-industrial Western psyche. Confronted with the death of identity based on heroic but unsustainable economic notions of unlimited growth and progress, the Western psyche is now undergoing a descent where it is being forced to comprehend its role in relation to the ecology of the whole.

Annabella's story

To illustrate these ideas about the contemporary initiation into vocation further, I would like to share Annabella's story of a pivotal episode in her life. Annabella currently works as a mindfulness and compassion educator at a university, where she brings myth, story and poetry into the practices of cultivating presence. This story which she generously shared with me is of a pivotal episode in her life. Indeed, I do not think it hyperbole to call it an epiphany. I do not suggest that Annabella's story is typical. Everyone's journey is unique. But like a good film, its particularities disclose larger archetypal patterns.

> *About five years ago, after I finished graduate work, I felt like if I moved a little bit to the left, I would be stepping into this deep river. I didn't know what that meant, moving a little bit to the left. But it kept coming up, this image – just a little adjustment, and then it would be . . . whoosh.*
>
> *It was a strong feeling, very palpable . . . through my whole body. It felt sensual, compelling, and such an invitation. . . . It was like a being, that filled me completely, but it was without me as well. . . . Someone in a different theology might have said it was an angel. I sensed it as a being, not just an idea that wouldn't let go.*

Might she call this presence her *daimon* – a mythical, soul companion that reminds us of our soul's purpose? "Yes, this was the daimon. It felt very much like love".

> *Around this time, I lost a lot in my life. My car blew up. I lost facial function through a virus that attacked my nerves. I lost my home. My twenty-year job teaching at high school fell apart. . . . My income went down. It was just alarming.*
>
> *I had been accepted at [University] as a postgraduate at the neuropsychological centre, and I tried to get part-time jobs but there was nothing. On a practical level I shouldn't be doing it [the postgraduate work]. It was expensive, I had lost my main income, I had these enormous debts from graduate school – and then I was going to postgraduate school?? It was crazy!! But the deeper this water – again, the image of water, needing to adjust – I knew if I went back and scrambled for security it would all fall – the centre wouldn't hold.*

Because of the virus which caused nerve and muscle damage, there came a time when Annabella could only see through one eye. It was winter and her head was swathed in a scarf:

> *I remember having this one eye I could look out of, and looking up at the sky, and thinking – ah, it's so beautiful! I have nothing, externally – I just have this one eye – but this one eye could see this beauty! I had this absolute felt sense that what is essential is unchangeable inside of us. So that was a huge thing. Partly the moving to the left was getting more aligned with that, the thing that was so essential and undying and unchanging in me – that would lead me and be the crumbs through a dark forest, even though it seemed more and more crazy, the way I was going.*

Already there are many layers and images to Annabella's experience. Literally she had suffered multiple losses and held grave concerns about money; metaphorically she felt a sense of needing to move to the left,[15] stepping into a river[16] and – like figures in folklore, mythology and Dante in the *Divine Comedy* – being lost in a dark forest in the middle of the journey of life. When she recounted being wounded by the virus, it was as if Annabella was finally swallowed by the whale, immobilised and left with nothing to do but surrender and look through the blowhole:

> *What was left was the beauty of nature, and being able to regard it, and have nature come back into me. It brought me into this lifeforce. I wasn't separate from it. . . . The sky was so beautiful. The sense of space. I was riveted by it. Beauty pulled me in.*
>
> *At the time, I used this koan: "Vast emptiness, nothing holy, I don't know". . . . It brought me into this indwelling, undying spaciousness of mind in everything.*

> *The soul's awakening is a process in beauty.*
>
> ~ Plotinus, 204–270 CE

The humility of being disabled opened Annabella's eye to the beauty of nature and to its vastness. Opening into the space of unknowing awakened a clarity and purpose in Annabella's vocational direction and what she would bring out of this as an educator. It transformed her life – not in the way her ego may have wanted, but in the way it was destined to be.

> *That's when I knew immediately that it had to do with my work. Immediately, I thought: I'm going to use this. It came from very much the personal and the archetypal. I remember thinking, I'm going to teach this. I know this now, for sure. I am going to tell people that they can lose everything and they're going to be okay. I can say that now. So it was completely about my work, and completely about myself.*
>
> *Then [X University] hired me, out of a class of thirty-five really amazing people. . . . There was no promise of that!*

Only a couple of days before this experience, Annabella recalled she had been in despair. She had been in the woods and heard an inner voice saying, "you must surrender". Surrender to what? The voice was very strong: "You need to surrender to life as it is".

> *I could feel myself in this deep river, fully in this luminous, numinous current of my life. . . . There were no barriers, no resistance. Everything became close, and everything shone.*
>
> *The end result was: this is what I was born to do. This is what my whole life has prepared me to do. This was the narrative when I knew I'd stepped left. It was a very big "aha" thing, that I integrated.*

The very strong spiritual, mystical quality of this archetypal moment awakened Annabella to an unshakeable sense of her vocation. This immediately translated through to her work as a teacher and then changed the way she approached her work. Annabella's experience was both completely unique to Annabella and, in its motifs and metaphors, clearly related to universal and archetypal experiences of initiation throughout folklore and mythology. The paradox that exists within any archetypal experience is that it feels incredibly 'other' – transpersonal – and yet particularly unique and apt to oneself and one's own circumstances.[17] The archetype is experienced as a numinous moment which constellates in the bridge between the universal and the personal.

I would describe Annabella's experience as a spontaneous initiation or "holy encounter",[18] precipitated by a numinous or sacred experience which carries its own authority to the individual who experiences it because of its emotional power.[19] If initiation is successful, the initiate emerges with a new myth, a set of guiding beliefs and assumptions to shape her awareness and actions in the community[20] and, specifically, "to restore harmony in the connection of all things through service to the community, both human and spirit".[21] It is this numinous quality of an archetypal experience which can foster a re-enchantment of one's experiences of work and calling and inspire creativity in many fields. I asked Annabella how her experience has informed her work as a teacher:

> *As a learning-styles consultant I am very prepared, even over-prepared. . . . What all this gave me was the ability to speak from presence, and that I could rely on that. . . . That's what my students and participants really want from me, to be completely present with them. "I see you". That can only come from the relationship I have with myself, that all of this gave me, being able to sit in the fullness of myself. Not how I self-identify, how my ego identifies – but in this larger, expanded consciousness.*

She is still constantly "straddling technique, structure and skill sets – because the thing can't fall apart". But in the educational environment, what difference does this sense of presence make?

> *There is the preciousness of connectedness, an awareness of impermanence. A deep kindness and warmth – the presence brings warmth and warms up the room. And rewiring neuropsychologically happens in presence – all the data shows that.*
>
> *Then there is the "third body" – what happens in the room. . . . That's when the teacher dissolves, when the third body arises, when the archetype steps in. . . . If we are in it too personally, this doesn't happen.*

> (Annabella)

Annabella's account of holding a space for the archetype to emerge reflects the real nature of sacrifice as 'making sacred', surrendering to the presence of the archetype (as other cultures sacrificed to the gods), humbling herself to the scheme of things. She shows how in contemporary life, sacrificial practice takes the form of remaining conscious of the patterns of the collective psyche.

A Copernican revolution of the psyche

It can be helpful to also conceptualise these experiences of initiation within a Jungian theoretical perspective. As I discussed in Chapter 5, **individuation** is the term Jung coined to describe the process of developing and maintaining a dialogue between the ego and the unconscious, with the goal of becoming our unique selves and living in integrity with the soul rather than in conformity with the collective. Individuation involves the dethronement of the ego as the centre of the individual's sphere and the cultivation instead of an ongoing dialogue with the whole of the psyche and the central archetype of wholeness which Jung called the *Self*. In this model, the ego is displaced from its assumed position of centrality: an ontological shift as revolutionary as the Copernican revolution in the 16th century that challenged the assumed centrality of the earth in the cosmos. "It once seemed obvious", wrote Whitmont, "that the sun rotated around the earth; it seems just as obvious to most of us today that our life is centered in or around our egos".[22]

The essential point about this ontological shift is the necessity (not only in relation to individuation but also in vocation) for the ego to relinquish exclusive control in repeated acts of surrender to an autonomous Other (or Others), by whatever name we call that Other. There is the feeling that our personal will, efforts and aspirations are joined or aligned with a much larger story – something larger and beyond our conscious awareness.[23] "An attitude of surrendering to psyche entails humility, and is a step towards mitigating the hubris, inflation and narcissism pervasive throughout modern culture", wrote depth psychologist Glen Slater.[24] This notion of surrender or relativisation of the ego is reiterated in traditions and perspectives other than Jungian psychology, for example, in the Hindu and Buddhist concepts of *dharma*.

Making this shift from an egocentric perspective changes the typical career question from "What do *I* want to do?" (which is often accompanied by a tremendous amount of angst and pressure) to "Who or what is calling? What is wanted at a level beyond and beneath consciousness? What is it within me that is seeking expression?" This relativises the idea that we are the omnipotent authors of our working lives (as promoted by the career constructivists) towards a sense that we are in collaboration or service with some larger field.

Invitation to reflection and journaling

- Recall an experience which might be regarded as initiatory in your own life. Perhaps it was something that you had no container for holding at the time, so you endeavoured to put it aside and get life 'back to normal'. Perhaps it was something that shook up everything you knew to be true, that broke you open to a different reality, and you are currently living the question of what that means for your life and your work in the world. Perhaps you presently feel yourself to be on the verge of an initiatory experience.
- Take some quiet time to recall and write down the nature of this experience.
- In what way(s) might this experience have awakened a calling?
- How might your vocation be envisaged as germinating from that initiatory experience?

Notes

1　Pratt 2007, p. 227.
2　Pratt 2007, p. 227.
3　Bogart 1994, pp. 24–25; Pratt 2007, p. 226.
4　Corbett 2007, p. 73.
5　Corbett 2007, p. 73.

6   Marohn 2011.
7   Bogart 1994, p. 11.
8   Mayes 2005.
9   Hollis 1996, p. 50.
10 Another way to contemplate what happens in an initiatory process is that the heroic ego is initiated away from certainty and literalism into metaphorical understanding (Hillman 1979, pp. 114–115). The ego becomes an "imaginal ego" (Hillman 1972, pp. 183–190; 1975, p. 37), adapted to the symbolic or imaginal world, as the individual develops 'double vision' (see Chapter 12), the ability to perceive both imaginal and collective or social realities.
11 Gill 1996, p. 236.
12 Rosen 2002, p. xxvi.
13 Hillman 1996, p. 251.
14 Jung 1934b CW17, para. 302.
15 Another woman I interviewed, Claire, also spoke about a feeling of moving to the left. During her mid-thirties, she would repeatedly say that she felt like her life was making a sweeping left turn, with no idea what that meant. In retrospect, she relates it to hemisphere specialisation in the brain. To turn left meant moving toward the intuitive side. The association across cultures of the left-hand side of the body with the feminine and associated modes of consciousness has been documented since antiquity (Hillman 1972, pp. 235–236).
16 The river is a timeless image for the currents and flow of life and an increasingly popular metaphor in career development.
17 Slater 2011.
18 Otto 1958.
19 Corbett 2007, p. 14.
20 Bogart 1994, p. 22.
21 Pratt 2007, p. 229.
22 Whitmont 1991, p. 265.
23 Bogart described this as *transpersonalization*, "a process in which personal will, efforts, and aspirations are felt by the subject to be joined or aligned with some larger field of activity" (1994, p. 30).
24 Slater 1996, p. 56.

8 Loving our fate so deeply it transforms into destiny

In career counselling, individuals are helped to identify their skills, interests and values, as well as their perceived constraints. These constraints include many factors, such as lack of money or education, the necessity to care for dependents, a disability, one's gender, age, ethnicity, geographic location and so on. A depth psychological view of vocation calls such constraints one's fate. As we will see, fate will often present individuals with a career obstacle or setback, which in hindsight is seen as instrumental in shaping a more extraordinary vocation. Two examples amongst many famous lives spring to mind.

As a young man, the French sculptor Auguste Rodin's application to study the human form was rejected three times by the prestigious Grande École. Rodin failed the school's sculpture exams with his unconventional approach, but he also suspected that his exclusion was due to his lack of family connections and his inability to supply letters of recommendation from renowned artists. Rodin finally gave up on art school and trying to win the academy's favour. But he did not stop making his art. Instead, he adopted a kind of "aesthetic of survival"; his art became grounded in lived experience, depicting the human form in all its raw and unexceptional misery.[1] In time, an acceptance of his fate combined with a fidelity to his calling led Rodin to become recognised as one of the world's and France's most famous sculptors.

Or consider Justice Ruth Bader Ginsburg, the second woman to be appointed to the Supreme Court of the United States. In 1959, she earned her Juris Doctor degree at Columbia and tied for first in her class. She was the first woman to be on two major law journals: the *Harvard Law Review* and *Columbia Law Review*. Yet at the start of her career, her applications for employment in the law were repeatedly rejected due to her gender. Squarely facing this aspect of her fate – a woman who simply wanted to be able to practice her profession – led Ruth Bader Ginsburg to argue for and successfully achieve the end of gender discrimination in many areas of United States law.

The Latin phrase *amor fati* means the love or embrace of one's fate. Fate, as Jungian analyst and literature professor James Hollis wrote, is the word we have historically ascribed to what is unavoidably given. *Amor fati* "is in the end a recognition that it is *here*, in *this place*, in *this time*, in *this* arena, that we are called to live our lives".[2] So there is a sense that fate is something inherent, something with which we are asked to work. Thomas Moore observed that "to take on one's fate is a necessary bondage" and that a refusal to submit to the actual limits of one's life and fate leads an individual instead to be bound by envy: the complaint that one is born in the wrong time, place or family, or wishing one was born with the gifts or talents of others.[3] Jung reinforced the connection between loving one's fate and the discovery of vocation when he observed that "it is the man without *amor fati* who is the neurotic; he, truly, has missed his vocation".[4]

Some psychologists and philosophers have tended to use the terms fate and destiny synonymously.[5] Yet conflation of these terms can give rise to disturbing ethical issues, such as a strongly masochistic or dangerously casual attitude to trauma, particularly childhood trauma.[6] Therefore I believe it is important and helpful to differentiate between these concepts of fate and destiny. In his evocative book, *Fate and Destiny: The Two Agreements of the Soul*, the mythologist Michael Meade describes fate as the thing which constricts our life, at least partially. Destiny, on the other hand, is something we pursue, the direction and arc of the arrow of our life. Although he draws a distinction between fate and destiny, Meade also perceives that these are irrevocably enfolded together, two sides of the same coin.

Jung has also used the word *destiny* synonymously with *vocation* to indicate "the growth of personality, the full realization of the life-will that is born with the individual".[7] Reflecting on the role of fate and destiny in his own life, Jung said:

> From the beginning, I had a sense of destiny, as though my life was assigned to me by fate and had to be fulfilled. This gave me an inner security, and though I could never prove it to myself, it proved itself to me. I did not have this certainty, it had me. Nobody could rob me of the conviction that it was enjoined upon me to do what God wanted and not what I wanted. That gave me the strength to go my own way.[8]

Ed Whitmont illuminated the nature of the relationship between fate and destiny when he argued that although we are all bound by the hand of fate in one form or another, it is the wise individual who can love their fate so deeply that it is transformed into destiny:

> *Amor fati*, then, includes an awareness of ourselves, of our inner and outer limitations, and the kind of acceptance and willingness to concern ourselves with them which makes the striving for adequate fulfilment within such limitations into a challenge to creative improvisation. Only by so accepting ourselves in the light of the overall pattern of our destiny can our sense of compulsive bondage be transformed into motivation.[9]

Destiny, as Whitmont portrays it, involves a quest for fulfilment according to our unique patterning, together with an acceptance of the limitations of our fate.

In the United States, I've noticed that people are often indignant about the idea of being bound by fate. Fate seems to represent an affront to Americans' sense of freedom and ability to make something of their lives, whereas in Australia, people incline to be more resigned to fate. Either position can be problematic. The latter can lead to victimhood and feelings of learned helplessness, dependence and passivity, whereas the former can lead to denial, inflation, hubris and a lack of empathy for any discomforting weakness or vulnerability.

There is a genuine relationship between *amor fati* and the discovery of the meaning of one's own life. This connection was evident amongst the people I interviewed for this work. Lying in bed with partial paralysis and able to see with only one eye, Annabella surrendered to what was and came to accept: "This is happening now". Her willing participation in what might appear as the full catastrophe of life opened her to a profound sense of the meaning of her life and a motivation to fulfil her perceived destiny within the limitations of her fate.

Many an important vocation arises in this way by working courageously and creatively with what life brings. In this respect, I often think of 2015 Australian of the Year Rosie Batty, who stepped into her role as a family violence campaigner after her son was murdered by his father. Of course, this was not a calling she would have chosen for herself (who would?). Yet it is important and socially transformative work which has done much to help victims and potential victims of domestic violence. Batty's calling in response to her fate has changed and saved the lives of many women and children who have existed in situations of fear and intimidation.

My family, friends and others with whom I've worked have often said I am a born teacher. As a very young child, I was known for saying, "I will show you", desiring to share my insights or discoveries about the way things worked with others. As a girl, I loved playing schools with my dolls or the other children in my street, and I imagined becoming a teacher. In my twenties I taught law, but soon felt that rather than teaching manmade laws, I needed to be studying and teaching more enduring truths of the human condition – the laws of the psyche, or the soul, if you will. Later in life, I learned that Jung called these laws 'archetypes' and that depth psychology was the field for which I had been searching so long. Yet depth psychology was not (and is still not) taught at any university or institute in my country. So I have long been a student and a teacher with no classroom in my home country for what I am called to learn and to teach. That has been part of my fate, and it has brought its share of suffering and difficulty. It has also necessitated ways to innovatively, persistently and courageously work with that fate, such as finding avenues to share my knowledge outside a tenured teaching position. As Abraham Maslow famously said, "A musician must make music, an artist must paint, a poet must write". And so – a teacher must teach.

In Chapter 6, I related the story of Jim's midlife crisis, precipitated by the deaths of his four closest people. The ancient concept of *amor fati*, said Jim, helped him deal with all the terrible things that happened to him. His daughters' mothers passed away, but that also enabled him to meet his current partner and step into his vocation. Michael was another whose sudden and traumatic death of his wife led him into a new life partnership and launched him in a particular vocational direction, writing a book about grief.

To lovingly embrace one's fate heralds the emergence of wisdom. Sherry Salman sees this emergence as the real goal of depth psychotherapy: "the transformation of fate or *heimarmene* (compulsion by the stars) into a conscious life which both rests in the containment of its boundaries and transcends them at the same time".[10] We are tasked with the paradox of both consciously surrendering to and actively struggling with the imperatives of our own fate.

Embracing our weirdness

Michael Meade draws a mythological and etymological connection between fate, being wise and being weird, which is relevant to our understanding of vocation. In Plato's Myth of Er in *The Republic*, it is the three sisters of Fate, known as the Moirai, who apportion each soul its 'lot' in life before birth. The first sister, Clotho, spins the invisible thread that is the web of each person's life. The second sister, Lachesis, bestows your positive and negative qualities and weaves the garment of your destiny. Then the third sister, Atropos, carries the "abhorred shears" which cut the thread of your destiny and determine the date of your death. The Three Fates are the daughters of Ananke (necessity) – suggesting that it is necessary that it be this way.

The Three Fates are also referred to in Norse mythology as the Norns and, in Shakespeare's *Macbeth*, as the Weird Sisters. So according to this myth, we are 'weirded' or given our particular lot in life by the sisters of Fate. "The original sense of *weird* involved both fate and destiny. Becoming weird enough to be wise requires that a person learn to accommodate the strange way they are shaped within and aimed at the world".[11] Furthermore, according to the *Oxford English Dictionary*, *weird* (n.) derives from the Old English *wyrd, meaning* "fate or destiny – the principle, power, or agency by which events are predetermined", and also the Fates, the three goddesses who determine the course of human life.

So Meade makes an imaginative connection between the way we are uniquely 'weirded' and our fate. To follow your *weird*, or your *wyrd*, is to embrace your fate. According to a personal conversation Thomas Moore recalled with Joseph Campbell in the 1970s, Campbell envisioned the original formulation of his famous adage "follow your bliss" to be something closer to "follow your *wyrd*", your fate, the core pattern and living story bestowed upon you from before birth, the "irreversible process of becoming from within".[12]

Attending to the insights offered by this ancient mythological wisdom suggests that it is by embracing our fate (*wyrd*) – in particular, the very particular way in which we are each 'weird' or uniquely formed – that the precise nature of our destiny, or calling, becomes manifest. In our weirdness, clues reside to our vocation. In *The Soul's Code*, James Hillman endeavoured to make a case for this by relating numerous anecdotes of the childhood idiosyncrasies of famous individuals and showing how these idiosyncrasies intimated their future work. Hillman attributed this weirdness to the compelling power of each individual's *daimon*, that mythic soul companion who accompanies us from before birth and which, by hints, intuitions and nagging symptoms, is always attempting to remind us of our calling in this lifetime. To be truly happy in life necessitates that we live true and close to the pattern woven into our soul, that we become content with our 'lot' and live in harmony with our *daimon* and ourselves. The ancient Greek word for this kind of happiness was *eudaimonia* – which literally means to have a well-pleased *daimon*.

> *Vocation acts like a law of God from which there is no escape. . . . Anyone with a vocation hears the voice of the inner man: he is* called. *That is why the legends say that he possesses a private daemon who counsels him and whose mandates he must obey.*
>
> — CG Jung (1934b CW17, para. 300)

This is, of course, a very different approach to that taken in mainstream career counselling, which tends to focus on and encourage the development of generic skills to fit the (existing, known) labour market. A normative approach to jobs may suit some people, at some times, but it will not suit everyone. At the very least, proper consideration might be given to each individual's 'weirding' – the way one has been shaped by fate, or one's particular obsessions or preoccupations, for example – as a vocational indicator. Such an approach may encourage more people towards occupations, businesses or careers (or particular ways of doing them) which have not been previously imagined but which feel authentic for that individual and which may also necessitate a degree of innovation and entrepreneurship.

An example of this is Jana, a PhD candidate who was born in Latvia. Although she has lived around the world and was studying in the United States, Jana thinks of herself very much as a Latvian. She described her feeling that being Latvian is:

> *sort of my uniqueness, and something that I need to use to bring something back to the world. Because there are only one, maybe two million Latvians in the world, so that must be for a reason then. I had grown up very close to Latvian folklore. I used to sing Latvian folksongs for hours and hours.*

Embracing the uniqueness of her cultural heritage, her *wyrd*, Jana chose Latvian legends as her thesis topic. In a way that was not yet completely clear to her, Jana anticipated this research would shape her post-doctoral career.

> *Even though it sounds as if I had a clarity about this research, I really didn't. It was like – taking me, and I was following it. It was as if the topic chose me. I think our research topics really do choose us. There could be many topics. The topics choose us, but it's also the people who happen to be around when we are choosing the topics. It also depends on the environment that we are in, and how people around us are supportive of who we are.*
>
> (Jana)

Jana's reflections on being chosen by her work as a researcher accord with imaginal psychologist Robert Romanyshyn's observation that research itself is a vocation: "A researcher is called into a work, claimed by it. He or she is chosen by a work as much as he or she or perhaps even more than he or she chooses it".[13] Loving one's fate means living the life one is summoned to, by the sense of some invisible agency, whether one might call that the gods, or the psyche, or forces transcendent to consciousness, but "not the life envisioned by the ego, by one's parents, by societal expectations".[14]

So contrary to the popular notion that we determine and direct our vocations through the exercise of personal will, in this chapter and the previous one, we have seen how vocation emerges as we surrender into a relationship and dialogue with the larger psyche. We do not choose our vocations; rather, we are *chosen by* our vocations.

In the next chapter, I will turn to look at how loving our fate involves the acceptance of our wounds, complexes and ancestral patterns and consciously working both with and through these in our vocations.

Invitation to reflection and journaling

- In what significant ways has Fate played its hand in your life? What are the limitations or constraints you have faced in your endeavours to self-actualise or express yourself?
- What other sensibilities, perhaps even gifts, have come into your life as a result of these difficulties?
- As we move into the next chapter, be open to the possibility that your destiny – and your calling – may reside in how you consciously and creatively engage with these aspects of your fate.

Notes

1　Corbett 2016, pp. 9–10.
2　Hollis 2001, p. 68.
3　Moore 1994, p. 128.
4　Jung 1934b CW17, para. 313.
5　See, for example, the writings of May (1989) or Whitmont (2007).
6　Hogenson 2007, p. 43.
7　Jung 1934b CW17, para. 313.
8　Jung 1989b, p. 48.
9　Whitmont 2007, p. 36.
10　Salman 2000, p. 82.
11　Meade 2010, p. 87.
12　Campbell 1991, p. 215. Campbell wrote that the roots of 'wyrd' can be traced to two German words (*warden*, which means to grow or to become, suggesting a sense of inward inherent destiny, and *wirtel*, or spindle, suggesting a spinning and weaving of destiny) (1991, p. 121). He also briefly discusses the similarities and differences between wyrd, kismet and fate.
13　Romanyshyn 2013, p. 320. See also Coppin and Nelson (2005).
14　Hollis 2001, p. 68.

9 A rough and uncommonly devious footpath

Complexes as pathways to vocation

I must find another way, in this new day, to let my demons sing.
And I must sing with them.

(Vanya)

According to Jung, the *via regia* (royal road) to the unconscious was not, as Freud thought, the dream, but "the complex, which is the architect of dreams and of symptoms".[1] A central theme of this book is the idea that our vocation arises from the deep psyche, or the unconscious. So if the complex is the royal road to the unconscious – or as Jung also put it, "more like a rough and uncommonly devious footpath"[2] – then our complexes may also be a pathway towards our vocation.

In this chapter and the next, I discuss the nature of complexes from a Jungian perspective, including how complexes derive from our personal wounds (often originating in childhood), the collective wounds of our culture or the traumas and patterns of previous generations. We will consider how callings may originate with, and be a way of transforming, our complexes. Complexes may provide a vehicle and vessel of transformation of **libido**[3] or 'psychic energy' from the unconscious towards individuation and the unfolding of vocation. Furthermore, an occupation or career which tends mindfully to our wounds or complexes holds the possibility of making a vital social contribution. As we will see, a more conscious understanding of our complexes can be revelatory for the discovery and conduct of our vocation.

Skeletons in the cupboard

What is a complex? Jung developed the concept of complexes through his experiments with the Word Association Test from 1904 onwards, though the term *complex* was used earlier by Sigmund Freud and Joseph Breuer. A complex may be described most simply "as an emotionally charged group of ideas and images that cluster around an archetypal core".[4] Jung's research into the nature of complexes and the power they exert in the psyche led him to assert that "complexes are in truth the living units of the unconscious psyche".[5] So important was the idea of the complex in Jung's psychology that he considered calling his approach 'complex psychology' (reflecting also the complexity of his psychological approach) rather than 'analytical psychology'.[6]

The existence of a complex is recognised by its strongly accentuated emotional affect. When something gets under your skin and you just can't seem to help yourself, when you have a strong reaction to something or someone and later think, "I don't know what came over me, why I said that, I really didn't mean to or want to" – then you've stumbled on an activated complex. Complexes can be recognised by the heightened emotional affect they trigger, often disproportionate to a situation. When a complex is activated, then a little disturbance takes place, where we are not fully in conscious control.

We typically meet complexes through projections. It is rarely the case that we first come across our complexes introspectively. They inevitably turn up in some projected form. We run into a complex because of someone or something we see 'out there' in the world that rankles or irritates us or gets under our skin – that we can't simply brush off. The things we continually talk about in our conversations will eventually point to our complexes. They are like little centres of gravity in the personal terrain of the psyche, which can show up in our moods, our habitual perspectives, our hopes, our dreams and our fears. Though getting to the root of the complex is another thing!

Phenomenologically, a complex may be thought of as an impulse, pattern of behaviour, recurring mode of imagination, obsessive thought or particular fantasy which keeps us in its grip. Where Jungian psychology uses the psychological term *complex*, vocational guidance has tended to speak of an individual's preoccupations, pains and problems.[7] Jung described complexes as the "vulnerable points", the "*bêtes noir*", the "skeletons in the cupboard", which frequently come back to mind unbidden and interfere with our lives in unwelcome ways.[8]

Our torments also may in length of time, Become our elements.
— John Milton, *Paradise Lost* (1667)

However, Jung also believed that complexes fuel libido or psychic energy and should not be missing, lest life comes to a fatal standstill. If the content of a complex is not made conscious, it can plague us with neurotic symptoms. But to the extent to which we can assimilate our complexes into consciousness, Jung suggested they may point to a "predestined vocation" which will support our individuation:

> Generally the psychic conditions that have caused the disturbance have to be made conscious with considerable effort. But the contents that then come to light are wholly in accord with the inner voice and *point to a predestined vocation*, which, if accepted and assimilated by the conscious mind, conduces to the development of the personality.[9]

Childhood wounds

A complex can frequently be traced back to a wound in childhood. Many people's vocational choices are, consciously or unconsciously, an attempt to heal these wounds and complexes. This is the vocational archetype or pattern of the 'wounded healer', ubiquitous in the lives of many who enter the helping professions. Typical examples are the man who becomes a family therapist because of his own experience growing up in a dysfunctional family, or the woman who becomes a lawyer because of her family or culture's experiences of injustice.

Claire described her sense of vocation as being "the thing which breaks your heart". One of Claire's deep wounds influencing her vocation was an early experience with a dance teacher. As a child, Claire longed to dance, but her family could not afford lessons. When she was 13, a modern dance teacher started a company in their town.

> *But the teacher taught no technique. It was "move however you feel" and as long as you're wearing a diaphanous white gown you're a dancer. I was just thrilled to be a dancer, and I didn't know what I wasn't getting. I remember a dance recital, where I was doing a solo and was moving the way that I felt. Afterwards, the teacher took me aside and said, "You have no business being in a dance group". That was the broken heart. I was devastated.*

Eventually, Claire continued her dance with another teacher who was able to develop her technique. She realised that the modern dance teacher who taught her nothing, and then proceeded to tell her she wasn't a dancer, was "a spectacular failure as a teacher". But the encounter with a teacher who projected her own inadequacies onto her students cut deeply:

> *I really hate it when teachers are full of themselves, narcissistic, egotistical and lift themselves up by putting their students down. I can't stand teachers who talk down and obfuscate. Sadistic, institutionalised behaviour. That has always bothered me. Students abused by a teacher for their own narcissistic needs. I've seen that all the way through to graduate level.*

This experience of having her heart broken by a teacher was a personal wound which profoundly influenced how Claire was to conduct her own future occupation as a university professor. Claire understands the tremendous importance of students receiving certain things from her in terms of evaluation, lest she, too, be the one who carelessly breaks their hearts.

So one way of discerning a call to vocation by tracing the path of one's complexes might be to ask, as Claire suggests: "Where does the broken heart show up?". Another way of putting this might be, "What am I sensitive to?" For Lynn, the broken heart showed up in conflicts around relationships.

> *So when I found my path and my calling, it's about relationship, because that was the bloodiest, hardest thing for me to understand. Finding the path of*

what I wanted to do, with eco-psychology, allowed me to understand what relationship is really about.

We all have woundings, we all have dysfunctions, as there is no sort of perfect life or perfect parenting. But then, what do we do with that? I think many times, if we work psychologically with these things, we will find that it does direct our vocation. Whether you choose to be a therapist, an eco-psychologist, a teacher, a lawyer, a doctor or a garbage collector . . . whatever. It informs what we do with our lives.

Lynn's story raises two important points. The first is Jung's belief that complexes cannot be controlled or eliminated but simply made conscious so that we *respond* rather than *react* to them. "Complexes are focal or nodal points of psychic life which we would not wish to do without; indeed, they should not be missing, for otherwise psychic activity would come to a fatal standstill".[10] It's humbling to think that we can never really be cured, or fixed, of that disturbing complaint that drives us to the therapist, as complexes fuel psychic energy (libido). The best we can hope for is to learn to live with the complex in a more satisfactory manner.

The second point is Jung's concern with the teleological function of the complex, as contrasted with Freud's focus on the developmental wounds that led to the complex. Whereas Freud regarded the complex only as a manifestation of illness to be transcended, rooted in the personal unconscious and symptomatic of a diseased psyche, Jung saw the complex as pertaining to a healthy human being. Far from being harmful, the complex may even be extremely fruitful, as the energy-giving cell from which psychic life grows. As Lynn said, "We all have woundings, we all have dysfunctions . . . but then what do we *do* with that?" A Jungian approach suggests that it is not simply that we are disturbed by what happened in the past and need to work on that so we can return to a 'normal' (or normative) level of functioning. Rather, it is as if the psyche itself, through the activated complex, has a hidden goal in mind. Perhaps our complexes also have a larger teleological purpose beyond our individual lives. For example, a complex around injustice, which may motivate a critical theorist or a community or environmental activist may also shift the collective for the greater good.

Jung considered that the complex has a dual aspect, "perhaps as an obstacle, but also as a stimulus to greater effort, and so perhaps, as an opening to new possibilities of achievement".[11] Jung's idea that the complex may take on a positive, prospective significance is relevant for the unfolding dynamics of vocation. If we consider our troubling complex or preoccupation as an unexpected ally instead of a pathology, it begs the questions: What fresh awareness or self-understanding is this issue inviting me towards? Where am I being pushed in terms of self-development? What aspects of the psyche have perhaps been relegated to my shadow, which I now need to reclaim and own as parts of myself? As Lynn suggests, if we work psychologically with our complexes, we may find that they *do* direct our vocation.

Lynn speaks of a positive outcome achieved through adequately integrating her complexes and personal wounds around relationships. The result has been fruitful for her life and work. Her whole being feels "in agreement with that", as conscious and unconscious pieces come together to affirm her vocational direction. Freud spoke of the possibility of shifting a large number of libidinal components towards professional work and the special satisfaction that may arise from this.[12] By keeping the libido theory in mind, one could say that when a person 'falls in love' with his or her work, the psychic energy which might otherwise be stuck in the eddy of a complex (preoccupation) is channelled by the release and progression of libido into a particular direction (occupation). The word *occupation* also means to be 'taken and seized', and in the past, it had strong sexual connotations. Our work may come to occupy us: "it can excite us, comfort us, and make us feel fulfilled, just as a lover can", wrote Thomas Moore.[13] Following the flow of eros, in this larger sense, may help one to notice when the libido is channelling itself in a particular vocational direction – be it a new interest, place or issue – where there is fuel for the creative fire.[14] In any case, we are obliged to trust eros, as (following the Greek myth of *Eros and Psyche*) eros' goal is always psyche, or soul-making.[15]

Joseph Campbell famously recommended to his students that they "follow their bliss", a term he derived from the Sanskrit *ananda*, meaning bliss or rapture.[16] Campbell's adage has been interpreted to mean identifying a pursuit about which one is truly passionate and then attempting to give oneself absolutely to it. Of course, it's optimal if we can develop our life's work by following our passions and doing what brings pleasure. However, as clinical psychologist Aaron Kipnis has observed, many people lack sufficient bliss to follow. Instead, Kipnis advises his graduate students to "follow their affect".[17] This means being true to the emotional currents running through them, including sadness, disappointment, anger and fear. Affect is invariably a sign that a complex has been activated. Jung tended to use *affect* as synonymous with emotional reactions, characterised by physical symptoms and disturbances in thinking.[18] So whether we are following our bliss or our affect, either way we are following the path of our complexes.

The danger of possession by a complex

> *Everyone knows nowadays that people 'have complexes'. What is not so well known, though far more important theoretically, is that complexes can have us.*
>
> – CG Jung (1934c CW8, para. 200)

Following complexes as a pathway to vocation may also be psychologically demanding and risky. There is a feeling of *possession* which accompanies a complex, where our reactions are overtaken by a force outside our conscious will and control. The problems associated with complexes occur when a complex becomes autonomous, due to the ego's inability to assimilate or integrate the complex.

A complex may quickly become problematic when we are unaware that our thoughts and actions are driven by the complex. This may lead to projection of the unintegrated complex onto others. Alternatively, if a complex is overcharged and becomes autonomous, it may take on any of the forms that generate neurosis and psychosis:

> Everything depends upon whether the conscious mind is capable of under-standing, assimilating, and integrating the complex, in order to ward off its harmful effects. If it does not succeed in this, the conscious mind falls a vic-tim to the complex, and is in greater or lesser degree engulfed by it.[19]

In Lynn's case, an education in depth psychology and mythology supported her to understand, assimilate and integrate her complex in the direction of a deeply fulfilling vocation. But for an individual who remains largely uncon-scious of a complex and its roots, his or her career may be unwittingly driven by the autonomous complex in a problematic fashion, marked by factors such as career tunnel-vision, a rigid work identity, high rates of burnout and deleteri-ous or negative relationships.[20] Jungian analyst James Hollis observed that indi-viduals whose careers appear successful and exemplary to others may in fact be driven by deep narcissistic wounds or an infantile need for external approval, resulting in a missed appointment with their own soul's vocation and "summons to personhood".[21]

Jim, the former Wall Street executive, reflected that the first "career-oriented" part of his life was "heavily driven by a lot of complexes. People thought that what I was doing and pursuing was normal". Complexes around power and money, which were also familial and cultural, were behind Jim's appetite for recognition and success. With the onset of individuation at midlife, and supported by his stud-ies in depth psychology, the grip of these complexes loosened. Ironically, as Jim left his former career and has become more psychologically mindful, exploring alternative work avenues with a greater social conscience, he comments, "Now, people look at me following my vocation, abandoning the cultural paradigms, and think I am going crazy". Jim's experience testifies to the ubiquity and strength of unconscious power and money complexes in his milieu.

An autonomous or untransformed complex may also inhibit us from following a vocational call. For example, Rose's compelling desire from childhood to be a writer has been constantly undermined by what she has identified as a mother complex:

> *I think I've got a big mother complex. Being an enabler. For some reason I feel like I need to be mother to everyone. That has kept me from writing, because I've always worried about having an income – through my marriages, worried about that, and ended up being the main breadwinner. So that wound, and again I'm not quite sure where it comes from – this is something I will be working through I think with my dissertation.*

(Rose)

Due to their archetypal core, complexes tend to have a bi-polar nature. This means that, according to the circumstances, a complex may be regarded as negative or positive. Rose's mother complex may in some respects have been beneficial, at least to those around her. However, in other respects, it is problematic and causes her angst regarding her frustrated vocation as a writer. Like Rose, we may find themselves stuck in the role of caregiver or provider and identification with the mother or father archetype, at the expense of other archetypes seeking expression in our lives. James Hollis states the situation plainly: "We remain stuck because beneath the surface our stuckness is wired to a complex".[22] An over-identification with one archetype or possession by a complex, the origins of which are often traceable to early childhood experiences, may at some stage become antithetical to further individuation and vocation. The archetype at the core of an autonomous complex takes hold in a totalitarian regime, and there is no democracy of the psyche.

In working with a complex, we need to reflect upon what the complex is asking of us. *What is the ethical response required?* This requires us to become more conscious of what is behind or at the root of our complex. It goes without saying that this is psychologically demanding and courageous work.

> *A complex can be really overcome only if it is lived out to the full. . . . If we are to develop further we have to draw to us and drink down to the very dregs what, because of our complexes, we have held at a distance.*
> – CG Jung (1938 CW9:1, para. 184)

The wounded researcher

Both Rose and Peter mentioned the possibility of working through their complexes in the process of writing their doctoral dissertations. The idea that researchers are called to their research work by their own wounds and complexes, which in turn may "give voice to the unanswered questions of culture and history",[23] has been advanced by depth psychologists, notably Robert Romanyshyn.[24]

Peter spoke about how his doctoral work was a means of consciously tending his complexes and crafting a new vocational direction with potentially wide-reaching benefits:

> *There were a lot of things that occurred in my life that I really couldn't account for. I thought it was just my nature, but in psychotherapy I found they went back to my interaction with my mother and siblings.*
>
> *As I looked into this in psychotherapy I found that the fact that I had a very traumatic infancy seemed to account for a lot of the problems I had later on. I was born with crossed eyes. They were severe enough. . . . Prior to the 1950s, crossed eyes, strabismus, was not treated in infants, only in adults. Infants were left on their own to deal with it. And really, they didn't know how*

> *to deal with it. . . . My surgeon revolutionised the field of modern paediatric ophthalmology by developing a surgical technique for re-attaching the musculature in the eyes to bring them into convergence.*

Peter had several operations in childhood and adulthood to correct his strabismus. One eye would wander out, and he was constantly being asked why he wasn't looking at somebody. But Peter wondered about the psychological aspects of strabismus. For a cross-eyed infant who sees two mothers, there is the possibility that when the eyes converge one mother disappears. What is the psychological effect of that?

> *Another possibility is that you see one mother, with an overlay of the other image that you see from the other eye. There are interesting ramifications from both these possibilities. It speaks of confusion, one way or another. Also, my mother couldn't make eye contact with her infant. How did that affect her and her affection for and bonding with me? All this forms the basis for my dissertation.*

Peter was able to address some of the wounding he experienced as a result of this condition through psychotherapy and through his studies in depth psychology. He also felt that his research work, though originating from and tending to a personal childhood wound, may have broader cultural implications, including a fresh insight into the nature of "bonding issues" (or what we might call a variation of the "mother complex").

> *I am doing it for myself, but I also see it as being able to help other people who have had similar experiences. Not just with crossed-eyes, but with any kind of vision-related or bonding issues. It brings that to the fore. This can also be translated to the culture, I would hope, in some way. . . . So I don't know where it's going to go, though I think it's beyond me. There are too many things that have come together than just to serve my own purposes. And that's a good thing.*

Peter's story illustrates a significant point, which is the link the complex provides between the personal and the archetypal, the individual and the universal. As Erel Shalit elaborated, Jung considered that all complexes have an archetypal core: "The complex serves as the vehicle that fleshes out the archetype, giving it human shape and personal body".[25] An individual who becomes conscious enough of a complex to trace its nodal point to the archetypal level "is then confronted with a problem which no longer represents solely his personal conflict but gives expression to a conflict that it has been incumbent on man to suffer and solve from time immemorial".[26] It is as if consciously working with our (ostensibly personal) complexes is indeed sacred work which assists in the collective evolution of humankind.

> We need complexes, for they are *the path and the vessel that give human shape and structure to archetypal patterns as they unfold in personal*

experience. The complexes provide the link between archetype and ego enabling the transformation of the archetypal into the personal. . . . The complex is, thus, the messenger of the gods, or the archetypes, rather than of the ego, though the personal life is its object.[27]

From an archetypal psychology perspective, we might also ask: What archetype or god is visiting here, and in what way or ways may that best be propitiated? Or as Hollis puts it, "The task is not the elimination of complexes, as if that were even possible, but redemption by honouring their power and autonomy".[28] Our vocational choices and the way we conduct our work may provide a vehicle for the redemption of our complexes (though of course the playing field of our complexes is not confined to the workplace). By becoming more conscious of our complexes, we can hope to collaborate with their forces more constructively and thereby serve our societies in a more psychologically mindful and ethical manner.

In this book, I've proposed the idea that vocation can be understood as a calling, not from the ego but from the *psyche*, the archetypal realm or the gods. The complex has been called the messenger of the gods, or the archetypes.[29] So in this chapter, we've seen how our complexes may indeed be the heralds of our vocation. Complexes reveal our preoccupations at a level below the conscious ego: preoccupations which, if responded to constructively and creatively, can point the way to *occupations* which hold profound meaning and rightness for us. The choice and conduct of an occupation may also provide a means of tending or healing the wound which triggered the complex. Yet an autonomous complex which overpowers the ego may be a pernicious derailer of our vocation. The task is to become more conscious of our complexes, to reflect not only upon their history but also enquire of their telos, or larger unfolding purpose. Through our complexes, we live in dynamic relationship with the archetypal basis of existence, which holds not only the dark and disturbing parts of our nature but also our unlived potential.

Invitation to reflection and journaling

- What does it feel like to be in the grip of a complex? Try to write about this in a way that captures the general qualitative state, without focussing on the biographical details. Use metaphor or draw an image to describe the feeling.
- Where does your broken heart show up? What are you sensitive to? What connection may there be between this and a) your choice of or approach to your past work and b) your sense of an emerging calling?
- What is the complex inviting you – perhaps pushing you – towards in terms of self-awareness or self-development?

Notes

1 Jung 1934c CW8, para. 210.
2 Jung 1934c CW8, para. 210.

3 For Jung, libido meant a "general life instinct", which may encompass but was not limited to a sexual dynamism, as it was with Freud (Jung 1928a CW8, paras. 54–56).

4 Singer & Kaplinsky 2010, p. 4.

5 Jung 1934c CW8, para. 210.

6 Jung 1948 CW18, para. 1129.

7 For example, career constructivist Mark Savickas emphasised the importance of concentrating on a client's enduring preoccupations and problems, for which "the solution, at least in the work domain, is the occupation. . . . Career construction revolves around turning a personal problem into a public strength and then even a social contribution" (2005, p. 59). But in speaking of personal preoccupations, Savickas might just as easily be speaking of complexes. Savickas' statements that "the heart of my counselling model is to identify a life theme by comprehending how clients *actively master what they have passively suffered*" (1997b, p. 11, italics added) and that "the archetypal theme of career construction involves *turning a personal preoccupation into a public occupation*" (2005, p. 59, italics added) are akin to saying that career constructivism endeavours to work with the individual's complexes as *prima materia*. Bringing a Jungian and archetypal understanding of complexes into career constructivism holds significant potential to enlarge our understanding of the dynamics of vocation – its libidinal drives and archetypal roots.

8 Jung 1933, p. 79.

9 Jung 1934b, CW17, para. 316, italics added.

10 Jung 1931a, CW6, para. 925.

11 Jung 1921 CW6, para. 925.

12 Freud 1961, p. 110.

13 Moore 1992, p. 182.

14 Coppin & Nelson 2005, p. 59.

15 Hillman 1972, p. 82.

16 Campbell 1988, pp. 113, 149.

17 Kipnis 2013, p. 201.

18 Jung 1921 CW6, para. 681; von Franz 2008, p. 16.

19 Jacobi 1959, p. 27.

20 Cardador & Caza 2012.

21 Hollis 2003, p. 61.

22 Hollis 2003, p. 43.

23 Butler 2013, p. 312.

24 Robert Romanyshyn (2007, 2010, 2013) explored the wounded healer complex in academia, creating the depth psychological research methodology known as alchemical hermeneutics. See also Yakushko and Nelson (2013), Coppin and Nelson (2005) for a depth psychological approach to research.

25 Shalit 2002, p. 8.

26 Jacobi 1959, p. 26.

27 Shalit 2002, p. 25, italics in original.

28 Hollis 2003, p. 29.

29 Shalit 2002.

10 Unfinished business

Callings arising from ancestral and cultural wounds

Due to financial limitations, I was the first person in the history of my family to graduate from high school, let alone attend university. As a young woman from a working/middle-class background, I worked hard to forge a career in the legal and corporate worlds. Initially, this included learning and adapting to workplace mores and crafting a professional persona. Throughout my career, I drew on my skills and training as a lawyer to advocate for various social, ethical, environmental and human rights causes. However, when I tried to give voice to my own questions and intuitive-feeling sense that there was a deeper soul-purpose underlying our working lives – that beyond the consensual rationale of material necessity and the bottom line, there was some kind of forgotten yet essential psycho-spiritual context and content to our labours – I experienced a sudden and fierce constriction at my throat. It was as if I was being choked by an invisible hand. Or as if a wire or rope was pulling tightly across my throat. There were things of which I could not speak. The very cells in my body seemed to know this.

Over the years, I have been surprised by the number of women I've met – friends, clients, students – who have confessed, often in tearful, hushed tones, that they too suffer from this same symptom: an incapacitating choking sensation at the throat. Inevitably it arises as we are trying to give voice to something we feel deeply, and know intuitively, but for which we struggle to account in rational terms. Beyond any specific recollected childhood events, the somatic symptom seems to have more distant roots. We remember our mothers struggling to speak *their* truth, becoming passive-aggressive and medicated or self-medicating into acquiescence with societal and family expectations and norms. Just how far back did the seeds of our symptoms extend?

In the last chapter, we considered complexes as stemming from personal wounds or childhood trauma. In this chapter, I will explore the idea that our complexes may also have much deeper origins, extending further back in time than our own lived experiences. New developments in biological science are confirming that the complexes from which we suffer may originate in the traumas suffered by previous generations, even when the events which occasioned the original trauma have been forgotten. Moreover, in recent years, some Jungian scholars have focused on the idea that complexes can also be *cultural*, or common to a people or nation. In this chapter, we will see examples of how a vocational calling may be tied up with these ancient ancestral traumas and larger cultural patterns, and furthermore, how our callings can arise as a potentially transformative and healing response to these wounds.

Mending ancestral patterns

The complexes from which we suffer today may well be a legacy of the psychological wounds or traumas of our parents, grandparents or even more distant ancestors.[1] Jungian career counsellor Sam Shaffer described this unconscious inheritance of an ancestral emotional pattern as a *miasma*:

> In vocational development, the unresolved dreams, expectations, and struggles of previous generations often come into play. Traumatic events that have threatened the safety and livelihood of the ancestors can leave a mark on succeeding generations. Even in the absence of actual contact with family forebears, emotional effects may appear in the descendants. Clients often carry the psychic burden of the ancestors in an attempt to create the potential for intergenerational healing.[2]

The search for an underlying cause or meaning of miasmal symptoms within the individual's life today will yield limited results, argued Shaffer, because the root of the pattern is contained in the experience of previous generations. The meaning of the symptoms predates the existence of the one who now carries them.

This relates to a core idea of Jung's, that the mind as well as the body has an evolutionary history, and that the work we undertake may in fact be a legacy from long ago.[3] Interestingly, this idea is now being affirmed by recent discoveries in the field of behavioural epigenetics:

> Traumatic experiences in our past, or in our recent ancestors' past, leave molecular scars adhering to our DNA. Jews whose great-grandparents were chased from their Russian shtetls; Chinese whose grandparents lived through the ravages of the Cultural Revolution; young immigrants from Africa whose parents survived massacres; adults of every ethnicity who grew up with alcoholic or abusive parents – all carry with them more than just memories.
>
> Like silt deposited on the cogs of a finely tuned machine after the seawater of a tsunami recedes, our experiences, and those of our forebears, are never gone, even if they have been forgotten. They become a part of us, a molecular residue holding fast to our genetic scaffolding. The DNA remains the same, but psychological and behavioral tendencies are inherited.[4]

To this list of examples, I would also add women, whose great-great-great . . .- grandmothers were tortured and executed in what has been called the women's holocaust – the European witch trials throughout the 15th to 18th centuries in which it is estimated between 60,000–100,000 women were killed, usually under the guise of Christian morality. It may be that with this example I am reaching more deeply than epigenetic research can presently verify; perhaps this example arises more from my imagining mind. My own ancestors were folk from those regions, though their stories have been long forgotten. Yet extrapolating from this research, is it not possible that the legacy of that monumental historical trauma continues to reverberate today in women? Women who feel a constriction in the throat chakra and an irrational embodied terror when it comes to 'speaking up' and giving voice to the feminine principle – particularly when our voices fly in the face of patriarchal or monotheistic traditions? Yet with the rise of the #Me Too movement, for example, in the 21st century, we are witnessing a resurgence of women who can no longer tolerate being silenced, and who are willing to risk speaking truth to power in service of their soul's calling. In the process of doing so, they are also remedying old karmic wounds.

CG Jung had a sense of answering to an impersonal family karma in his own life's work. In his autobiography, he wrote:

> I feel very strongly that I am under the influence of things or questions which were left incomplete and unanswered by my parents and grandparents and more distant ancestors. It often seems as if there were an impersonal karma within a family which is passed on from parents to children. It has always seemed to me that I had to answer questions which fate had posed to my forefathers, and which had not yet been answered, or as if I had to complete, or perhaps continue, things which previous ages had left unfinished.[5]

So there's this idea that perhaps one of the clues to our life's work or soul's purpose, our deepest vocational calls, may have something to do with mending the threads with our families, our ancestors and the things in our past and those of our families and cultures that have been left unfinished. That in some way the work we are called to do in the world is about completing the unfinished business of our ancestors.

This topic of ancestral complexes also connects with the discussion in Chapter 8 on *amor fati*. Fate, as Michael Meade wrote, "involves the inevitable and indelible threads of family heritage as well as the unique and oracular inner voice of our own lives".[6] From a depth psychological perspective, to become conscious of and to creatively and courageously embrace our fate is the task, rather than living out that fate unwittingly in the grip of family, ancestral or cultural complexes. We see this tragedy most famously played out in the Greek myth of Oedipus. As Jung stated, "The psychological rule says that when an inner situation is not made conscious, it happens outside, as fate".[7]

Callings arising from histories of colonisation, war and exile

In a lecture Jung gave in New York in 1925, he said many interesting things about the ancestors. In particular, he spoke about how "they seem to be in the land". Sandra Easter has drawn upon Jung's definition of ancestors to include "those who continue to live in the nature and memory of [the] land".[8] Of course this understanding is prevalent in many indigenous cosmologies. However, this definition of ancestors has interesting vocational implications, I suggest, for those who live on colonised country.

For example, over years of talking with people about work, I have on occasion noticed, particularly amongst certain individuals of European descent born on Australian soil, a passionate calling towards what might be described as indigenous healing and reconciliation, or reviving indigenous ways of knowing. A great-great-great-grandfather of my husband was Sir Henry Ayres, after whom the sacred aboriginal site Uluru was appropriated and re-named Ayres Rock in the 19th century. Throughout his career as a publisher, my husband was particularly concerned with providing a platform for the voices of aboriginal women, although he made no conscious connection between this work and redeeming his ancestor's legacy until recently. He was also motivated by Henry Ayres' treatment of miners in the Burra copper mines to focus on health equity for vulnerable populations. Perhaps for an increasing number of individuals today, vocation is experienced as a calling to tend the trauma and wounds of those indigenous ancestors who live in the nature and memory of the land? Or to atone for the actions of their colonial forebears?

Alyce was an American woman who had thought a great deal about how her work as a mediator was related to addressing the wounds and unanswered questions of her ancestors:

> *I come from a background of warriors. For years I gravitated towards wanting to work with soldiers. My dad rarely talked about his experience, but he spent six years in World War II in Europe. It wasn't a big part of me growing up, but it's always been a background. . . .*
>
> *In mediation, there were times when I worked with soldiers. And I was always so deeply touched by that population. Then when I ended up with a brain injury, and realised we had soldiers coming back from Iraq and just feeling so sorry for what they had to contend with . . . that goes directly back to the fact that my dad came back from World War II with PTSD [post-traumatic stress disorder] and it was absolutely undiagnosed. I grew up with a bit of a tyrant for a father . . . very volatile, and totally exhibiting PTSD symptoms. So it might be for the children that I want to work with that, more than anything. And that's definitely my wound.*
>
> *As far as the other ancestral piece, my grandfather who was in World War I, probably my great-great-great-grandfather who was in the Civil War . . . I'm not sure what I bring to the healing table with that. Except that maybe even going into mediation was something about resolving conflict differently. Without weapons. That could be part of why I resonated so deeply with that. Could be the ancestral piece that is unspoken. Like – what is an alternative to this?*

What is an alternative, Alyce has asked herself, to that particular problematic place of conflict and war where her ancestors were continuously caught? Alyce dreams of founding a healing sanctuary on a piece of land she owns, a healing arts centre for soldiers. In what way might her own life's work be a means of addressing, as Jung wondered, the unanswered questions of her forefathers, the places where they were stuck?

For a deeper insight into vocational impasses and imperatives, a useful question to ponder may be: Where were your parents stuck? In career counselling, the use of genograms has been adopted as a qualitative technique for supporting an individual to resolve career impasses and barriers.[9] A genogram describes an individual's family tree and occupations over three generations. In particular, an Occupational Transmission genogram can include the scripts and patterns developed in the family of origin and transmitted through generations, including the meaning of success, failure, strength and weakness, which have been shown to have significant influence on the career choices and personal relationships of individuals.[10] A genogram can help to bring to light unconscious factors in the choice and conduct of one's career, which have stemmed from our parents' and grandparents' occupations and attitudes to work.[11] Therapeutic intervention for a miasma (unconscious ancestral pattern) may require a release of the pattern through the Jungian technique of **active imagination.**[12] This is a method of voluntary involvement or dialogue with the ancestral figure followed by some form of self-expression (such as writing, sculpture or ritual) to assimilate the awakened insights into consciousness. Family constellation work, which is a healing modality used to address trans-generational wounds and entanglements, may also provide a release.[13]

Michael was another who felt that his life had been about working on the unfinished business of his ancestors, particularly on his father's side. Michael grew up listening to his father's stories:

So the story is my father was an orphan. If there is one archetypal image or theme that has followed me it is the theme of the orphan. It appears in all of my work. I felt like an orphan in psychology, because it wasn't really the psychological thing I was looking for. So it's threaded itself all throughout my life.

What does that mean to be an orphan? It means you are always on a journey of homecoming. . . . That was something my father deeply experienced in his life. Where's my home? Now he made a home, but I remember sitting with him and he always had a far-away look in his eye. Rilke's poem, "Sometimes a man stands up" – that's about that. . . . He was the most responsible man you would ever meet. But there was something missing for him. . . . He left something behind.

That's what I do – I hold workshops on "left by the side of the road", who's waiting for us – the return. I tie that to Jung's notion of individuation as homecoming.

I think that all the work I've done is work that has been the unfinished business of my own ancestors. That whole gypsy thing, all of that wandering, and what's in a name. . . . Even my first name.

Michael reflected upon the meaning of his family name, which he links with the orphan's continuous search for home. Michael felt that his life's work around the theme of the orphan is in some sense linked to that ancient ancestral line. Even his first name ('Michael' is a pseudonym) has been significant in his vocational journey, as it carried certain meanings linked with parental aspirations and projections for what he might do with his life:

> *It took me a long time in analysis to really deal with following someone else's prescription for my vocation. . . . So there I was, fighting my whole life to escape the destiny they wanted for me, in the name. What's in a name? I guess a part of that for me was saying: that's not my name. I never thought of that connection before. But I reached back to older ancestors.*

Michael then related a story about consulting a physician for a medical problem, who treated him for a period of time in the Western medical tradition. Michael knew this doctor was from South Africa and that he was also trained as a *sangoma* (a traditional healer and diviner who throws the bones and stones to access the advice of ancestors).

> *After a while I said to the doctor: I'd like you to take a look at this problem from the point of view of your sangoma treatment. He does this with people on a select basis, and he says fine. He knows the insides of my body as a Western doctor, but he knows nothing about my life and its psychological depths.*
>
> *So he throws the bones, and he says, "There it is. Your problem now that you're experiencing, that I've treated from a Western medical position, is rooted in the fact that you've been too far away from your ancestors". And this was in my sixties, when I was feeling lost. And he said, "Except one". He throws the bones again and says, "The one who has stayed by you all these years is your father's mother". He suggested this be the start of a daily ritual.*

Michael described how he found some very old family photos to perform this daily ritual. This connected him with his grandmother and with another male ancestor on her side, whose name he discovered was Michael. Through tracing the family ancestry, he discovered another more distant ancestor named Michael who led the family line into Eastern Europe in the 16th century. Knowing nothing previously about these ancestors, Michael recalled how when he started school, aged 5, he had felt very centred, and when the teachers called the roll, he announced that his name was Michael. This was not the name his parents chose for him. He had no idea where this name came from.

> *But knowing, with a certainty, at age 5, that I had come from elsewhere. So there is a lineage which goes back to that name. There is something about that ancestral line, that for me is a vocation. Unfinished business.*

Like Jung, Michael has a sense that his evolving vocation is in some sense tied up with the unfinished business of his ancestors. Although this idea may be strange to Westerners, the belief that a consciously sustained relationship with the ancestors is critical to one's well-being is more common in cultures still connected with their indigenous roots, such as the Sioux in North America, the Dagara in West Africa and the Māori in New Zealand. Both Michael and Alyce found that their particular vocational calls became more apparent with maturity, as they contextualised their life's work within a larger and continuing story that reached back to previous generations. Shaffer emphasised this importance of attending to larger ancestral patterns to psychologically liberate vocational counselling clients to express their authentic purpose:

> In Jungian terms, the release of the miasmal pattern can be understood as a multigenerational, collective event. It frees vocational counselling clients from the dimly understood but extraordinarily powerful psychic inheritance of previous generations. It provides these clients with a stronger opportunity to pursue their own life purposes.[14]

In Chapter 5, I mentioned a dream I had immediately prior to embarking on my PhD for the research which led to this book. It seemed to me that the PhD was the 'big stick' I needed if I was to be heard as a woman who could speak with some authority in (the still-present if dying throes of) a patriarchal era, particularly regarding the ways we conceive of the greater purpose of our work. If I was to speak for the appreciation of a more soulful sensibility, a sensibility that is inclusive of the feminine principle. The dream indicated that, on this career path, I was to follow my great-grandmother's dog, a breed known as the 'blue heeler'. It has seemed as if travelling this path has necessitated following the lead of my animal-soul and healing the blue throat chakra. On this journey, I have felt supported by various integrative practices. One has included sleeping with a smooth flat piece of lapis lazuli under my pillow for years, a semi-precious stone reputed to assist with self-expression and all forms of deep communication. Whether or not there is any scientific basis to this belief doesn't really concern me. I can feel strengthened by the qualities of the stone by appreciating it with a symbolic and aesthetic sensibility. Who says that the presence of nature and beauty, combined with subtle imaginative intention, isn't intrinsically healing to the soul?

Of course, healing our voice is also related to living our vocation, from the Latin *vocare*, to call, and *vox*, meaning voice. Attending to vocation is not only about listening to the inner voice, it is also about how we express our voice in the world too.

To summarise, we can be open to the possibility that the troubling symptoms or complexes we experience in our lives today may have their roots or drivers in traumas experienced by our ancestors, even many generations before. We can view this as an invitation to mend old ancestral patterns and release future generations from the karmic burden we have inherited from the ancestors. Rather than being viewed as obstacles to successful lives and careers, our complexes stemming from trauma in other times and places may indeed be the unbidden heralds of an authentic calling.

Cultural complexes

We've already explored the idea of a complex as a personal wound, triggered by a childhood trauma or by an ancestral trauma or pattern. However, in recent years some Jungian analysts and scholars have focused on the idea that complexes may also be cultural, or common to a people or nation.[15] In this section, I will outline the general theory of cultural complexes and show how these can influence individuals' vocational callings. Any number of cultural examples could be explored to illustrate this theory, such as the Hero archetype within North American cultural complexes or the Sage/Guru archetype in India. Drawing on my own culture of origin, I will offer an analysis of Australia's cultural complexes, at the root of which I suggest is the archetype of the Orphan.

Like any complex, the complexes of a person's culture can influence his or her vocation either detrimentally or constructively. An awareness of cultural complexes is particularly significant for those who are called to become leaders or change agents in our society. We will consider some further anecdotal stories of how individuals' careers and vocations can be either unconsciously driven by, or a creative response to, the complexes of the culture in which they live.

Jung understood that the psyche is not just interior but also collective and social, and that archetypes "seem to belong as much to society as to the individual".[16] Cultural complexes carry the same characteristics as complexes pertaining to individuals, but they are experienced by the collective (as a whole) as well as by individuals within that group. We are all affected – indeed, infected! – by the complexes of our culture, for cultural complexes aren't just 'out there'. They tend to be activated in the psyches of all the individual members of the culture.

> Cultural complexes can be defined as emotionally charged aggregates of ideas and images that tend to cluster around an archetypal core and are shared by individuals within an identified collective. They accumulate experiences that validate their point of view and create a store house of self-affirming, ancestral memories which are based on historical experiences that have taken root in the collective psyche of a group and in the psyches of the individual members of a group. The complexes of a given culture are built up over time and multi-generational experience, some of which have been traumatic.[17]

So the complexes from which we suffer may also arise from the collective psyche of a culture or group of which we are part. Just as the endeavour to heal our personal wounds can lead us to a vocation, the pain of our cultural wounds may initiate a vocational direction that enables us to, in our own particular way, tend the complexes of our culture. The culture or group suffering the complex may even be a profession. For example, Michael spoke about his particular vocation as a poet as being a response to the gap between his profession of psychology (with its scientific bias) and "the eros of being in the world in an embodied way".

Many people are unconsciously driven by the complexes of their culture, especially in their choice and conduct of work and career. Previously I have mentioned Jim, who reflected on how his first career in the financial sector was heavily driven by ubiquitous cultural complexes around power and money.

However, if we are sensitive to the complexes in our culture, there is the potential to move from being a victim of them, or unconsciously complicit in them, to more consciously healing and transforming these complexes through our work. For example, Jana perceived a connection between her country of origin, its cultural complexes and her emerging vocation:

> *I believe that as a Latvian, which puts me in a unique position, I am called to do something that is relevant to Latvia. . . . This is linking to the cultural complexes, and most probably also with the ancestral complexes that I am living with as well. . . .*
>
> *Latvians are extremely good at arts and culture – that's what's very alive – and really lousy when it comes to the practicalities of life, financially. Even running a shop. Latvians would typically not be in the shop, instead they would be singing, and weaving . . . and at the same time having this very intense relationship with money.*

In midlife, Jana felt that her life and work experiences were constellating around a calling to bring consciousness to a particular complex of her Latvian culture, which she identified as a complex connected with money. Shortly after her birth Jana's family moved to a small village in Latvia whose name translates to 'Money', though Jana made no connection between the village name and her vocational interests until someone recently pointed it out to her. Some cultures such as the African Dagara believe that one's name is programmatic for one's destiny.[18] Like a fairy tale heroine, one might imagine that Jana's life project was intimated by the unusual name of the village in which she spent her childhood years.

> *Then I worked in [a United Nations organisation] that deals with money. Now I'm researching Latvian folklore and legends [passed down to her by her grandmother] which turn out to be about money, which I hadn't realised at first. I first thought they were about complexes. The more I researched the more I understood they were about complexes related to money. So there is clearly something going on there which is very unconscious.*

Having worked in environments focused on dealing with money in a very literal way, Jana is now starting to understand money in a depth psychological, symbolic and mythic sense. She believes that this is what has been missing in our personal and collective relationships with money. Her innovative research looks at what Latvian legends reveal about cultural complexes related to money.

> *I think that by doing my research, I might be able to articulate that there is this tension, that there is this complex. My talking about this complex, bringing it to light, there may appear some ways of working through this complex. . . .*
> *If I do that, I think I will have answered my calling.*

Money complexes of one sort or another afflict most people. They are especially constellated in the context of work and careers. I discuss the money complex (and Jana's reflections on this as her calling) in detail in Chapter 11. Jana found that the Latvian money complex, also connected to her ancestral complexes, is pervasive in Latvian folklore and fairy tales. She feels that her vocation as a researcher responding to this complex may also make a vital contribution to her society. As Jana says, perhaps by talking about this cultural complex and bringing it to light, ways of working through it may appear. There is the potential for cultural transformation and healing to take place, which may profoundly influence the psychological well-being of future generations in that culture.

The orphan archetype within Australia's cultural complexes

In the same way that some people are born into families in which they feel like an outlier, I have long been perplexed by many common behaviours and attitudes in my culture of birth. And just as some people find it is not easy to separate from their incompatible or dysfunctional families, try as I might, I have not been able to escape from my culture! While in many material respects, mine is a fortunate country and culture in which to be born, being consigned to live and work in Australia has also been a major aspect of my fate with which I have been obliged to wrestle. When I had the opportunity to embark on postgraduate studies in the United States, I felt much of this 'cultural baggage' fall away. I began to participate in a different culture with some regard for imaginal and mythic perspectives, as well as for concepts like spirit and soul. Immersing myself in the northern hemisphere traditions of Jungian psychology gave me a new language and perspective to reflect on the confusion and ambivalence of my experiences in Australia. I applied the concept of cultural complexes to the Australian context and began to map out my thoughts. It soon became apparent to me that there was not just one Australian cultural complex but a web of interacting symptoms and complexes. To elaborate, I developed the schema in Figure 10.1, which offers a kind of landscape of the cultural psyche rather than a cause and effect diagram.

Like the famous parable of a group of blind men each trying to describe an elephant by touching only one part, what we see of the whole depends upon where we are standing. Different facets of Australia's complexes come to the fore according to different psychographic, demographic and geographic perspectives. David Tacey has written at length about what he has identified as

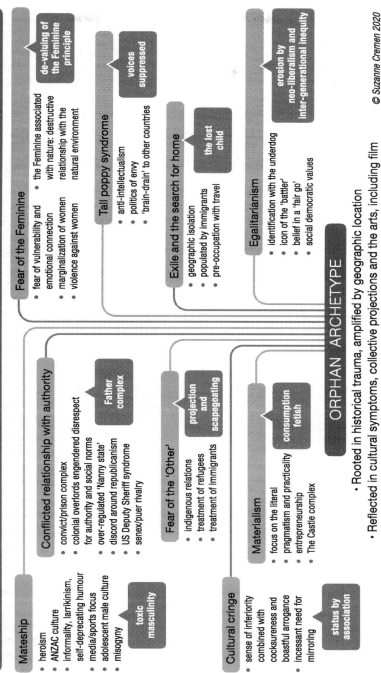

Symptoms of the Orphan Archetype within Australian Cultural Complexes

Mateship
- heroism
- ANZAC culture
- informality, larrikinism, self-deprecating humour
- media/sports focus
- adolescent male culture
- misogyny

toxic masculinity

Conflicted relationship with authority
- convict/prison complex
- colonial overlords engendered disrespect for authority and social norms
- over-regulated 'Nanny state'
- discord around republicanism
- US Deputy Sheriff syndrome
- senex/puer rivalry

Father complex

Fear of the Feminine
- fear of vulnerability and emotional connection
- marginalization of women
- violence against women
- the Feminine associated with nature: destructive relationship with the natural environment

de-valuing of the Feminine principle

voices suppressed

Tall poppy syndrome
- anti-intellectualism
- politics of envy
- 'brain-drain' to other countries

the lost child

Cultural cringe
- sense of inferiority combined with cocksureness and boastful arrogance
- incessant need for mirroring

status by association

Fear of the 'Other'
- indigenous relations
- treatment of refugees
- treatment of immigrants

projection and scapegoating

Exile and the search for home
- geographic isolation
- populated by immigrants
- pre-occupation with travel

Materialism
- focus on the literal
- pragmatism and practicality
- entrepreneurship
- The Castle complex

consumption fetish

Egalitarianism
- identification with the underdog
- icon of the 'battler'
- belief in a 'fair go'
- social democratic values

erosion by neo-liberalism and inter-generational inequality

ORPHAN ARCHETYPE

- Rooted in historical trauma, amplified by geographic location
- Reflected in cultural symptoms, collective projections and the arts, including film

© Suzanne Cremen 2020

Figure 10.1 Symptoms of the orphan archetype within Australia's cultural complexes.

the spirituality complex in Australia and the Australian resistance to individuation.[19] However, most Australians will be familiar with, for example, the revered masculine value of mateship (and its offshoot of misogyny); the notion of egalitarianism (which in recent years has been rapidly eroded by neo-liberalism); the 'tall poppy' syndrome (a recognised social phenomenon where people of genuine merit are resented, attacked and cut down because their talents or achievements elevate them above others); and the Australian cultural cringe or inferiority complex.

According to some authors, an inferiority complex is common to many colonised countries, such as Mexico and Brazil.[20] It is generally attributed to traumatic events in their colonial past. However, Australia's founding as a penal colony in 1788, where Britain sent its felons and petty criminals who were crowding the rotting hulks on the Thames, as well as other undesirables such as the poor, the Irish and political dissidents, carried a specific kind of wounding: not only for the Australian aboriginal people but also for the European newcomers. From the start, the nation was tainted with a convict stigma. This strange and often terrifying land at the farthest edge of the known world was also very harsh. Much was sacrificed, including high culture and principles, in the struggle to survive. David Russell wrote about how the early decades of settlement in Sydney were by all accounts one long nightmare, such that the experience became literally, and metaphorically, unspeakable. This experience of embryonic psychic pain may help us to understand foundational elements of the cultural psyche. Russell suggested that the metaphor that connotes the presence of this psychic pain, both then and today, is "a certain type of silence: a silence, not of words for talking was everywhere, but of reflective language".[21]

As a white Australian woman, I have long struggled to comprehend the deeper roots and telos of recurrent patterns and symptoms in my culture. So it has been tremendously insightful and healing for me to identify the Orphan (also described in the organisational context as the Everyperson)[22] as the dominant underlying archetype in Australian culture. Life is tough. I am alone. I have to band together with other orphans ('mates') to survive. Australia is in many ways "the scorned and reviled offspring of the parent culture".[23]

I discovered that the Orphan archetype at the core of Australia's cluster of cultural complexes can be traced through numerous aspects of Australian culture and history. The archetype is suggested by Australia's remote geographic location as well as its historical place as a colony of the British empire. It is also apparent in Australia's role in the futile battle of Gallipoli in 1915. This was an epochal moment in the Australian psyche, where the nation lost its innocence and was confronted with a betrayal from the motherland and the death of its heroes on a massive scale. The Orphan archetype is activated when we feel "abandoned, betrayed, victimized, neglected, or disillusioned".[24] The Orphan is also suspicious of people in any kind of position of power or authority; hence we see the archetype activated in Australia's revered ethos of egalitarianism (and its negative pole, the 'tall poppy' syndrome), as well as in the nation's history of political and trade union movements. "In politics, the Orphan stage is the time when we begin to develop the capacity to identify with the oppressed and seek solutions in unified, populist actions".[25]

The unmothered child can be seen to lie at the root of the nation's psychological need for mirroring, such as the obsessive curiosity to see how Australia is reported in the world's media. What do they think of us? What are they saying about us? Mirroring is where children have their talk and accomplishments acknowledged, accepted and praised by others, particularly parents. According to Heinz Kohut, who developed this theory, children who receive insufficient mirroring in terms of approval and admiration are considered to be at risk of developing a narcissistic personality later in life.[26] Bravado and boastfulness compensate for the wounding.

The Orphaned child is also found behind the nation's collective projections. Singer and Kimbles explain that "Cultural complexes also tend to be bipolar, so that when they are activated the group ego becomes identified with one part of the unconscious complex, while the other part is projected out onto the suitable hook of another group".[27] As long as the Orphan complex remains collectively unconscious, it is projected outwards, visible in white Australia's traumatic and forcible orphaning of the Stolen Generation (see for example Mary Terszak's autoethnography *Orphaned by the Colour of my Skin*) as well as in more recent incidents of the forcible separation of the children of asylum seekers from their parents.

The Orphan also features in the artefacts of Australia's indigenous and contemporary culture, including its films. "Art", wrote Jung, "is that most delicate of all instruments for reflecting the national psyche".[28] The arts give expression to the deeper psyche of a culture, and we can see clear inflections of the Orphan archetype in several iconic Australian films.[29] *Rabbitproof Fence*[30] tells the story of the quest for home of three young Aboriginal girls snatched from their mothers' arms as part of the Stolen Generations; while *Australia*[31] features an orphaned Aboriginal boy who is 'adopted' by an English aristocrat and an Australian drover before returning to his grandfather in the Outback. In *Walkabout*,[32] two English children are abandoned and orphaned in the Outback. *Oranges and Sunshine*[33] continues the orphan theme, unveiling the disturbing true story of thousands of British children, many of whom were wrongly told they were orphans, who were exported to Australia for child labour as recently as the 1960s.

I have endeavoured here to provide a succinct case to show how the Orphan archetype lies at the core of Australia's web of cultural complexes. Connected with the orphan are themes of primal loss, self-worth, vulnerability, abandonment and rejection, together with the longing for home and an ambivalent relationship with the archetypal feminine and Mother.[34] To identify the archetypal pattern which lies at the core of a complex, and to bring this into consciousness, is to support the individuation process and the path towards healing – at an individual or a cultural level.

Particularly relevant for the purposes of this book, which promotes a symbolic perspective towards work and career, there is another fascinating yet seldom noted aspect of the Orphan archetype. Clinical and Jungian research indicates a link between those who identify with the Orphan archetype and *an excessive focus on the literal, which precludes the capacity for symbolic thinking*. Jungian analyst Melinda Haas observed from a clinical perspective that "there seems to be something inherent in the precocity of the orphaning experience that has the effect of blocking the imagination and the capacity for symbolic thinking".[35] Haas attributed this to the developing child's need to apply all his resources to surviving a difficult environment, "focusing exclusively on the literal".[36] The literal perspective of the Orphan complex becomes habitual, following one into adulthood. If we apply this theory to Australian culture, it gives significant insight into the qualities of rationalism, pragmatism and tough-mindedness, borne of adverse beginnings, which have become identified with the national character, and how these continue to impede the capacity for imagination and symbolic thinking. It also affords insight into why depth psychology has failed to find a foothold in Australia, stubbornly resisted by the concretism of the Orphan complex.

In a nutshell, white Australian culture remains overly focused on the literal and pragmatic to the detriment of the healing wellspring that comes from opening to the imaginal and the symbolic. This is particularly ironic when Australian aboriginal culture, one of the oldest on earth, is infused with an imaginal, mythological consciousness, alive for generations with the Dreaming. Some indigenous elders, particularly women, have urgently tried to share this understanding with the broader culture before the ancient aboriginal Songlines are broken forever under the weight of Western rationality and colonisation.[37] Yet only a few Australians seem to appreciate the value of these offerings as a window into a numinous, restorative dimension for our re-engagement with this place. In general, the Australian proclivity for rationality, logic and literalism throws sensibility of the numinous into the cultural shadow – part of what David Tacey has written about as the nation's 'spirituality complex'. Perhaps this also explains why Jung's notion of archetypes, which are recognised by their numinous character, is ignored or treated disdainfully in Australian academia and even amongst many Australian Jungians. A volume of essays by Jungian contributors exploring cultural complexes in Australia rarely mentioned the word 'archetype'.[38] This seemed an odd omission to me, given Jung's fundamental understanding that all complexes have an archetypal core.

Is there a therapeutic remedy for the Orphan complex? The task persists in moving from the intransigence of the complex towards an archetypal perspective, "which as metaphor for the truths of the soul, holds the redemptive potential".[39] As Judy Isaac discovered in her research on individuation and the orphan archetype:

> For many who identify with the orphan, the search for one's own fairy godmother often begins and ends with the unconscious psyche, the matrix out of which all consciousness has sprung, the source from which one's deepest secrets of identity might be discovered. Herein lies . . . the possibility of connecting with the archetypal or "Great Mother," *through one's capacity for imaginal and symbolic dialogue.*[40]

Isaac's words speak to the necessity of Australians cultivating an imaginal and symbolic mode of consciousness if we are to engage constructively with our cultural complexes. Cultivating an imaginal, mytho-poetic sensibility in a culture where this has been discouraged and stunted is an essential ingredient of any pre-scription for collective healing. "An imaginal consciousness would give Austral-ian society the numinous dimension that it obviously lacks and needs", observed Tacey.[41] He discussed the potential activation of the **transcendent function** in Australia, arising from the tension between white rationality (*logos*) and the Abo-riginal dreaming (*mythos*). The transcendent function is a term coined by Jung to describe the emergence of a third position which arises through the holding of the tension of opposites in the psyche. The synthesis of "white rationality" and "black animism" in Australia could give birth, Tacey suggests, to a "discerning or watch-ful mysticism, a mysticism on the alert for improbable claims and a capacity to detect nonsense, yet always open to wonder and revelation".[42]

Jennifer Selig offered further insight into the operation of the transcendent function at the cultural level:

> If a group can understand the complex they're living, and challenge it by activat-ing the other pole of the archetype, the transcendent function can occur, and cul-tural transformation and healing can take place. That will profoundly impact the psychological health of those yet to be born into the culture. In this way, the cul-ture can heal the individual just as much as the individual can heal the culture.[43]

It can be tremendously liberating to discover that some of the things we have struggled with throughout life are not just particular to us but are in fact cul-tural complexes. There are many ways, directly or indirectly, in which our voca-tions may be a way of tending or healing the complexes of our culture. There is no singular prescription. For Jana, and in my own life, the sensitivity to cul-tural complexes led us each towards academic research, writing and teaching to bring the unconscious complex further into group consciousness – what we have respectively described as the Latvian Money complex and the Australian Orphan complex. Others will find themselves working with cultural complexes on their vocational paths in more oblique ways. For example, Steve was a 38-year-old Australian filmmaker who took various other jobs to support his filmmaking inter-est. He reflected on how the interweaving of both personal and cultural complexes had informed his calling towards filmmaking:

> *My experience thus far is that my wounds are wrapped up in my pur-pose. . . . What emerges from your wounding . . . in terms of expression, is what you give to the world. My own experience is that working through the wounds of the past is intrinsic to my exploration of vocation.*

I asked Steve whether he saw his work, and the subject matter of his film, as tending to wounds and complexes in collective Australian culture:

> *Definitely. I don't have an intellectual or academic understanding of what those wounds are. It is more of an intuitive thing. But it is definitely coming through. . . . One of the themes of my film is the disconnect from the feminine*

(or whatever that concept is). I experience this lack in myself, and I also see it in Australian society. I guess the colonial setting in my film is quite apt to explore this – because there actually was a lack of women in the colony.

Steve describes the wound or complex which he perceives in Australian culture and in himself as "a disconnect from the archetypal feminine". Steve also shared several dreams which communicated to him how other aspects associated with the archetypal feminine have been repressed in pragmatic Anglo-Australian culture. The dreams raised Steve's awareness of how his vocation in filmmaking could be a response to this collective wound or complex.

Steve experiences the archetypal feminine as a mode of consciousness akin to a more mythic sensibility, or the sense that there is wisdom in the non-rational, in contrast with a more literal, rational way of looking at the world. This accords with what I've referred to as the Orphan complex, and it also accords with the "fear of the feminine" (and its associations with the unconscious, the chthonic earth, the indigenous and women)[44] implicit in Australia's cultural complexes. Steve perceives his calling as a storyteller/filmmaker as a potentially healing response to this Australian cultural complex. And this is what infuses his life and work with meaning and purpose. So by tending our own wounds and complexes, we may find ourselves following vocations which also tend the complexes of our culture and which thereby make a vital social contribution.

To summarise, in this chapter and the previous one, we have explored how an individual's complexes may provide a pathway to vocation. A complex reveals itself in heightened emotional affect, projections or troubling disturbances. The first step in treatment entails the individual understanding and acknowledging that a complex has become activated in certain situations and beginning to get some perspective on it. Our complexes may stem from personal wounds (often originating in childhood); the collective wounds of our culture; or the traumas and patterns of previous generations. Rather than treating the complex merely as a historical wound or pathology that needs to be fixed, a Jungian approach suggests that the complex may have a teleological function, whereby the psyche leads the individual towards new horizons and a particular vocational direction. In the last two chapters, we saw examples of how bringing complexes into consciousness and working with them ethically and imaginatively can lead individuals to interesting and fulfilling vocational pathways. In the next chapter, we will look at complexes around money, which may arise from personal, cultural, familial or ancestral wounds, and which are commonly foregrounded in the context of work.

Invitation to reflection, conversation and journaling

Ancestral patterns

- Where were your parents stuck vocationally? Where have these stuck places shown up in your own life?
- Where were your grandparents stuck vocationally? Where have these stuck places shown up in your own life?

- (If you know about them): What about your more distant ancestors?
- If possible, interview your parents, grandparents or other relatives for details about family occupations, vocational hopes and dreams, and also traumatic events and difficulties. You may be surprised by the unexpected healing effect of such conversations.
- Draw a genogram to organise what you have learned about your ancestral history. A genogram is essentially a family tree, which can include other information, such as occupations, significant life events and even complexes.
- In what ways are you repeating the patterns of your parents or more distant ancestors, or trying to overcome them by compensation? Notice too the good that your ancestors have left you, and appreciate their legacy.

Cultural complexes

- In this chapter, I have offered an analysis of Australia's cultural complexes. Reflect on your own experiences, of this or another culture. If you are part of a different culture, how would you describe the symptoms and complexes of that culture? Following the model outlined in this chapter, in what traumas did those complexes originate? Can you discern an archetypal basis to the cultural complex?
- In what ways has your work or career been shaped or limited by the complexes of your culture?
- How might your calling be envisaged as a more conscious and transformative response towards your ancestral and/or cultural complexes?

Notes

1 Easter 2016; Fromm 2012; Hollis 2001, pp. 71–75. See also Hirsch (2012) and the concept of 'postmemory', which describes the relationship that the generation after bears to the personal, collective, and cultural trauma of those who came before.
2 Shaffer 1999, pp. 162–163.
3 Yakushko & Nelson 2013.
4 Hurley 2013, paras 14–15. Bombay, Matheson and Anisman (2014) also examined the effects of trauma in indigenous peoples reaching across generations through DNA. See also *Lost in Transmission: Studies of Trauma Across Generations*, edited by M. Gerard Fromm (2012).
5 Jung 1989b, p. 233.
6 Meade 2010, p. 23.
7 Jung 1951 CW9:2, para. 126.
8 Easter 2016, p. 87.
9 Di Fabio 2010; Kakiuchi & Weeks 2009; Malach-Pines & Yafe-Yanai 1999; Okiishi 1987.
10 Kakiuchi & Weeks 2009.
11 Bedi & Matthews 2003, pp. 143–149.
12 Shaffer 1999, p. 164.
13 Fidyk 2016b; Payne 2006.
14 Shaffer 1999, p. 164.
15 Fidyk 2016a; Henderson 1984; Kimbles 2000; San Roque, Dowd & Tacey 2011; Singer & Kaplinsky 2010; Singer & Kimbles 2004.
16 Jung 1964 CW10, para. 660.

17 Singer 2010, p. 234.
18 Somé 1994, p. 1.
19 Tacey 1993, 2009, 2011.
20 Gerson 2004; Ramos 2004.
21 Russell 2012, pp. 161–162.
22 Corlett & Pearson 2003.
23 Tacey 1993, p. 35.
24 Pearson 1991, p. 83.
25 Pearson 1991, p. 86.
26 Kohut 1971.
27 Singer & Kimbles 2004, p. 6.
28 1989a, p. 66.
29 Waddell (2019) has also traced the recurring motif of the 'lost child' in Australian cinema and art.
30 Noyce 2002.
31 Luhrmann 2008.
32 Roeg 1971.
33 Loach 2010.
34 Isaac 2008. See also Norris (2015); Rothenberg (1983).
35 Haas 2000, p. 5.
36 Haas 2000, p. 50.
37 Neale 2017.
38 San Roque, Dowd & Tacey 2011.
39 Isaac 2008, p. 257.
40 Isaac 2008, p. 256, italics added.
41 Tacey 2009, p. 154.
42 Tacey 2009, p. 155.
43 Selig 2011.
44 Tacey 1993, 2009.

11 Money and the dark side of vocation

Who amongst us does not think (or fret) about money? Certainly one of the most ubiquitous complexes is the money complex. Complexes around money affect nearly all of us, whether rich or poor, in one way or another, and they are often constellated in the context of our working lives. Indeed, throughout the years of writing this book, which has been the fulfilment of a soul calling, hardly a day has passed where I have not had to manage concerns and anxieties about money. As anyone knows who has written a book or completed a thesis, like raising a child, it is most often a labour of love for which tremendous financial and other sacrifices are made.

Yet money remains one of the most neglected issues psychologically. The thorny subject of money is often overlooked in depth psychology, including in writings on work and the exhortation to follow one's true calling. While we are encouraged by Jung to individuate, to emancipate ourselves from the herd and its well-worn paths; by James Hillman to heed our *daimon* or guiding spirit and follow the soul's calling; and by the mythologist Joseph Campbell to follow our bliss, the truth is that many people lack the means to follow or fulfil the work of their choice.

Vocation and privilege

We are living in a time of exponentially escalating economic inequity. A report by Oxfam published in January 2019 showed that the world's twenty-six richest billionaires (overwhelmingly men) now control the same wealth between them as the poorest 50% of the global population. Wealth in the hands of billionaires has become dramatically more concentrated in just the last three years: in 2017, it was forty-three people, and in 2016, sixty-two people, who owned the same wealth as half the world's population. By 2018, the wealth of the world's billionaires was increasing by $2.5 billion *per day*.[1] Reports in Australian media highlight the increasing economic inequality for those under thirty years of age who "find themselves saddled with mortgage-sized education debts, no chance of ever buying a home and shrinking employment opportunities in their chosen field of study".[2] Money and work continue to top the list of significant stressors for adults overall, tracked annually by the American Psychological Association.[3]

These kinds of burgeoning collective problems are of the greatest concern. Our personal difficulties and anxieties around money exist in the context of national and global economic policy, in which rapidly escalating inequity is systemic. As Rabbi Michael Lerner observed:

> Much of people's suffering is rooted in the hidden injuries of class and capitalist values – not only in the economic inequalities, but also in the psycho-spiritual crisis that the capitalist marketplace generates.[4]

Financial hardship affects many people, and this may necessitate taking any job for immediate survival. In Chapter 1, I discussed how the concepts of *career, work* and *job* are generally associated with making a living and earning money, whereas *vocation* may or may not be income-producing. While most of us would love to prosper financially from our vocations, this ideal may not always be realised. For many, the notion of vocation as calling has been effectively conscripted for service within the dominant neo-liberal economic paradigm.

So is vocation an elitist concept? Does the modern emphasis on meaningful work as an avenue for self-fulfilment reflect a strong bias of class privilege, given the less than ideal reality of working life for many under social and political conditions? Well, if we assume that a person needs a higher education, or a PhD in depth psychology, to understand or hear a vocation, then in countries where education is unavailable or unaffordable – yes, to have a vocation could be a privilege of the elite. But while education is invaluable for providing a language and conceptual framework to understand vocation more deeply, over millennia, people of different cultures and often with little or no education have experienced compelling callings from the deep psyche in the ways in which I describe in this book – through dreams, synchronicities, symptoms, ancestral patterns or cultural trauma, initiatory experiences, vision quests and other non-ordinary experiences. In this sense, vocation is highly democratic and available to all, in that any one of us is capable of dying to the world of the ego and being reborn into a transpersonal sense of the larger world.

Addressing vocation in any depth does imply the ability to reflect upon and explore one's life process. This ability may well be augmented by educational background and occasioned by privilege but not necessarily so. The question of vocation can arise independently of one's job and may occur to those in the crafts or trades just as much as those in professional careers.

Indeed, if there is any distinguishing factor between those who grasp and actualise a calling and those who do not, it is more likely to be the psychological mindfulness and courage of the individual.

> *It has nothing to do with your wealth or your status or your ancestry or your educational level. If anything, those things can sometimes get in the way of vocation. Because if you've invested that much in your persona, it might be harder to let it dissolve, and go through the nekyia, the death, that's necessary to begin the possibility of living a life of vocation.*

(Claire)

Likewise, if we assume that vocation must be what supports us financially, or that we must have a certain amount of money in order to follow our vocation, then yes, the notion of having a vocation could be elitist. But let's recall the distinction made in Chapter 1 between a job, a career and a vocation. The vocational anhedonia which many people experience today may be attributed to conflation of these terms and confusion about their respective places in one's life, with the idealised expectation that we will 'have it all' in one perfect package and that it is our vocation which should support us financially if we are doing it right. It is worth re-stating that our work, or job, or career is not necessarily the same as our vocation – *and neither need they be the same.* Vocation is not 'doing what I want'. It is about heeding the calling that arises from the psyche or soul and not being overly fixed or prescriptive about the form this may take. Vocation may be indeed found through doing what one loves, but it may also be found through engaging with the areas in life where we are sensitive, including to the inequities and injustices life delivers. In light of escalating global economic inequity and the depletion of resources, most people today will not experience the same kind of prosperity and abundance that was taken for granted by many in the 1980s. It may be, then, that how we respond to economic inequity and injustice becomes an aspect of our vocational calling.

> *Listening for, or feeling where, we can participate in the* anima mundi *(world soul). Feeling where our heart is broken and where we can make a difference. Honestly, somebody can have a vivid, satisfying, rich vocational life and spend half an hour a week at it.*
>
> (Claire)

Claire's comment grounds some of the more inflated notions about vocation and calling: that it's this great thing the world has to recognise us for, for which we need to receive acclaim and monetary reward. It might also be said that a serious reflection on vocation provides a braking mechanism for outlandish and unrealistic fantasies of success. In other words, when there's no process of real reflection on work and meaning, a compensatory idealism sets in. At this point it is worth noting Thomas Moore's definition of vocation as "a calling from a place that is the source of meaning and identity, the roots of which lie beyond human intention and interpretation".[5] This is subtly but critically different from stating that vocation is about *having* meaning and identity, a position which may easily morph into an ego-directed life project. Moore is saying that vocation is *a calling from a place that is the source of* meaning and identity. This may well result in meaning, identity and purpose, but vocation is the *calling from that place*. In depth psychology, this place is called the psyche, the soul, the unconscious or the imaginal realm.

In this respect, a depth psychological view of vocation is *incredibly egalitarian*, because everyone has access to this place. One may lose everything, like Viktor Frankl, who found his specific vocation or mission in an Auschwitz concentration camp, yet one can still have a relationship with the psyche, the unconscious or soul, from which stems meaning, purpose and identity. One will still have vocation. Indeed, that may be all one has.

So while it is important to acknowledge that our personal struggles and anxieties around money exist in and (for the majority) are exacerbated by an inequitable macro-economic context, I do not purport to offer an analysis of that macro-economic situation. Instead, my intention is to focus on the nature of our inner relationships with money and to offer some ideas which I hope will expand our thinking about money in a symbolic, mythic and depth psychological sense. The stories and anecdotes in this chapter illustrate some of the paradoxical relationships which individuals have with money as both a motivator and a complex, and how family, gender and cultural influences are complicit in money complexes. Whether we consider ourselves to be wealthy, poor or somewhere in between, we can become aware of what our particular financial situation and our relationship with money is asking of us on our journey of individuation.

The nature and mythic origins of money

Money has long been something of a puzzle to me. From a depth psychological perspective, I've wondered: What's really going on with money? To begin to explore the deeper nature of money, it can be helpful to consider how money originated.

Money is commonly defined as "a condensation of value, a sign of wealth, and a medium of exchange".[6] However, such definitions overlook money's origins in connection with the earth and with the wealth of nature. The word 'economy' derives from the Greek word *oikos*, meaning home or dwelling place. Originally, the word economics had nothing to do with money but rather meant the management of one's home or dwelling. For the human species, our home is this planet and the land on which we live. Rather than assume that the role of the earth is to serve economic ends, it is time our political leaders and governments acknowledged that the economy is in fact a wholly owned subsidiary of the natural world.

Let us remember that money originated in connection with the earth and the wealth of nature. Cattle were the oldest form of money, and the word 'capital' derives from the Latin *capitale*, which means cattle. Traditionally currencies were minted from or backed by the wealth extracted from the earth, such as gold and silver. Today, as pieces of paper, plastic or coins minted from base metal, money itself has little intrinsic value – even less so as it has become increasingly abstract and ethereal in form, shifting to digitised transmissions of light in the electronic banking system. Yet who would deny that money has real power, including some of the powers our ancestors ascribed to gods?

What exactly *is* money, from a depth psychological perspective? James Hillman described money as an "archetypal psychic reality".[7] He invoked the metaphor of the ocean, the primordial unconscious, to convey the mysterious, fluid, powerful and potentially overwhelming nature of money. Amongst the many metaphors that arise in connection with money,[8] the language of water (cash flow, liquidity, flush with funds) is a frequent one, to which I will return at the end of this chapter.

According to Hillman, money is both protean and polymorphous, with the capacity to take us into great depths of the psyche:

> Money is a *psychic reality*, and as such gives rise to divisions and oppositions about it, much as other fundamental psychic realities – love and work, death and sexuality, politics and religion – are archetypal dominants which easily fall into opposing spiritual and material interpretations. Moreover, since money is an archetypal psychic reality, it will always be inherently problematic because psychic realities are complex, complicated. . . . Money is devilishly divine.[9]

There is a natural ambivalence that most people feel towards money. This is due to the paradoxical and irresolvable nature of money; what Hillman underscored as its profanity as well as its sacredness. Economic psychologists have observed that money has a translucent character rather than an inherent meaning, which is a reflection of the sacred or profane meaning of the processes in which money participates.[10] As Hillman says, money is both devilish *and* divine.

Depth psychology often draws on myth (the sacred stories of cultures) as a method of amplification and way of knowing, so it is worth noting a few of money's associations in the Western mythic tradition. In Greek mythology, Plutus was the god of wealth and of the riches mined from beneath the earth's surface. Plutus (from whose name we derive the word plutocrat) was also known to the Greeks as Hades, god of the underworld. Associations between money, power and the underworld (and mining) persist today. Money matters can easily transport us into a chthonic realm.

The Greek god Hermes was, amongst other roles, the patron of trade and merchants (also of thieves). Hermes is also a trickster figure. He reminds us that in mercurial matters of money, it is often necessary to take risks, to be creative, confident and resourceful, and to exercise guile. On the other hand, it was the god Saturn who invented coining and hoarding to begin with. The word *money* itself originates from the Roman goddess Moneta, also known as Juno, who was the goddess of memory and protector of funds, in whose temple money was minted and kept.

According to Hillman:

> Money in the hand awakens imaginal possibilities: to do this, go there, have that. It reveals the Gods which dominate my fantasies – Saturnian tightness, Jupiterian generosity, Martial show, Venusian sensuality.[11]

Taking an archetypal psychology perspective suggests that at the core of our various money complexes – to hoard, to posture, to gift, to consume – bubble the energies of various gods or archetypes seeking propitiation. If you want to know which gods or goddess you are really serving in your life, notice in which directions you feel pulled to spend your money. Is yours a Promethean fantasy, about investing in innovation and industry? Or a Dionysian fantasy, spending on wine, revelry, and other escapist past-times? Are you in service to Aphrodite, with trips to the beauty salon, or to Artemis, going on nature retreats, or to Chronos or Saturn, as you save all your money away and don't tell anyone about it? In this respect, money is a genuinely polytheistic phenomenon. Money makes the gods come alive.

Hillman emphasised the essential character of money as imaginative and suggested that "to find imagination in yourself or in a patient, turn to money behaviours and fantasies".[12] This connection between money and imagination is a crucial theme amongst depth psychologists who have written on this topic. "Money brings fantasies out of the depth and locates them in human time; money provides the means through which imagination takes root in the world", wrote Robert Sardello.[13] Thomas Moore likened money to sex, in that "money is so numinous, so filled with fantasy and emotion and resistant to rational guidance, that although it has much to offer, it can easily swamp the soul and carry consciousness off into compulsion and obsession".[14] Moore suggested that an alternative to responding to money apotropaically or compulsively is "to *enter into* the particular fantasies that money gives us and see what messages they might offer".[15]

Turning to money behaviours and fantasies is a technique used by some career counsellors and coaches. Asking about money fantasies (or constraints) may offer an unexpected window into a client's vocational interests and desires. *On what do you like to spend your money? What would you do if money were no obstacle?* Nevertheless, for most of us, as well as sparking imagination, money also limits what is possible; it defines what we can and cannot do in our lives. In my career counselling practice, I observed that money is often experienced as a decisive constraint inhibiting a person's longed-for vocational fantasy, or as a rationale for an unfulfilling career choice. Mainstream approaches to career development and vocational guidance continue to treat issues of money in a predominantly literal and pragmatic fashion. There is, however, a lack of awareness about how money's character, as a conduit of the imagination, has a great deal to do with the condition of the soul.

> Money is not just a rational medium of exchange, it also carries the soul of communal life. It has all the complications of soul, and, like sex and disease, it is beyond our powers of control. It can fill us with compelling desire, longing, envy, and greed. The lives of some people are shaped by the lure of money, while others sense the temptation and take an ascetic route, in order to avoid being tainted. Either way, money retains its powerful position in the soul.[16]

Money as a motivator and a complex

Freud understood money to be the carrier of anal erotic associations as well as a practical necessity of social and economic life. Freud himself had a self-acknowledged "money complex", and his personal letters to Jung and others reveal he was obsessed with generating more of it.[17] For example, Freud wrote to his friend Wilhelm Fliess that: "My mood also depends very strongly on my earnings. . . . Money is laughing gas for me".[18] I think we all know what Freud means by this: that absolute power which money has to inflate our spirits and dispel anxiety. As a German Austrian Jew, it may be that Freud was psychologically disposed to worry about the uncertainties of his times and money. Whether the origin of Freud's complex was personal, ancestral and/or cultural, it would certainly have been exacerbated by valid fears about his personal security in light of the scape-goating of Jews for the collapse of the economy and their persecution and geno-cide through two world wars.

Jung also regarded money as a vital issue and motivator in his personal life and professional work. As a pastor's son, the family's poverty was a significant factor in Jung's early career decisions. His money worries were later alleviated by his marriage to the wealthy Emma Rauschenbusch, but this then raised doubts for Jung regarding his self-worth and professional viability.[19] In one of his letters to Freud, Jung lamented the problem of being married to a wealthy woman. Freud advised: "Give your charming, clever, and ambitious wife the pleasure of saving you from losing yourself in the business of money-making". He encouraged Jung to give himself instead to his true vocation (which Freud hoped would be to fol-low in his own footsteps). "On the whole, it will prove to be good business if you forego ordinary pursuits. Then, I am sure, extraordinary rewards will come your way".[20] Jung later parted ways with Freud to follow his own calling. However, extraordinary rewards and wealth *did* come Jung's way as he shifted his focus from the ordinary pursuit of building a practice to develop his true calling and engage in reflective and imaginative work, research, travel, writing and lecturing.

Although money was not the dominant factor in Freud's and Jung's choices of occupation, neither was it insignificant. In my interviews with people who experi-ence a sense of vocation, irrespective of their economic background, nearly all described money as of secondary or less importance, although not something that could be ignored. For example:

> *Money has definitely been a secondary consideration when it comes to the choices I've made regarding career and vocation. . . . I've just turned 38 and matters of security and stability are more present in my mind. . . . I've prob-ably been absent-minded or neglectful to that reality. I can live fairly simply. On the other hand, money can enable abundance, it can enable joy, it can facilitate creativity, compassion and love and warmth. . . . I'm opening up more to this potential that money has.*
>
> (Steve)

> *Money hasn't been my driving impetus for doing my work in the world. It hasn't constricted my vocation. But at the same time, I don't intend to starve doing my work in the world. . . . Money has been secondary to almost tertiary for me. That's been both positive and negative.*
>
> (Lynn)

The negative for Lynn was not knowing her "deep mythological misunderstandings" around money. Her father had few scruples around money, and this caused many family problems. So Lynn thought she didn't need money, because she "didn't want to be like that".

> *But to think that you don't need it in your adult years is problematic, because you do.*
>
> *Not knowing what those associations are, psychologically, or even what the long family narrative is – then you continue to basically live out that narrative unconsciously.*
>
> (Lynn)

Michael was another who spoke about the powerful legacy of his family's complexes around money:

> *My father worked two jobs. He liked to say "I know how to hold on to a buck. I can squeeze it so hard that you can hear George Washington fart".*
>
> (Michael)

This colourful phrase is an image Freud might have appreciated, given his views that money and the handling of money were unconsciously associated with excrement. Michael described money as being a real challenge for him: in his earlier years he was totally obsessive about it. He believed this could have become a real problem for him, and he had to "educate the feminine side of his own psyche" to pull him out of that. Later in this chapter, I will share a story from Michael which illustrates that process.

For Jana, the decision about what to study when she left school was very practical. Her focus was on having a job. Although artists were prominent in Latvia, Jana thought it was important to study something that would make money, as opposed to the arts, because she was told that was not where the money was. As Thomas Conklin observed:

> With the lens of calling applied to career decisions, it is quite possible that many of our choices would be significantly different. Currently, the economic paradigm drives many of the decisions people make regarding their careers. Where can I make the most money? What is going to be the hot career in demand in the next 10 years?[21]

On the other hand, in hindsight, Jana saw that her various work opportunities arose not because of her degree but through synchronicities and personal connections: "So in the end, my assumptions about money weren't right". Jana felt that the influence of money on her career choice was strong not only because the outer world told her to consider it but also because of an unconscious predisposition in her own psychological makeup, also revealed by the strong Saturnian influence in her natal (astrological) chart.

As I discussed in Chapter 10, money complexes may also be cultural complexes. Consider for example the paradox of the Protestant work ethic, which exhorts hard work and acquisition at the same time as altruism and asceticism. Gender differences have also been found to exist, not only in continuing gender pay gaps but also in the meaning and use of money. One study found that, while women are no longer structurally or legally blocked from the power granted by money, "women do not think of money as power as frequently as do men; instead, women think of money in terms of the things into which it can be converted, while men think of it in terms of the power its possession implies".[22]

Nikki articulated how her challenges around money were related to gender, intertwined with personal, ancestral and cultural wounds. Her undergraduate degree was in writing, and when she was younger she wanted to pursue a creative life:

> *There were always the voices that writers don't make money – but I made a lot of money as a writer. There were associations that doing what you love and what nourishes your soul is not viable, it's a luxury.*
>
> *This came from my culture, but particularly my parents. And also my inner parents – my inner masculine and feminine – patriarchal/matriarchal figures.*
>
> *My actual parents never had vocations. They had jobs that made them money, and that was what you did. I think a vocational call can be selling shoes, it doesn't have to be something grand – but I never saw either of my parents express any joy, passion or fulfilment from their work – not even any frustration. Really, kind of nothing . . . just "doing duty".*

Nikki perceived her family's response to the idea of vocation as very "fear-based", which she traced back to her grandparents' generation and the particular economic vulnerability of women:

> *Neither of my grandmothers or my mother were ever able to leave the marriages they were in, and probably all three of the women should have, had they had the resources and independence to do that. So I started working when I was 15, and I've been financially independent my entire life. I've been the opposite of all the women in my family, where I've been very driven and motivated to provide for myself and not be vulnerable to a husband or a man partner to have to provide for me. . . .*
>
> *On that same note I did my PhD. I think I'm the only one in my family with any education after high school. Living out the parents' shadow, like . . . have to work, have to be independent, have to be educated.*

Let's not negate the magnitude of complexes around money that traditionally have affected men, such as the pressure to be a breadwinner and the sense of identity associated with that. However, women will often experience deep personal anxieties around work, vocation and money which they associate with their mothers' and grandmothers' lack of economic independence and agency. This is exacerbated today where, for example, in Australia, women over 55 are now the fastest growing group of homeless people.[23] The 2019 Oxfam report emphasised that the impact of global wealth inequity is felt disproportionately by women, as men own more than 50% of the total wealth, and women are still left to fill the gaps in public services with many hours of unpaid care.[24]

Annabella described herself as never driven by money, and as having a diversified sense of vocation where some streams brought in income. However, at age 65, Annabella also had real concerns about providing for herself financially:

> *I am the first generation of women in my family who didn't have husbands, and didn't have security. I'm the first generation of women having to do this alone. I don't know how to do it.*

If, as I suggested in the previous chapter, vocation is about partly completing the unfinished business of our ancestors, then perhaps an aspect of the vocational task for many women is to attend in our own lives to the places and ways in which our mothers and grandmothers were caught by money and to develop an increased sense of agency and personal sovereignty in money matters – and not to abrogate this to our menfolk.

As I discussed in Chapter 10, to release a miasma (the unconscious inheritance of an ancestral emotional pattern), a useful question to ponder may be: Where were your parents stuck? Rose recalled how her mother was limited by her financial dependence:

> *My mother was stuck being a mother, because she didn't have any income of her own, so she was also stuck in her marriage, though I never heard her voice that.*

> (Rose)

In contrast to her mother's financial dependence, Rose's career in IT has been focused on making money, to the extent that she is the main breadwinner in her family. However, Rose's focus on money has come at the cost of her calling to write, which causes her continuing anguish. When she was younger, Rose was encouraged by teachers who saw her talent for writing to apply to an expensive women's liberal arts college. However, Rose did not see how this could prepare her for a career, and she felt guilty using her parents' limited money for that purpose:

> *I didn't know any writers in my life, so I never had any kind of role model. . . . Whenever my parents or anybody would talk about a career or vocation that was not ever mentioned other than it was something to do if you wanted to live in a tent and drink a lot. It was always associated with negative things. So I never seriously entertained it as something that I would be able to do and have a family. If I was going to do it I'd have to be a hermit. That was the story I told myself about being a writer. . . . I couldn't envisage it as a*

vocation. I still don't know how writers do it. I am always amazed that they are able to support themselves.

Rose's seemingly pragmatic decision to focus on a career that makes good money has ironically come at a high cost, for Rose now feels trapped by her high earning capacity:

I'm stuck with the infrastructure of a life with high overheads. . . . The hardest thing really is being stuck in the income bracket that everyone is used to, and that I can't just walk away from.

Rose's story illustrates the paradoxes inherent in our relationships with money. On the one hand, money facilitates Rose's vocational interests: her high income pays for her postgraduate study and allows her to take writers' courses. On the other hand, her high income obstructs her vocation. Rose fears the possible effect that giving herself to her calling to write may have on her income and the infra-structure of a life built around it. As Bryan Dik and Ryan Duffy observed, "High-status work may, in fact, discourage or obstruct the pursuit of calling and vocation to the extent that such work creates an internalized demand to maintain a high baseline of wealth or power".[25] The questions arising for Rose revolve around a sense of duty to work, career and family. The feeling that her soul's vocation is passing her by is also strongly expressed in her story.

The shadows of vocation

Rose's fears that following her vocation could be financially detrimental are not entirely unfounded. While there are many stories of creative or innovative indi-viduals who are blessed with riches through the courage to follow their unique callings, another line of research suggests that following a calling can also be financially detrimental. Although it is generally expected that calling and voca-tion correlate positively with job satisfaction,[26] some studies have suggested that individuals oriented towards calling and vocation often sacrifice aspects of job satisfaction (such as pay and comfort) for the sake of others (such as making a difference in society).[27] For example, a qualitative study of zookeepers who exhibited a greater sense of calling found that they were also "more willing to sacrifice money, time, and physical comfort or well-being for their work, and were therefore more vulnerable to being exploited by management".[28] These zookeep-ers described the sacrifices made for $9 per hour in the name of the care, commit-ment, love and moral duty they felt towards the animals, including working two or three jobs and living on food stamps. Jung's allusion to the dark side of vocation is often overlooked by one in the grip of a calling: "The fact that many a man who goes his own way ends in ruin means nothing to one who has a vocation".[29]

To go the distance on this journey we call life, finding ways to serve and express a vocational calling will always be tempered by a degree of ground-ing pragmatism. This is no different from responding to any inner voice or drive: total identification with the call leads to *puer* (idealistic, youthful) flights, whereas the realisation of the call always involves a digestion into the restrictions of life. Steve described the financial challenges and tensions inherent in his call to storytelling:

> *Filmmaking and storytelling require capital, and the opportunities to secure this capital are finite and extremely competitive. It is not something that pays a reliable weekly salary. You won't get money in a conventional way. It's feast or famine.*
>
> *The reality is that you are most likely very talented, skilful, lucky and extremely single-minded if you manage to make enough money from this pursuit to also live comfortably. . . . You have to be a business-person as well to protect your rights and not be exploited. It's quite a skilful individual who can make all of that happen. That's not to be negative. I'm just more coming to terms with the reality. It's a lifelong commitment.*

(Steve)

Steve is consciously grappling with the ambiguous financial nature of his vocation and opening to more lateral ways going forward to answer the essence of his calling. The individual who follows his calling and passion in life but who is unable to come to terms with financial reality (the figure of the starving artist) *may* be a genius, but he may also be "ill in a money-archetypal sense of monetary rewards".[30] Sometimes what is needed in such instances is more of Hermes' imagination, resourcefulness, persuasion and even guile around money. "The art of convincing people", observed Joel Covitz, "is an important part of the art of affluence".[31] This is where the traditional career counselling methods discussed in Chapter 2, focused for example on the cultivation of persona, self-marketing and salary negotiation, can provide a necessary supplement to a soul-focused, depth psychological approach to vocation.

In *The Gift*, Lewis Hyde explores this problem of the disconnect between the practice of art and the usual ways of earning a living. He notes that the artist's fidelity to his or her gifts generally draws energy away from the common activities by which men become rich. The artist, of any medium, must find a way to negotiate a double economy: the modern market economy and the "gift economy". The latter, Hyde shows, has a long lineage in traditional cultures and is the creative cultural commons in which the source and inspiration of the gift comes forward. One way or another, whether by taking a second job, or finding a patron, or managing to place his work on the market, the artist is tasked with sufficiently straddling this double economy to resolve the problem of sustaining his livelihood. But if the artist does not sacrifice his labour in service of his own *daimon* or *genius*, reserve a protected gift-sphere in which the work is created or alternatively allows all his talents to be converted into commodities, then the gift can disappear. The artist's path is easier if the culture appreciates the debt it owes to those who dedicate their lives to the realisation of a gift, and has institutions (whether private philanthropic, or government funding) which convert market wealth towards the gift economy. Nevertheless, financially, the artist's path is more likely to be a way of getting by than a way of getting rich.

On the other hand, for those who do not hear or respond to the artist's calling, a different shadow of the frustrated vocational impulse may be consumerism. Some commentators have wondered whether the idea of work as vocation is the privilege of the elite, whereas the masses are "too often locked into meaningless or degrading jobs that offer little opportunity for notoriety or fulfilment". The sole vocation available to everybody then ironically becomes the "vocation of the consumer" – "fulfillment not through working, but through the fruits of work in an endless cycle of working and spending".[32] While Western society is certainly infected with the black plague of consumerism, for reasons that I canvass throughout this book, I am not convinced that the statement that most people are necessarily "locked into meaningless or degrading jobs" is indisputable. If the right attitude towards the work is there, then even a humble job can hold the dignity of a vocation.[33] Nevertheless, addictive behaviours such as workaholism and consumerism may be viewed as attempts (generally with fleeting success) to satisfy some inner need with some external thing. From this perspective, consumerism becomes an attempt to palliate the loss of meaning associated with the drudgery of work that is *not* a calling, through the unconscious projections of the soul's quest for meaning onto money and objects.

Such struggles may also be our invitation to attend more deeply to our own money complexes, whether their roots lie in personal, family or cultural experiences. That process in itself may lead us in unexpected vocational or career directions, as Jana's career story illustrates. Consciously or unconsciously, we may be troubled or conflicted about following a calling which appears incompatible with our family or cultural beliefs about career and money and what these represent (status, security, power or honour). As Jung expressed, vocation "destines a man to *emancipate himself* from the herd and from its well-worn paths".[34] It may require much soul-searching, shadow-work and external support (such as therapy) to differentiate our own authentic values from those of the collective and then to choose how we will conduct our life and work to honour our deepest values in relation to the collective.

Money and values

> *The deeper part of this question about money has to do with value. What we place value on. We don't place value on those type of vocations that really make a difference in the world. . . .*
>
> *Doing things for the money is probably many times a misalignment of your own values, because you don't know what you really value in yourself.*
>
> (Lynn)

In Chapter 2, we saw that career counsellors typically ask questions which probe a person's values so that career goals may be pursued with those values in mind. Responses often include values such as 'wealth' or 'financial sustainability', though usually many other values emerge too, unrelated to money and often taking precedence over a high income, such as health and emotional well-being. Unfortunately, one of the problems with this kind of self-assessment report is that usually little deeper inquiry is made into what extent the conscious values, particularly regarding money, are driven by or compensating for unconscious complexes.

One of the preliminary tools I used with clients in career counselling was a journaling activity called "Things I most enjoy doing". The types of activities that individuals would frequently list included time spent in nature, with family or friends, reading, creating art, listening to music or making a difference in some positive way to the lives of others. Reflecting on their lists, people were often surprised to discover that many of the things they most enjoy doing in life involve little or no cost at all. But is this really so surprising? There is an extensive body of empirical and sociological research on the correlation between money and happiness.[35] This research confirms what most people know intuitively: that while an increase in income matters a great deal to people living in poverty (just as more food is satisfying to a hungry person), there is a real limit to the degree of happiness that money can buy. Beyond a certain point, additional wealth and income do not result in increased well-being. Reflecting on his work with a high socioeconomic status client base, clinical psychologist Aaron Kipnis writes, "The formula that more is always better is false. Moreover, it becomes easy to see that when one sacrifices relationships, health, and psychological well-being for the pursuit of more, then not only is the formula false it is toxic".[36]

The experience of wealth is in many ways a subjective thing. Claire is mindful that having more money does not necessarily equate with wealth. In her work as a teacher and writer, Claire does not earn a lot of money, but she says she's been "blessed with the ability to manage money well". She doesn't spend more than she earns. From a middle-class background, the messages around money from Claire's family were: save, live within your means and money in the bank is freedom. An expensive car or house is not freedom (if anything, she views those things as a form of slavery):

Wealth for me is health, a fabulous husband, a peaceful and sweet home, two cats I adore and work that I love (teaching and writing). I have hobbies – I work with horses, I draw mandalas, I sing in a choir. I have the freedom, and the energy, and the flow to repair the world – 'tikkun olam' – because I am constantly being repaired by the world.

(Claire)

Claire attributes her sense of freedom to the sensible management of the flow of currency in her life. Money has not been a primary, nor even secondary, consideration in her work choices, maybe third or fourth.

But I have a very clear set of values about what I want to spend money on. I couldn't care less about shoes, but I do love travel. And books. But I'm very proud of the fact that I have three library cards in my wallet, and only one credit card. Money has not motivated me – if it did, I'd still be working in technology (and be a multi-millionaire by now).

Moreover, Claire spoke about the fulfilment she received from her volunteer work as a grief counsellor.

I wasn't getting paid, but I knew death very well. I loved that work. That's vocation.

Alyce also spoke about her love of her volunteer work in the field of mediation. Alyce's other sources of income allow her some financial freedom to pursue non-remunerative vocational calls. To some degree, Alyce regards her *pro bono* work as part of her career portfolio. However, Alyce was adamant about the importance of being paid for her work as a depth psychologist.

I feel really strongly about that. I might donate to a non-profit, but I want to be paid for the work I have done in depth psychology. I want this field to be recognised. . . . So If I can get paid for leading a dream group, then that tells me that the work is being respected, it's being acknowledged.

(Alyce)

For Alyce, money signifies an affirmation of the work's value by the culture. Her determination to have her work recognised by the culture is reminiscent of Joseph Campbell's mythic structure of the hero's journey, which entails three separate stages, of departure, initiation and return. Applying the hero's journey model, Alyce has embarked on a journey through her years of study in depth psychology to retrieve something that has been missing, in herself and in the consciousness of her culture and community. This is a very difficult task, but the final and most difficult part of the hero's journey, said Campbell, was often the hero's return.

The whole point of this journey is the reintroduction of this potential into the world; that is to say, to you living in the world. You are to bring this treasure of understanding back and integrate it in a rational life. . . . Bringing the boon back can be even more difficult than going down into your own depths in the first place. . . . The point is that what you have to bring is something that the world lacks – that is why you went to get it. Well, the daylight world doesn't even know that it needs this gift you are bringing.[37]

Being paid for her work is one sure sign by which Alyce knows she has completed her journey and brought the boon back. That people are prepared to pay money for her services shows that her work in depth psychology is now recognised and valued in the community.

Inspired by the potential of money, Alyce also articulates her vocational vision arising from a call to tend suffering and trauma traceable to the lives of her military ancestors:

> *My dream is to have a healing sanctuary – a healing arts centre – for soldiers to come to this lovely piece of land on their healing journeys. . . . I want to build a barn that's going to have movement space on top, accommodations beneath. And I want to have seminars and workshops where people are paying me. But on the other hand, if I have group of soldiers come and there's no money to pay me, I'm not going to stop them from coming. So I'll have to find a balance between that.*

(Alyce)

Although money and soul are frequently dichotomised, Alyce's approach shows that money can be an integral part of work without loss of soul. According to Moore, "The crucial point is our attitude. In most work there can be a close relationship between caring for the world in which we live (ecology) and caring for the quality of our way of life (economy)".[38] While Alyce doesn't take her financial ability or stability for granted, because "it all turns on a dime", she also seems comfortable with the flow of money in her life. She has a sense of trust and competence in her ability to work with money and to cultivate and channel its creative potential. Guided by her vocation, Alyce also holds a vision beyond herself and her self-interests regarding what her money can do. As the Norwegian economist Per Espen Stoknes said:

> Money allows the images of desire to put down roots so that they can start sprouting in our common life. Money gives the images substance and sets them off in the direction of new changes in society and the world. Your commitment to money is, viewed in this way, also a commitment to the world.[39]

What is also of interest is that in Alyce's simple statement, "I'll have to find a balance between that", she does not abort or cripple her calling with rigid ideas about the need to make money from it. Instead, she views it as part of a larger ecosystem of currency. The part of Alyce's client base that can pay for her services will support another part of her client base that is unable to pay. This is similar to the way in which Alyce's earlier *career* choices, focused more consciously around money, have supported her later *vocational* choices.

A shifting paradigm: decoupling work and money

While it may seem strange to modern Western minds, the contemporary fusion of work and money has not always been regarded as 'just the way it is'. Before the

13th century, activities involving the exchange of currency incurred the oppro-
brium of the medieval Church:

> Although money occupied an essential role in economic development, it was
> tolerated as an undesirable necessity. The exchange of money for labor or
> credit involved the purchase of time. From the perspective of the early medi-
> eval Church, time was a gift from God and therefore could not be sold.[40]

It was only with the rise of the professions and trades that the exchange of
currency gained a new theological acceptance. But by 1854, Henry Thoreau was
already decrying American society's growing enslavement to economics: "Most
men, even in this comparatively free country, through mere ignorance and mis-
take, are so occupied with the factitious cares and superfluously coarse labors of
life that its finer fruits cannot be plucked by them".[41]

In more recent times, James Hillman, Michael Sipiora and Per Espen Stoknes
are amongst those who have argued that work is an idea that has fallen prey to the
oppressive dynamic of economics.[42] From a depth psychological perspective, "the
Economy" is a modern myth.[43] "The economy is God. And there is only one God",
observed Stoknes. Ideas about money and business are taken as literal truths about
reality – "that's the way life is". Instead of being a consideration, economics has
come to shape the way we talk about and look at everything, the only measure
of reality. Because the internalisation of its ideas is so pervasive, the Economy is
where the "contemporary unconscious" resides.[44] The problems we experience in
connection with work have to do with ideas of the economy usurping the place
of any other imagination. We don't know we have these ideas because we're only
conscious of them as literal facts. Therefore, these ideas have us. Ideas about the
Economy have become internalised as monotheistic thinking and then rule by
psychological means.[45]

Hillman argued for the re-visioning of work in an aesthetic way, apart from the
Marxist economic view of it as drudgery. He advocated that we reimagine work
as an activity of soul or psyche rather than chaining work predominantly to an
economic paradigm.

> We have to make that move because that link between work and money is
> precisely what makes us feel like slaves. . . . People are desperately looking
> for work that really *pays* – work that give them credit, that has interest and
> value, that gives them shares. . . . Money-pay is a substitute for these soul
> needs. The language of economics has usurped all the soul terms for richness
> and worth.[46]

Indeed, even the word *vocation* has been now hijacked by the dominant economic paradigm, where the phrase 'vocational education and training' now commonly refers to the development of technical skills for the purpose of getting a
particular job with an industry and trade focus.

Like Alyce, Nikki was also experiencing the breakdown of assumptions that money will – and should – flow directly from her work. Nikki admitted that she would prefer it if the relationship between vocation and money was linear, a cause and effect paradigm. But that has not been a reality for her for six years now. A dream and a synchronistic encounter with a builder prompted her to build her own home. Then, within seven months, the equity in that house paid for her postgraduate studies.

> *So the money came from somewhere else entirely, and it came through synchronicity. And then it flowed so fast – it was so effortless, everything was aligned to make it happen. . . .*
>
> *It means stepping out of the assumption that the money only comes from a direct exchange for the service offered, and allowing the creative universe to provide for me. Which really is how my life has unfolded the last six years. My ego consciousness was initially very afraid, wondering how the unknown would open up financially. And yet it has and it continues to. However, the paradigm of how that happens has broken. It is not a black and white equation of fair trade any longer. There is a third now, psyche, which is the force that ultimately guides where the money, the sustenance, comes from.*
>
> (Nikki)

Nikki wants to say something more about money that has been very, *very* important for her vocation. With a child to support and unable to access student financial aid, she finished her dissertation quickly because:

> *Money was the wolf at the door that made me sit down and write. That was really helpful. I was very conscious of it the whole time . . . it is the driving force that's very real in keeping me grounded. Other than running out of money, it's created the tension, the pressure that means I can't just crawl under a rock and hope it's all going to work out, I have to keep moving forward. . . . I'm at the point where I don't go into the fear about money as much as it's a catalyst for energy.*
>
> *. . . So money actually has a very interesting role for me at the moment in vocation. It's not about the direct return for services offered, it's not that black and white, fair exchange. But it is very important in propelling me forward into the next thing, whatever that is.*
>
> (Nikki)

Instead of blaming money for imposing constraints on her vocation, Nikki has reframed her need for money as that which now propels her full throttle into her vocation. Neuroses and fears around money are transformed instead into a "catalyst for energy".

Michael was another who found that when he followed the psyche's call to vocation, "money comes in weird ways". Earlier I mentioned Michael's family complexes around money, and that he felt that money could have become a real problem for him had he not "educated the feminine side of his own psyche" to get past it. Like many people, Michael acknowledged that money is often the last obstacle inhibiting one from responding to a calling.

> *Money is something you can't ignore. So here is a perfect example of when I had to deal with this issue. Thirty years ago I had a dream where I go to the Arctic. I forgot the dream, until a friend sent me photos from the Antarctic, which awakened my earlier dream. . . .*
>
> *I said, "I've got to go to the Antarctic". I wanted to go on a nature cruise. When I figured out the whole package, it came to $25,000. I said, I can't do this. So that was going to be the end of it: a dream that came back after 30 years, something about the ice. My wife said, "No. You're saying 'we can't do this'? What's all of this 'we can't'? Do you want to do it? Then we'll find a way. If you really want to do it you open it up, you give it to the universe. . . ".*
>
> *Well what happened was, about two weeks after the conversation, the Social Security office (I was 67) says, well you've applied for social security, so we owe you some back-money. I figure it would be $500. You know what the lady told me? She said, "You're going to get a cheque for $24,500". I said, "I can't believe this!" I made other calls and everyone I talked to said, "This has never happened to us". It was a desire, and then the world answered. It was a piece of synchronicity. And that changed my life, because I went down there and it was a spiritual transformation [and now I'm engaged in work that emerged out of that trip]. . . . So it's changed my life.*
>
> *If I had said no in the beginning – this goes back to the money question – if you start with that, then you can limit yourself prematurely, and then your life shrinks. But it's not then to disregard it. There might be occasions where I say: I want to do that, but I can't do it right now. But I'm not going to let that dream die.*
>
> (Michael)

A cynic might put Michael's financial windfall down to luck or an example of New Age, magical thinking, that somehow the universe will provide. However, Michael's reflection on the meaning of this "piece of synchronicity" is more nuanced and complex than such a critique allows. This experience deepened Michael's trust that there is something larger of which he is part and which is not solely tied to his ability to earn money through work, which will provide him with the essential resources that he needs to serve his vocation.

The metaphor of flow

> *The question of money – that is the ultimate leap into the arms of psyche. Follow your vocation with the belief that psyche will sustain you. You may not be living at the top of the hill anymore: you may be living at the bottom of the hill. But maybe that's where you need to be. Now I go more with the ebb and flow of money.*
>
> (Jim)

At the beginning of this chapter, I mentioned how the language and metaphor of water – liquidity, currency, circulation – is frequently connected with money. People talk about freezing funds, liquidating assets and how money can run through the fingers or down the drain. Money matters draw us into the waters of the unconscious (water also being a common metaphor for the unconscious). Yet without water, or when our circulation stops, we die. Archetypal psychologist Robert Sardello described cash flow as "the river which moves imagination into the world and in which the world becomes shaped according to the needs of imagination".[47] What might we learn by viewing our relationships with money through the metaphor of ebb and flow?

Annabella described her relationship with money as "very fluid". She has a diversified sense of vocation, where some streams have brought in income. She is not frivolous, but she tends to use her money to help in her family's lives and doesn't save it for herself. Annabella related to the archetype of the Magician because she found that money comes when she needs it in unusual ways (for example, she wrote a hiking guide and made money out of that). She admitted, laughing, that she was not good with money on a practical level.

> *I just kind of depend upon it to come (which I also think is a folly). It's very fluid. But I keep thinking – well that's not going to last forever!*

Annabella tries to have a different relationship with money, more grounded in the realities of being an ageing woman alone. But she also feels she is not good at doing that. She uses water metaphors as she talks, which suggest that while money flows through her life, she is also aware of a need to conserve it like water, as a resource and a source of life. I ask her if she simply trusts that the rain will come again?

Living in drought-stricken California, Annabella thinks we are at a stage (both in the world and in herself) where it's not necessarily going to rain much again. She thinks about her use of water as a metaphor for money and the personal implications of this:

> *I'm the first generation of women having to do this alone. I don't know how to do it, just like I don't know how to conserve water in my house to the degree that we need to, because we think it's always going to be there. It's a paradigm shift I haven't made. Because it's completely new – a woman alone at my age, and what's happening with water right now.*
>
> (Annabella)

The associations Annabella makes between water and money cause her to ponder the scarcity and stewardship of both essential resources at this stage in her life. Jungian analyst Russell Lockhart argued that the talismanic nature of money also "turns us, forces us, moves us into confrontation with our telos . . . our final end, our purpose"[48] – and, I suggest, towards our vocation. Lockhart described this power that money has in terms of Jung's notion of the Self, the guiding archetype of wholeness in the psyche, or the *Imago Dei*, the god image. "When we confront the power of money in our lives", wrote Lockhart, "we are confronting the power of the 'other' in us, a power that works its will in and through money".[49]

To advance this idea further: how we relate to money is one way by which we relate to the psyche as a whole. Furthermore, *money may be a means by which the psyche or the Self relates to us*. This means that rather than thinking about money as an inconvenient obstacle or impediment to the fulfilment of our ideal life or work, an alternative is to embrace the shadows of money instead, as an inescapable part of our own journey of individuation.

In conclusion, psychological growth may come from working with the psychic content money offers, especially in the context of our daily lives and work. As we do this inner work, to understand the deeper psychology of money in our own lives, we can know that this work too has a deeply transformative effect on the collective of which we are part.

We can do this work by becoming more conscious of the projections money carries for us. We can see how our own money complexes and behaviours may be deeply rooted in our families of origin or in our culture. We can notice where the ancient gods and goddesses, and mythic stories, are alive today in our money behaviours. We can remember money's origins, connected with the wealth of the natural world. Most of all, we can appreciate the inevitably problematic, paradoxical nature of money, as devilishly divine. And remember that money is more than a literal, 'real-world' concern but is also an imaginal, archetypal, psychic reality which, if we engage with it more consciously and creatively, can tend us towards individuation and soul-making work.

Invitation to reflection and journaling

- What saying was inscribed on your Family's 'invisible money crest'?
- In what directions do you like to spend your money? What archetypes, or Gods and Goddesses, are you in service to with your various money behaviours?
- What self-betrayals have you committed in the name of economic and social survival?
- Consider the metaphor of money as flow in your life:

    - How are you using, treating or conserving this essential resource at this stage in your life?
    - How clean – or polluted – are your sources of income? Perhaps you have a diversified sense of vocation, with only some streams bringing in income?
    - Are there areas in your life where money is rushing wastefully down the drain?
    - Where does the money passing through your hands go back into circulation?
    - What vision of life is the money that you steward helping to water, shape and sustain?

Notes

1 Lawson et al. 2019.
2 Verrender 2015, para. 4.
3 American Psychological Association 2018.
4 Lerner 2017, para. 32.
5 Moore 1992, p. 181.
6 Sardello 1983, p. 2.
7 Hillman 1989, p. 173, italics in original.
8 Kipnis, for example, offers a long list of metaphors associating money with mental health and psychopathology: words like depression and inflation, lows and highs, slumps and peaks, losses and investments (2013, p. 88).
9 Hillman 1989, p. 173.
10 Belk & Wallendorf 1990, p. 61.
11 Hillman 1982b, p. 39.
12 Hillman 1989, p. 174.
13 Sardello 1983, p. 5.
14 Moore 1992, p. 192.
15 Moore 1992, p. 195.
16 Moore 1992, p. 190.
17 McCreary 2000, p. 22.
18 McCreary 2000, p. 76.
19 McCreary 2000, pp. 22–28.
20 McGuire 1994, p. 192.
21 Conklin 2012, p. 311.
22 Belk & Wallendorf 1990, p. 51.
23 Perkins & Boseley 2018.
24 Lawson et al. 2019.
25 Dik & Duffy 2009, p. 437.
26 Wrzesniewski et al. 1997.
27 Dik & Duffy 2009, p. 438.
28 Bunderson & Thompson 2009, p. 52.
29 Jung 1934b CW17, para. 300.
30 Covitz 1982, p. 75.
31 Covitz 1982, p. 70.
32 Bauman 1998; Dawson 2005, p. 226.
33 Csikszentmihalyi (1990) gives examples of an old woman who farms in the Alps, a welder in South Chicago and a cook from ancient China.
34 Jung 1934b CW17, para. 300, italics added.
35 Hamilton 2003; Hamilton & Denniss 2006.
36 Kipnis 2013, pp. 28–30.
37 Campbell 2004, pp. 119–120.
38 Moore 1992, p. 189.
39 Stoknes 2009, p. 49.
40 Shaffer 1999, pp. 58–59.
41 MacIver 2006, p. 35.
42 Hillman 1983, 1995; Sipiora 2012; Stoknes 2009.
43 Hillman 1995, pp. 2–6; Sipiora 2012.
44 Hillman 1995, p. 4.
45 See also the documentary *Money and Life* (Teague 2013), which traces the history and invention of money and considers how individuals may participate more consciously in its continuing evolution as a system.

46 Hillman 1983, p. 171.
47 Sardello 1983, p. 23.
48 Lockhart 1982, p. 18.
49 Lockhart 1982, p. 15.

12 Living on the edge between worlds

I know now that the psyche is something that I cannot not consider. Sometimes I do forget to talk to the psyche. I always remember when I can't figure out the answers. Then I ask for dreams, I ask for visions. I just talk to the psyche and say – I just don't know; can you tell me? And in a strange way, something always comes. It definitely doesn't come from my brain, it comes from somewhere else. But I definitely like to translate it into practical reality which can be carried out.

(Jana)

Being alive in the 21st century evokes the dizzying sense of rapidly moving between diverse realities. Our locus is constantly shifting, between circles of family, friends, colleagues, bureaucracies, social media, mainstream media, other cultures, places, tribes, local and global economies, political manoeuvres, spiritual practices, the plant and animal worlds and so on. As late 20th century postmodernism's rejection of modernism's master narrative showed, it seems as if there are multiple fragmenting worlds which we are continuously negotiating and transitioning. In this concluding chapter, I want to bring this multiplicity into a different focus, at least initially. I want to refocus our attention on two ever-present realms of which we are all citizens: our awareness of both inner, imaginal *and* collective, social realities.

Finding and following a vocational calling is a practice which challenges us to engage with and bridge both the symbolic, soulful, unconscious *and* the rational, material, practical dimensions of life. In Jungian terminology, as we have seen, this entails honouring paradoxical imperatives: of the ego, to be secure and sustainable in the world; and of the psyche, or soul, to be engaged in work which holds resonance and meaning.

In previous chapters, we've seen how a person may be initiated into a profound and fulfilling sense of meaningful vocation through experiences which relativise the ego into relationship with a much larger whole, which I have called the psyche. As we saw in Chapter 5, 'psyche' in the depth psychological sense is both inner and outer, in oneself and in the world. When the human ego submits to a dialogic relationship with the psyche, a relationship which heeds both the voices within and is inclusive of a sense of deep kinship and shared fate with the more-than-human world:

> One discovers both a sense of individuality and uniqueness and a deeper, humble sense of one's participation in the mysterious drama of life, of which one is not the author. This . . . is a religious sense whether or not any orthodox religious dogma is held.[1]

This "religious sense" which Roger Brooke describes is implicit in the re-imagining and re-enchantment of our working lives. By re-enchantment, I mean that we approach our work in the world not only from the perspective of consensual, material reality but also that we are mindful too of another mythic, imaginal or psychic reality running alongside this.

Engaging *mythos* and *logos* perspectives

Throughout this book, we've seen how a fundamental premise of depth psychology is the importance of being able to live symbolically, to have a symbolic life, and to be capable of finding the symbolic, the psychological, that exists within concrete behaviours or thinking. This is not to forsake the concrete or literal; rather, it is to cultivate a kind of 'double' or 'binocular vision' that embraces what the ancient Greeks called *logos* – which is the principle of speech, discourse, reason and judgment, or logic, if you like – as well as *mythos*. For the pre-Socratic philosophers, the word *mythos* did not mean a fiction, fallacy or falsehood; it was a term which meant 'breathed from the divine', a divinely inspired sacred truth. *Mythos* is a worldview, or way of seeing reality, which embraces "the poetic, metaphoric, the symbolic, the affective, and the imaginal".[2] In the pre-modern world, as well as in traditional and indigenous societies, both *mythos* and *logos* were valued as complementary ways of arriving at truth, each with its special area of competence.[3]

To apply these concepts to our working lives – the *logos* side is our résumé or CV. It represents the verifiable facts of what have occurred, where we have worked and when, and what we accomplished, in an external kind of way. The *mythos* side is the mythic, inner story which we have lived and are living alongside this. Rooted in the unconscious, myth is not concerned with practical matters or what happens literally but with the meaning of what occurs.

This intriguing relationship between *logos* and *mythos* is beautifully illustrated in the 2012 film *The Life of Pi*.[4] This is the tale of a young Tamil boy from Pondicherry who survives 227 days after a shipwreck while stranded on a lifeboat in the Pacific Ocean with a zebra, an orangutan, a hyena and a Bengal tiger. After his rescue, Pi is interviewed by Japanese insurance agents for the shipwrecked freighter, who simply do not believe his fantastical story. They insist on knowing what *really* happened. So Pi relates another story, in which human beings take the place of the animals. The anguish on Pi's face as he tells this second version suggests that it may indeed correspond to the horrific external realities of his experience.

This second story represents the *logos* perspective. The animal story, with which we have been enthralled throughout the film, conveys the *mythic* perspective. The question that Pi then asks is, "Which story do you prefer?"

The writer to whom Pi relates his life story chooses the mythic version with the tiger because (as all good writers know) it is the better story. But so, too, it transpires, do the fact-seeking insurance agents ultimately prefer the mythic version. They conclude their report with a remark on the feat of "surviving 227 days at sea . . . especially with a tiger". It is the mythic, metaphoric story which is replete with the more psycho-spiritually satisfying meaning, even for those whose occupations, like insurance assessors, are ostensibly in service to *logos'* concerns with external facts. The lingeringly ambiguous ending to the film leaves us, the audience, to ponder which story we prefer, with the dawning realisation that the fullest and most compelling picture emerges from the interplay and synthesis between these *logos* and *mythos* worlds.

To further illustrate the way in which these two worlds weave together, clinical psychologist and Jungian analyst Donald Kalsched has offered the image of a mask of a human face, with one eye open and one eye closed. Carved by an unknown Inuit from the vertebrae of a humpback whale, the mask is called "The Storyteller".[5] The closed eye focuses on the inner world of dreams and the mythopoetic images of the imagination, while the open eye focuses on the harder edges of material reality and human relationships. Thus the image of the Storyteller gives dramatic expression to the "two worlds" which must be kept in view if a genuine and compelling story of our lives is to be told. In other words, one is able to hold both *mythos* and *logos* perspectives simultaneously.

In the tradition of visionaries, theologians and artists such as William Blake and Abraham Heschel, Kalsched uses the term "binocular vision" to describe this perspective. Binocular vision sees both the sensate, material world of outer reality and a second, spiritual world which lies alongside ordinary reality, the latter being an idea which is "not widely accepted in scientific circles, and yet it is as old as the human race".[6] This is what the 19th century Romantic visionary William Blake called "double vision": the ability to perceive a thing in at least two ways simultaneously. When Blake looked at the sun, he reported seeing not only "a round thing somewhat like a guinea" but also "an immeasurable Company of the Heavenly Host crying Holy, Holy, Holy is the Lord God Almighty".[7] Jung referred to this as living in the spirit of the times and the spirit of the depths.[8] Rabbi Abraham Heschel considered that "Citizens of two realms, we all must sustain a dual allegiance: we sense the ineffable in one realm, we name and exploit reality in another".[9]

To draw this book to a conclusion, I want to suggest that consciously cultivating this kind of double vision is now essential if we are to re-awaken to a deeper sense of our lives and work as vital and meaningful in these collectively precarious times. To be able to see with this double vision enables us to hold not only the literal but also the enriching imaginal, mythic and archetypal perspectives on our lives and our work. It allows us to hold the present and the possible at the same time. It leads to respect for other ways of knowing, beyond intellectual reasoning, to encompass *eros*, *pathos*, imagination and intuition, qualities traditionally associated with the archetypal feminine. Today, the rational, pragmatic, scientific thrust of the *logos* principle predominates in our society. Yet the crisis of meaning and imagination, which many people experience today in connection with their work, may well be due to an excess of *logos'* literalism, the dearth of a mythic perspective and a commensurate absence of imagination. An antidote to this lies in the reunion of *mythos* and *logos* perspectives.

Walking the borderland between *logos* and *mythos* perspectives is where 'soul-making' happens. I began this book with the proposition that *soul* was a quality missing in many people's experiences of work. Yet we have seen that a sense of soul and of soul-making is fundamental to the experience of authentic vocation. In contrast to Jung's notion of *individuation*, which implies a move *away from* collectivity or the group mind to attend to what arises from the unconscious, the notion of *soul-making* emphasises bringing an imaginal, mythic, archetypal perspective towards all aspects of existence and towards our creative engagement with the world.[10] According to Hillman, soul-making is not a treatment or therapy but "an imaginative activity or an activity of the imaginal realm as it plays through all of life everywhere and which does not need analyst or an analysis".[11] Annabella's story (presented in Chapter 7) is but one illustration of how soul-making happens, as a person lives into a vocation that arises from the meeting of inner and outer worlds, seasoned too with the quality of *eros* (respectful relationship and loving care). Of her work as a teacher, Annabella said:

> *Coming from a deep presence inside of myself has been a journey. And from that, to now creating an environment where people find that inside themselves . . . so they can find the richness, the value, and the beauty that is inherent. . . . So they want to keep living.*

> (Annabella)

Another way of appreciating the relationship between a vocation or calling and a job or career is to consider these notions as the *mythos* and *logos*, the yin and the yang, of a life at work. When it is necessary to make things happen, to get something done or to persuade people to adopt a particular course of action (the 'yang' aspects of career), the practical focus of *logos* is important. Yet regarding the receptive 'yin' aspects of a vocation, it is the intuitive insights of *mythos*, closer to those of art, music, poetry or sculpture, which provide the context of meaning which makes such practical activities worthwhile.

So it is as if the notions of calling and career are the yin and the yang of a life at work. It is about a dialogue – a dance – between these two perspectives, and between the ego and the different parts of the psyche.

Waiting in the midst of ambiguity

Yet there is an undeniable tension being in this place. As the imaginal psychologist Robert Romanyshyn wrote:

> On the edge, one has to learn to think differently . . . outside the box of either/ or dichotomies. One has to learn how to be able to tolerate waiting in the

midst of ambiguity. . . . Between reason and dream, between fact and idea, between conscious reflection and unconscious dynamics, one has to be careful and patient enough to linger in 'uncertainties, Mysteries, doubts, without any irritable reaching after fact and reason,' which is the poet Keats' description of negative capability.[12]

When we allow the psyche, the soul, to guide our vocation, we embark on a journey with no pre-determined destination and which may not necessarily lead towards an existing occupation. We may find ourselves in the process of creating a new, hybrid or niche occupation, unique and responsive to our particular combination of interests, aptitudes, experience, complexes, fate and environment. This may not be an occupation which others recognise or understand until it is brought into existence. Or we may be called to conduct or reimagine our existing occupation in new ways. The vocational counsel which Rainer Maria Rilke offered a young poet and military student in 1903 is just as timely for seekers today:

> Be patient toward all that is unsolved in your heart and to try to love the questions themselves like locked rooms and like books that are written in a very foreign tongue. . . .
> Live the questions now. Perhaps you will then gradually, without noticing it, live along some distant day into the answer.[13]

If new occupations are to emerge which are responsive to the social, economic and ecological crises our planet faces today, it is essential that we develop the capacity to tolerate ambiguity – what Keats described as "negative capability". Repeatedly, the people I interviewed for this research spoke about their patience and trust with actively and consciously being in this place of uncertainty:

> *I don't know exactly how it looks. . . . It's more that I'm just following my calling, this vocational pull that is in me and I just follow it right now. . . . It really involves a lot of trusting, a lot of submission to the calling. When I have gone through this period . . . then that will be my next career, my next way of giving back.*
>
> (Jana)

> *When I picked my career [in] engineering, to some degree I was trusting that I could do it. . . . I really don't know where I'm going with this one, but I've come to trust the psyche . . . to lead me in the direction that is best for me, as well as for whatever particular aims it has for me or for the culture at large.*
>
> (Peter)

> *I trust that if it doesn't work out I will figure it out, one step at a time. . . . That willingness to be very moment to moment and responsive to the present moment – that's been an integration of what I have worked with as the*

wild woman archetype in my dissertation. It's that instinctual knowing that responds to each moment.

(Nikki)

The kind of "instinctual knowing" to which Nikki refers is also developed by attention to **synchronicity**. A synchronistic experience, such as an unexpected encounter or exchange with a pivotal person, or a book falling open at a page which presents us with just the words we need to read at that time, can feel akin to an act of grace, offering vocational guidance and breakthroughs from a source beyond the conscious mind.[14] Due to the psychologically edgy nature of synchronicity, we are wise to bring a reflective consciousness to such experiences. Yet as we track our unfolding soul's calling through shifting landscapes where there is no pre-existing path, a synchronicity may provide compelling affirmation of a vocational calling signalled by some other psychic commentary, such as a dream or reverie.

Furthermore, depth psychology's polycentric, polytheistic[15] approach acknowledges the multiplicity of voices within us. Rather than insisting on pigeon-holing these into a unity (a singular 'I', a 'perfect career'), we can adopt a posture of welcoming and endeavouring to integrate each fragment according to its own principle.[16]

I have . . . more energy now for coming back to take action in the world. I'm not at a stage yet where I know what form that will take. I'm trying not to be prescriptive about it. I'm trying to let go of my ideas about filmmaking in case they are something my ego dreamed up. I'm willing to let deeper voices have their say.

(Steve)

As Steve suggests, the practice of holding council with the various parts of ourselves that demand voice in our lives may evolve into creative occupational directions beyond the neat fantasy of a 'perfect career'. It may lead to portfolio work (wearing a number of different hats simultaneously). It may lead to serial work-projects that invigorate and satisfy the *puer* (eternal child) temperament for variety and new horizons, rather than serve the *senex* (wise old man) disposition to work in one occupation or for one company for a lifetime. If we are psychologically many persons, each may make their claim on us at various points.

Vocation's historical links with monotheism and Christianity tend to bias thinking about vocation towards ideals of unity, integration, transcendence and wholeness. Even Jung's psychology, with his attention to unifying symbols of wholeness, such as the mandala, and an emphasis on the Self as the archetype of wholeness, has been critiqued for having a monotheistic bias.[17] Perhaps even the word 'career' is covertly monotheistic, based in assumptions of advancement and ascent.

By contrast, the polycentric, polytheistic perspective of archetypal psychology, which sits more comfortably with postmodernism, acknowledges that consciousness is located in multiple figures and centres in the psyche.[18] There are:

> no preferred positions, no sure statements about positive and negative. . . . When the idea of progress through hierarchical stages is suspended, there will be more tolerance for the non-growth, non-upward and non-ordered components of the psyche. There is more room for variance when there is more place given to variety.[19]

A polytheistic perspective encourages us to look at all the jobs and vocations within us: the work of being a good son or daughter or sibling or parent, the work of citizenship or neighbourliness, and our inner work as having a place alongside our outer work. To me, this is the art of life which, as Jung observed, is "the most distinguished and rarest of arts. Whoever succeeded in draining the whole cup with grace?"[20] Depth psychology provides a frame for our many personalities, for holding the many paradoxes and valences of our work and careers. Bringing these other layers and perspectives to career development expands the playing field for the creative unconscious to find expression through work.

Dancing with the psyche

All the people I interviewed for this research on vocation and calling spoke of their trust in the process of staying close to and being guided by the psyche. They evidenced a capacity to tolerate ambiguity, even when it was acutely discomforting. A few described this as a feeling of 'dancing' with the psyche.

> *For me, Psyche is a dance partner. The key is knowing when to lead and when to be led. I'm comfortable being led by factors so ambiguous they would scare most people to death. I'm comfortable being in the chaos, the not-knowing, living with ambiguity.*
>
> (Jim)

> *Over six years I have come to trust the process, the psyche, the daimon very much. . . . I listen to the dreams. I listen to the synchronicities, the feelings. . . . Today, I was going around looking for a space to lease . . . and just feeling – what kind of images come up? Do I get a rush of yes? Of no? Do I hear any words? One place I was in I actually heard the words "not a fucking chance" [laughter]. Listening to the quiet voice inside, listening to my body. . . . Sometimes in life things can just unfold and it can just be effortless. This particular part of this transition requires that I do a lot of networking and turn over a lot of stones. Part of me would just like to crawl under one of those rocks. It's taking a bit of work to go out and network and look and*

research and feel: Where do you want me to go? It feels like this kind of dance.

(Nikki)

Claire also thought of the psyche as not just a dance partner but as a choreographer in her life and work:

It's a very interesting dance. . . . How much authorship can we claim, and how much is a gift coming through us? Both are necessary. Authority and humility.

(Claire)

Although a person may (even surreptitiously) move to be the controlling figure in this dance with the psyche, Joe Coppin and Elizabeth Nelson suggest that a "more psychological approach is to treat the work as an autonomous partner by entering into a lively, dialectical relationship with it, fully prepared for the unexpected and the synchronistic".[21] Regarding the manifestation of her vision for a healing sanctuary for war veterans, Alyce likened this to "a marriage of listening to the psyche and exercising will":

I've never been someone to say, "I will just put this out to the universe and the universe will take care of it for me". Manifesting this, in part, is really being in a calm place and allowing the other to speak. Holding the dream really clearly. What is it? Not what is it for me, but what is it in its entirety? Certainly what is it for me is really important. But what does the whole thing want to be?

(Alyce)

Alyce's comments raise two significant points for the reader who seeks to take the insights from this book into application in the world. The first is the radical implication, from Jung's more inclusive definition of the psyche, that "any work a person undertakes has as much psychic reality as the worker. It is an active, autonomous participant in its own development, with legitimate demands and desires, on the path of its own individuation".[22] This idea positions the human ego in a relationship of attentive service towards the overall emerging vocational direction and, indeed, towards the work itself. It is not only the person who is individuating by virtue of being engaged in work that is a calling. The work itself is individuating and is in the process of becoming. Our role is to be aware of and in service to that too.

The second point is the necessity to apply our personal will behind things as well. Once we hear a calling and trust it, it is necessary to act in service of manifesting it.

There really is that which I can take care of, the nuts and bolts. I can see if we can get permits, I can get an architect, I can figure out the finance – but the thrust behind it is Psyche. She is the one who is helping it to happen. And seeing that dream materialise: that is very energetic.

(Alyce)

I absolutely believe that vocation is meaningless without work, unless you're willing to – well, in my case – put the seat of my pants to the seat of my chair and write. You're required to be engaged.

(Claire)

So the conscious personality becomes the agent of the larger psyche, or transpersonal will. To elaborate on this idea, Claire gave an example from an interview she conducted years ago with the woman who re-introduced the labyrinth to the modern Western world:

Her feeling about that was that if she had not said yes to that vocation (she clearly saw it as a vocation), at that moment, the daimon might have asked a few more times but then would have said, "Okay I'm not hearing a yes. I'll find someone else". I believe that the gods are looking for our yes, and it needs to be real, it needs to be manifest.

(Claire)

Realising these deeper vocational impulses into new occupational or entrepreneurial directions is then where the development and application of specific career or business skills may be useful and necessary; for example, around marketing, strategic planning and financial management.

Another way we might imagine this dynamic dance with the psyche is again as the yin and yang of work. The yin is the ability to receive the vocational inspiration, the vocational moment, however it turns up; whereas the yang is the ability to act on it and integrate it. There is an ongoing, cyclical relationship between the movements of yin and yang.

Repairing the world

Throughout this book, we have considered ways in which vocational callings are initiated and guided by the psyche, which includes various psycho-spiritual dimensions beyond the conscious mind. In the tradition of depth psychology, I have called this source the psyche, but it might also go by other names, such as the unconscious, the Self or (in mythological and religious traditions) the gods and goddesses, or God. But we might also imagine a vocational calling as arising from and as a response to the world soul, the *anima mundi*. This is an idea first proposed by Plato, affirmed by the Christian mystics, Renaissance philosophers, German and British Romantics and American transcendentalists, amongst others, and revived in more recent times by the archetypal psychologists.[23] Jung described the *anima mundi* as "a natural force which is responsible for all the phenomena of life and the psyche".[24] In other words, it is as if the *anima mundi* gives birth to the human psyche and nurtures its growth and development. From this perspective, a vocational calling extends beyond an individualistic, self-promoting activity to call forth actions which bring one into a more harmonious relationship with the interdependent web of creation.[25] The idea of vocation as a response to the *anima mundi* has profound implications for the creation of new occupational directions which are responsive to the economic and ecological crises our planet faces today.[26]

Are some occupations riper than others for vocation? Ecological or environmental work in particular would seem to be a fertile area for the discovery of calling.[27] Hillman extended a responsiveness to the *anima mundi* to reinvigorating work in areas such as energy policy, nourishment, hospital care and even the design of interiors.[28] In my research, teaching and practice, I have seen individuals bring a depth psychological sensibility towards advances in educational design, therapeutic approaches, community development, leadership, organisational development, economics, architecture and urban planning, ecological sustainability, literary analysis, working with indigenous cultures, mindfulness, sexuality, healthcare, rehabilitation and more, via channels including teaching, writing, filmmaking, counselling, consulting, art and performance, volunteer work and entrepreneurship. Once we begin our dance with the psyche, new horizons open up for intelligent and soulful innovation in a myriad of fields.

Claire also linked these emerging vocational directions to the Hebrew idea of *tikkun olam* – the notion of repairing the world:

> *This is a very important idea for me: that god (or the gods) want us to participate in the ongoing repair and creation of the world, and that no one individual can do it all, or even a lot, but each of us is called in a very particular way to repair what we can.*
>
> *So we are both crucially important, and we are part of something much, much larger than ourselves.*

(Claire)

When vocation is envisioned as a response to the *anima mundi*, it becomes released from the values of a utilitarian economic ideology and re-situated in a more interconnected and ecologically rooted paradigm. This allows the return of a very natural and vitalizing sense of how the world itself is continuously speaking to us. However, this sense is primarily psychological, not metaphysical, and it turns on a metaphorical and poetic vision (of course, the *anima mundi* is itself a perspective).

This sensibility supports us to feel deeply inspired by and committed to our relationship with our calling, even in challenging times. Despite the inevitable vicissitudes of life, we can find ourselves graced with the state of happiness and contentment which the Greeks called *eudaimonia* because we have truly 'shown up' in our lives and fulfilled the soul's contract with our own *daimon*.

We may begin to navigate our careers as a journey of soul simply by making a space for the psyche in the conversations we have about our work. Being able to speak about and reflect on our careers and work experiences in a context where the reality of psyche is honoured is in itself surprisingly therapeutic. The people I spoke with made the following comments about our interviews:

> *The conversation was rich and spontaneous, and I found myself thinking in new ways, articulating ideas that had not yet come into form.*
>
> (Claire)

> *Having this talk about psyche and vocation is giving me much more clarity than I had ever imagined. I could never have expected anything like that.*
>
> (Jana)

Bearing witness to another's mythos/logos story of vocation can be a significant source of healing and soul-making. As *The Life of Pi* so aptly conveyed, telling one's story to a respectful witness creates "a vision of the life, an imagining of the life, that wraps it in meaning and significance", leaving all with "a feeling of sacred happiness".[29]

Jana commented that while our interview covered the usual external story of what she did in her life and career, it felt different because it made space for the psyche at the same time.

> *It wouldn't be so difficult really to make the space for psyche, if we wanted to – in all kinds of conversations about all sorts of topics. And the benefits are great. We get to better understand our own path, in this very practical world, in this very mundane way. At the same time we can also start seeing the teleological aspects of whatever we are doing . . . because we allow the psyche into the conversation.*
>
> (Jana)

The point of this quote, and of this book as a whole, is also the essential tenet of depth psychology. It is that we begin to invite and host what has lingered on the margins, below the level of consciousness, into our conscious awareness. This hosting includes the imagination, the synchronicities, the symptoms, the ancestors, the *genius loci*, the *daimon* . . . – because these things make up the landscape of lived experience. They are part of the soul of life. The alternative is for vocational guidance to be captured by the values and demands of external, economic principles and dying industrial processes. The re-enchantment of work means that soul and imagination are taken seriously, though not literally, as we each work towards the ongoing repair and creation of our world.

> *The great events of world history are, at bottom, profoundly unimportant. In the last analysis, the essential thing is the life of the individual. . . . This alone makes history, here alone do the great transformations first take place, and the whole future, the whole history of the world, ultimately spring as a gigantic summation from these hidden sources in individuals. . . . In our most private and most subjective lives we are not only the passive witnesses of our age, and its sufferers, but also its makers. We make our own epoch.*
> – CG Jung (1964 CW10, para. 315)

Invitation to reflection, conversation and creative practice

- In his autobiography, Jung reflected that "The meaning of my existence is that life has addressed a question to me . . . or, conversely, I myself am a question". If life has addressed a question (or questions) to you, what would it be? How might your unfolding calling be envisaged as a creative response to that question?
- If you have a leadership role (in any context), in what way(s) are you making space for the psyche in the conversations people have about their work and lives? A simple way to start may be by inviting others to reflect, without fear of judgment or reprisal, on the difference between a job, a career and a vocation (as discussed in Chapter 1), and to share how these ideas play out in their own lives.

- **Create a collage** of your personal myth. To make the collage, you'll need a canvas or large piece of light cardboard (minimum A3 size); some paints, coloured pens, crayons or pencils; glue and scissors, and possibly some magazines (or access to a colour printer to print from your computer). Although you can make the collage on a computer, it is better if you craft it by hand, activating the tactile senses too.

  The collage can take any form you like. It could be a mandala, a river, a spiral, a tree, a question mark. As you review your reflections at the end of each chapter, you'll find many clues regarding the larger mythic story you are living.

  You've thought about your most important values, identified resonant symbols which hold a feeling of soulfulness for you and observed the figures and images showing up in your dreams.

  You've become acquainted with your shadow and how that relates to your vocation – the shadow of your persona and the glowing coals under gray ashes. Don't forget to acknowledge the shadow in your collage!

  You've reflected on your sensitivities and complexes and where the broken heart shows up and on the ways your unfolding calling may be shaped by ancestral history and cultural patterns.

You've considered various metaphors for money in your life and what gods/goddesses you are serving with your money behaviours.

Perhaps you've underlined or noted significant passages in this book that speak directly to you. Any of these words or images may find a place in your collage.

Perhaps there is an image or symbol that has surfaced for you that remains mysterious, yet somehow it feels important. All the better to include it – you may be surprised at how its significance reveals itself over time.

The purpose of this creative activity is not to produce an artwork for anyone's judgement or aesthetic appraisal, but psychically this is a very powerful activity. By using your hands to make something from the symbols and ideas that have surfaced for you, you are demonstrating to the psyche that you are listening. The collage works as a kind of vision board from the psyche to propel you into your future, your destiny, your calling.

When you've finished your collage, place it somewhere where you can notice it every day. Allow the words and images to continue their work with you as you navigate your career as a journey of soul-making.

Notes

1 Brooke 2015, p. 20.
2 According to Leonard and McClure, *logos,* to pre-Socratic philosophers, represented a kind of everyday transactional discourse which could be true or false, "a means of arguing propositions, tricking someone, or accurately describing reality" (2004, p. 3). Both *logos* and *mythos* were later translated into English as *word* or *story*. However, the definition of *mythos* was permanently complicated by Plato (427–347 BCE), who was perhaps the first to conscript the political power of myth, using the word *mythos* ambivalently to mean both lie and truth. The confusion was furthered by campaigns of the Christian church to discredit the stories of other religions (Smart 1999, p. 71). The term *logos,* at least in the New Testament, came to mean something like transcendent truth, and *mythos* was associated with fiction, or worse, "outright falsehoods designed to damn souls to Hell" (Leonard & McClure 2004, p. 7). The connotative meaning of *logos* and *mythos* had switched places, and the "negative Platonic/Christian definition of myth prevailed for the next 1500 years" (Leonard & McClure 2004, p. 7) – and indeed, continues to prevail today.
3 Armstrong 2001, p. xv.
4 Lee 2012. Based on Yann Martel's 2001 novel of the same name.
5 Kalsched 2013, p. 6.
6 Kalsched 2013, p. 7.
7 Avens 1980, p. 22.
8 Jung 2009, pp. 229–230.
9 Heschel 1976, p. 8.
10 Slater 2012, pp. 27–31. While differentiating between *individuation* and *soul-making*, Slater notes that they converge around the task of recovering values that have been obscured by collective trends.
11 Hillman 1972, p. 7.
12 Romanyshyn 2013, p. 318.
13 Rilke 1986, pp. 34–35.
14 Bogart 1994; Guindon & Hanna 2002.

15 Although Hillman uses the term 'polytheistic' to describe archetypal psychology, thereby locating the discipline within a religious framework, we could also adopt the terms 'polycentric' (many centres) or 'polyvalent' (many sided).
16 Hillman 1971, p. 197.
17 Hillman 1971, 2005b.
18 Hillman 1975, p. 26.
19 Hillman 1971, pp. 197–198.
20 Jung 1931b, para. 789.
21 Coppin & Nelson 2005, p. 55.
22 Coppin & Nelson 2005, p. 55.
23 Hillman 1982a.
24 Jung 1969 CW8, para. 393.
25 Bogart 1992, p. 210.
26 Turner 2014.
27 Conklin 2012, p. 312.
28 Hillman 1982a, p. 87.
29 Garay 2013, pp. 121, 122.

Glossary of Jungian terms

Active Imagination   A method developed by Jung of voluntary involvement or dialogue with a dream or fantasy image to assimilate it into consciousness using some form of self-expression, such as drawing, painting, writing, sculpture, dance or music (Jung 1956 CW14, paras. 706, 753–756).

Amplification   Amplification involves seeking parallels of a symbol or image in text passages, mythology, religion, fairy tales and so on, and if these resonate, then collecting and using them as ways of perceiving the meaning of the word or image. Amplification is essentially looking for ways in which the collective unconscious has manifested and used a symbol or image.

Anima/Animus   The contra-sexual archetypes in the psyche. Jung used the term *anima*, which means soul, to describe the feminine aspect of a man's psyche; and *animus*, which means mind or spirit, to describe the masculine element in a woman's psyche. The general direction of modern post-Jungian thought has been to recognise that the archetypes of *anima* and *animus* are available to everyone, not only pertaining to those who identify with one pole of a traditional gender binary. We each have within us both feminine and masculine qualities, though historically those qualities which an individual has associated with the opposite sex have frequently been unconscious or repressed.

Archetype   Jung revived the ancient Platonic idea of archetypes as structuring principles of the collective unconscious (1940 CW9:1, paras. 5, 88–90). An archetype is a principle or agency which organises and structures psychic imagery into specific patterns, motifs or constellations. Archetypes may also be described as 'partial personalities' appearing in myth, religion, legends, fairy tales, art, cinema and literature, as well as in dreams, visions, family roles, emotions and pathologies. "The archetypes . . . are the ruling powers, the gods, images of the dominant laws and principles, and of typical, regularly occurring events in the soul's cycle of experience" (Jung 1960b CW7, para. 151).

Archetypal Image   An archetypal image is the form or representation which an archetype takes in consciousness. Archetypes themselves are unrepresentable, but their effects appear in consciousness and throughout culture as archetypal images, motifs and ideas. The archetype is "a dynamism which makes itself felt in the numinosity and fascinating power of the archetypal image" (Jung 1954a CW8, para. 414).

Collective Unconscious A term coined by Jung to describe a field of fundamental possibilities inherited from the long history of experiences of the human species (1969 CW8, para. 342), which finds expression through various cultural and personal filters, such as myths and dreams. The Jungian unconscious is both vast and inexhaustible, including not only thoughts and emotions that have been repressed but also contents that may or will become conscious. It is populated by archetypes as inherent structuring principles. What Jung called the 'objective psyche' is essentially equivalent to the collective unconscious. See also **Unconscious**.

Complex An emotionally charged group of ideas or images that cluster around an archetypal core (Jung 1934c CW8).

Depth Psychology Depth psychology is a discipline that acknowledges the continuous interaction of conscious and unconscious influences on human behaviour (Coppin & Nelson 2005; Ellenberger 1970). In particular, it values what Jung called the collective unconscious or the objective psyche – a realm which is beyond conscious knowledge and personal will – as a source of wisdom and guidance. Depth psychology may be described as a psychology of metaphor and imagination, in which the most important words are "it is *as if* . . .". Its methods encompass the study of myth, dreams and symbols.

Depth psychology emerged as a discipline in the late 19th century, and although it was originally equated with Freudian psychoanalysis, it later came to designate more broadly a number of psychological approaches related to the unconscious. These included the development of theories and therapies pioneered by Pierre Janet, William James, Sigmund Freud and Carl Jung. In more recent times, the term depth psychology has come to be more closely associated with the downward, soul focus of the movement in post-Jungian psychology known as archetypal psychology.

Dream According to Jung, a dream is "an expression of an involuntary psychic process not controlled by conscious outlook" (1933, p. 5), which offers a compensation for the dreamer's conscious attitude. By this, Jung means that dreams reveal latent and unconscious aspects (such as the shadow) which the psyche needs tended in the process of individuation.

Ego The ego is the centre of our subjective identity and consciousness. It is the originator of personal will which translates our decisions into actions towards specific goals.

Feminine/Masculine The 'masculine principle' (also 'archetypal masculine' or 'masculine consciousness') refers to a psychological orientation emphasising logical thought, objectivity, planning, assertiveness, detachment and a goal-orientation. By contrast, the 'feminine' refers to countervailing qualities such as feeling, intuition, receptivity, relationship, empathy and a process-orientation. The term 'feminine' has been extended to encompass all that the Western masculine mind has projectively identified and repressed as 'Other', including imagination, emotion, instinct, body, nature, mystery, ambiguity and woman (Tarnas 1991, p. 442). It is important, however, not to conflate women and the feminine nor men with the masculine. Jung recognised the androgynous nature of the psyche and that we each have within us both feminine and masculine qualities. See also *Anima/Animus.*

Individuation   A term coined by Jung to describe the process of developing and maintaining a dialogue between the ego and the unconscious, having for its goal the development of the individual personality, or becoming one's own self (1921 CW6, paras. 757–761). Jung considered that individuation was usually triggered around midlife, although it is indeed the work of a lifetime (1970 CW18, para. 1099).

Intuition   One of the four basic psychological functions which Jung identified, along with Sensation, Thinking and Feeling. Like Sensation, Intuition is an 'irrational function', but in contrast to Sensation, Intuition perceives via the unconscious (for example, via flashes of insight) and is not dependent on concrete reality. Intuition is the function that perceives possibilities inherent in the present.

Libido   For Jung, libido meant a general life instinct or psychic energy, which may encompass but was not limited to a sexual dynamism, as libido was with Freud (Jung 1928a CW8, paras. 54–56).

Numinous   A term used by Rudolph Otto (1958) to describe the direct quality and experience of an encounter with the sacred. It comes from the Latin *numen*, meaning a divinity, and the verb *nuere*, meaning to nod or beckon.

Persona   The persona is the sense of the role we play in the world and how well we play it. This may include our occupation or profession and social position. "The persona is a complicated system of relations between individual consciousness and society, fittingly enough a kind of mask, designed on the one hand to make a definite impression upon others, and, on the other, to conceal the true nature of the individual" (Jung 1928b CW7, para. 30).

Projection   The process whereby the contents of one's own unconscious are perceived to be in others. Frustrated expectations indicate the need to withdraw projections in order to relate to the reality of the other.

Psyche   In Jungian psychology, the psyche is radically different from the Cartesian notion of the personal mind, which is something interior and separate from the outer world. Jung came to describe the psyche as something that surrounds us, inside and out. According to Jung, the psyche is no more 'inside us' than the sea is inside the fish (Jung 1967 CW13, para. 75).

   Jung introduced the term *objective psyche* to stress that the psyche is not to be confused with or limited to the boundaries of the individual person, whose personal psychology or *subjective psyche* is organised around the ego (Jung 1960b CW7, para. 103). The 'objective psyche' is essentially equivalent to the unconscious, and in particular to what Jung called the collective unconscious. The 'subjective psyche' equates to the personal level of the unconscious, equivalent to Freud's notion of the 'subconscious'.

Self   In Jung's model of the psyche, the Self is the central archetype of wholeness, also known as the *Imago Dei*, or internal God image. Jung described the

Self as "the totality of the psyche. The self is not only the centre, but also the whole circumference which embraces both conscious and unconscious; it is the centre of this totality, just as the ego is the centre of consciousness" (1974, p. 115). Jungians have taken to capitalising the term *Self* to distinguish it from the commonplace use of the word *self*, which is equivalent to the personal ego or 'I' (though Jung himself did not capitalise the term in his writing, which has led to some confusion).

Sensation   Sensation, or Sensing, is one of the four psychic functions. It is a process of perception directly through the five senses, which emphasises realism, concrete detail and practicality. See also **Intuition**.

Shadow   The shadow is the hidden or unconscious parts of ourselves which the ego has rejected or failed to recognise. Jung described the shadow as "the 'negative' side of the personality, the sum of all those unpleasant qualities we like to hide, together with the insufficiently developed functions and the content of the personal unconscious" (1960b CW7, para. 103).

Symbol   The word *symbol* is used in a specific way in Jungian psychology as distinct from semiotics. Jung described a symbol as being: "the best possible expression for a concrete fact not yet clearly apprehended by consciousness" (1916 CW8, para. 148). A symbol has a mysterious quality, as it stands in for something relatively unknown or ultimately unknowable; this is in contrast to a *sign*, which points to something known or knowable, typically with a meaning given by culture

Synchronicity   Synchronicity is a term coined by Jung to describe an acausal connection between inner and outer states which has meaning to the person who experiences it (Jung 1952b CW8). The numinous quality and emotional affect inherent in a synchronistic experience suggests the underlying presence of an archetype.

Transcendent Function   The *transcendent function* is the emergence of a third position which arises through the holding of the tension of opposites in the psyche. Conscious and unconscious data are brought together so as to arrive at a new attitude. "The transcendent function manifests itself as a quality of conjoined opposites" (Jung 1916 CW8, para. 189).

Unconscious   In Jungian psychology, the term *unconscious* has an expansive meaning. It denotes both contents repressed or inaccessible to the ego (the personal unconscious or subjective psyche) and a psychic arena with its own properties and functions (the collective unconscious or objective psyche), the latter populated by archetypes as inherent structuring principles (Jung 1934a CW9:1). The collective unconscious does not derive from personal experience but is universal to all people.

Bibliography

Abrams, D 2017, *The spell of the sensuous: Perception and language in a more-than-human world*, Vintage Books, New York.

Aizenstat, S 2009, *Dream tending: Techniques for uncovering the hidden intelligence of your dreams*, Spring Journal, New Orleans, LA.

American Psychological Association 2018, *APA Stress in America™ Survey*, viewed 15 October 2019, www.apa.org/news/press/releases/2018/10/generation-z-stressed.

Amundson, NE 2003a, *Active engagement: Enhancing the career counselling process*, 2nd edn, Ergon Communications, Richmond, Canada.

———— 2003b, 'Applying metaphors from physics to career/life issues', *Journal of Employment Counseling*, vol. 40, no. 4, pp. 146–151.

———— 2003c, *The physics of living*, Ergon Communications, Richmond, Canada.

———— 2005a, 'Adjusting career counseling methods to fit with a changing labor market', *Proceedings of the career counseling and the global labor market conference*, Petru Maior University, Târgu – Mures, România, 31 May–2 June, pp. 14–19.

———— 2005b, 'The potential impact of global changes in work for career theory and practice', *International Journal for Educational and Vocational Guidance*, vol. 5, no. 2, pp. 91–99.

———— 2010, *Metaphor making: Your career, your life, your way*, Ergon Communications, Richmond, Canada.

———— 2011, 'Active engagement and the use of metaphors in employment counseling', *Journal of Employment Counseling*, vol. 48, no. 4, pp. 182–184.

Armstrong, K 2001, *The battle for god: A history of fundamentalism*, Random House, New York.

Atwood, GE & Stolorow, RD 2004, *Faces in a cloud: Intersubjectivity in personality theory*, Rowman & Littlefield, Lanham, MD.

Avens, R 1980, *Imagination is reality: Western nirvana in Jung, Hillman, Barfield and Cassirer*, Spring, Putnam, CT.

Bauman, Z 1998, *Work, consumerism and the new poor*, Open University Press, Buckingham, UK.

Beaton Consulting 2007, *Depression in the professions survey: Research summary*, Beaton Reserch + Consulting Pty Ltd, South Yarra, Victoria, Australia.

Becker, C 2004, *The heart of the matter: Individuation as an ethical process*, Chiron Publications, Wilmette, IL.

Bedi, A & Matthews, B 2003, *Retire your family karma*, Nicolas-Hays, Berwick, ME.

Beebe, J 2004, 'Understanding consciousness through the theory of psychological types', in J Cambray & L Carter (eds), *Analytical psychology: Contemporary perspectives in Jungian analysis*, Brunner-Routledge, Hove, UK, pp. 83–115.

———— 2007, 'The spine and its shadow', *Australian Psychological Type Review*, vol. 9, no. 2, pp. 11–20.

Belk, RW & Wallendorf, M 1990, 'The sacred meanings of money', *Journal of Economic Psychology*, vol. 11, no. 1, pp. 35–67.

Benjamin, GA, Darling, E & Sales, B 1990, 'The prevalence of depression, alcohol abuse and cocaine abuse among United States lawyers', *International Journal of Law and Psychiatry*, vol. 13, pp. 233–240.

Berkelaar, BL & Buzzanell, PM 2015, 'Bait and switch or double-edged sword? the (sometimes) failed promises of calling', *Human Relations*, vol. 68, no. 1, pp. 157–178.

Bettelheim, B 1992, *Freud and man's soul*, Knopf, New York.

Bezanson, L 2004, 'The hero's journey: Stories and strategies for seekers – Using myth, metaphor and narrative in career development', Queensland Guidance and Counselling Association, Brisbane, Australia, 15 September 2004.

Black Dog Institute n.d., *Going south: Depression and the law*, Black Dog Institute, Randwick, NSW, Australia.

Bloch, DP 2005, 'Complexity, chaos, and nonlinear dynamics: A new perspective on career development theory', *Career Development Quarterly*, vol. 53, no. 3, pp. 194–207.

Bloch, DP & Richmond, L (eds) 1997, *Connections between spirit and work: New approaches and practical perspectives*, Davies-Black, Palo Alto, CA.

Bogart, GC 1992, 'Initiation into a life's calling: Vocation as a central theme in personal myth and transpersonal psychology', PhD thesis, Saybrook Graduate School and Research Center, Pasadena, CA.

———— 1994, 'Finding a life's calling', *Journal of Humanistic Psychology*, vol. 34, no. 4, pp. 6–37.

Boldt, LG 2009, *Zen and the art of making a living: A practical guide to creative career design*, 3rd edn, Penguin, New York.

Bolles, RN 2019, *What color is your parachute? A practical manual for job-hunters and career-changers*, Ten Speed Press, New York.

Bombay, A, Matheson, K & Anisman, H 2014, 'The intergenerational effects of Indian residential schools: Implications for the concept of historical trauma', *Transcultural Psychiatry*, vol. 51, no. 3, pp. 320–338.

Bordo, S 1986, 'The cartesian masculinization of thought', *Signs*, vol. 11, no. 3, pp. 439–456.

Bosnak, R 1986, *A little course in dreams*, Shambala, Boston.

———— 2007, *Embodiment: Creative imagination in medicine, art, travel*, Routledge, London.

Bowles, ML 1991, 'The organization shadow', *Organization Studies*, vol. 12, no. 3, pp. 387–404.

Bright, JEH, Pryor, RGL, Chan, EWM & Rijanto, J 2009, 'Chance events in career development: Influence, control and multiplicity', *Journal of Vocational Behavior*, vol. 75, no. 1, pp. 14–25.

Bright, JEH, Pryor, RGL & Harpham, L 2005, 'The role of chance events in career decision making', *Journal of Vocational Behavior*, vol. 66, no. 3, pp. 561–576.

Brooke, R 2009, 'The self, the psyche and the world: A phenomenological interpretation', *Journal of Analytical Psychology*, vol. 54, no. 5, pp. 601–618.

———— 2015, *Jung and phenomenology*, Routledge, New York.

Brown, D & Brooks, L (eds) 2002, *Career choice and development*, 4th edn, Jossey-Bass, San Francisco.

Bunderson, JS & Thompson, JA 2009, 'The call of the wild: Zookeepers, callings, and the double-edged sword of deeply meaningful work', *Administrative Science Quarterly*, vol. 54, no. 1, pp. 32–57.

Butler, JA 2013, 'Alchemical hermenutics: Differentiating the polyphony of voices in the work', *International Journal of Multiple Research Approaches*, vol. 7, no. 3, pp. 306–313.

Campbell, J 1988, *The power of myth*, Doubleday, New York.

—— 1991, *Reflections on the art of living: A Joseph Campbell companion*, HarperCollins, New York.

—— 2004, *Pathways to bliss: Mythology and personal transformation*, New World Library, Novato, CA.

—— 2008, *The hero with a thousand faces*, 3rd edn, New World Library, Novato, CA.

Cardador, MT & Caza, BB 2012, 'Relational and identity perspectives on healthy versus unhealthy pursuit of callings', *Journal of Career Assessment*, vol. 20, no. 3, pp. 338–353.

Colman, W 2015, 'A revolution of the mind', *Journal of Analytical Psychology*, vol. 60, no. 4, pp. 520–539.

Colvin, S (ed.) 1925, *Letters of John Keats to his family and friends*, Macmillan, London.

Conklin, TA 2012, 'Work worth doing: A phenomenological study of the experience of discovering and following one's calling', *Journal of Management Inquiry*, vol. 21, no. 3, pp. 298–317.

Coppin, J & Nelson, E 2005, *The art of inquiry: A depth psychological perspective*, 2nd edn, Spring, Putnam, CT.

Corbett, L 2007, *Psyche and the sacred: Spirituality beyond religion*, Spring, New Orleans, LA.

Corbett, R 2016, *You must change your life: The story of Rainer Maria Rilke and Auguste Rodin*, WW Norton, New York.

Corlett, JG & Pearson, CS 2003, *Mapping the organizational psyche: A Jungian theory of organizational dynamics and change*, Center for Applications of Psychological Type, Gainesville, FL.

Covitz, J 1982, 'Myth and money', in RA Lockhart et al. (eds), *Soul and money*, Spring, Dallas, TX, pp. 63–82.

Cremen, SN 2019, 'Vocation as psyche's call: A depth psychological perspective on the emergence of calling through symptoms at midlife', *International Journal for Educational and Vocational Guidance*, vol. 19, no. 1, pp. 41–61.

Csikszentmihalyi, M 1990, *Flow: The psychology of optimal experience*, HarperPerennial, New York.

Dawson, J 2005, 'A history of vocation: Tracing a keyword of work, meaning, and moral purpose', *Adult Education Quarterly*, vol. 55, no. 3, pp. 220–231.

Deng, C-P, Armstrong, PI & Rounds, J 2007, 'The fit of Holland's RIASEC model to US occupations', *Journal of Vocational Behavior*, vol. 71, no. 1, pp. 1–22.

Di Fabio, A 2010, 'Life designing in 21st century: Using a new, strengthened career genogram', *Journal of Psychology in Africa*, vol. 20, no. 3, pp. 381–384.

Dik, BJ & Duffy, RD 2009, 'Calling and vocation at work: Definitions and prospects for research and practice', *The Counseling Psychologist*, vol. 37, no. 3, pp. 424–450.

Dobrow, SR 2013, 'Dynamics of calling: A longitudinal study of musicians', *Journal of Organizational Behavior*, vol. 34, no. 4, pp. 431–452.

Downing, C 2007, *Psyche's sisters: Re-imagining the meaning of sisterhood*, Spring, New Orleans, LA.

Duffy, RD 2006, 'Spirituality, religion, and career development: Current status and future directions', *Career Development Quarterly*, vol. 55, no. 1, pp. 52–63.

Duffy, RD, Allan, BA, Bott, EM & Dik, BJ 2013, 'Does the source of a calling matter? External summons, destiny, and perfect fit', *Journal of Career Assessment*, vol. 22, no. 4, pp. 562–574.

Duffy, RD & Dik, BJ 2013, 'Research on calling: What have we learned and where are we going?' *Journal of Vocational Behavior*, vol. 83, no. 3, pp. 428–436.

Easter, SL 2016, *Jung and the ancestors: Beyond biography, mending the ancestral web*, Muswell Hill Press, London.

Eaton, WW, Anthony, JC, Mandell, W & Garrison, R 1990, 'Occupations and the prevalence of major depressive disorder', *Journal of Occupational Medicine*, vol. 32, no. 11, pp. 1079–1087.

Edinger, EF 1972, *Ego and archetype*, Shambhala, Boston.

————— 1978, *Melville's 'Moby-Dick': A Jungian commentary: An American nekyia*, New Directions Publishing, New York.

Ellenberger, HF 1970, *The discovery of the unconscious: The history and evolution of dynamic psychiatry*, Basic Books, New York.

Fidyk, AL 2016a, 'Unconscious ties that bind – Attending to complexes in the classroom: Part 1', *International Journal of Jungian Studies*, vol. 8, no. 3, pp. 181–194.

————— 2016b, 'Unconscious ties that bind – Attending to complexes in the classroom: Part 2', *International Journal of Jungian Studies*, vol. 8, no. 3, pp. 195–201.

The Foundation for Young Australians 2015, *The new work order: Ensuring young Australians have skills and experience for the jobs of the future, not the past*, Melbourne, viewed 15 October 2019, www.fya.org.au/2015/08/23/the-new-work-order-report.

Frankl, V 1984, *Man's search for meaning*, Washington Square Press, New York.

Fredericksen, D 2005, 'Why should we take Jungian film studies seriously?' *Spring: A Journal of Archetype and Culture: Cinema and Psyche*, vol. 73, pp. 31–40.

————— 2012, *Bergman's Persona*, Adam Mickiewicz University, Poland.

Freud, S 1952, *On dreams*, trans. J Strachey, WW Norton, New York.

————— 1961, 'Civilization and its discontents', in J Strachey (ed), *The standard edition of the complete psychological works of Sigmund Freud*, Hogarth Press, London, vol. 21, pp. 74–85.

————— 1969, 'Fourth lecture', in J Strachey (ed), *Five lectures on psycho-analysis*, WW Norton, New York, pp. 42–53.

————— 1973, *New introductory lectures on psychoanalysis*, vol. 2, Penguin, Harmondsworth, UK.

————— 1995, 'The future of an illusion', in J Strachey (ed), *The standard edition of the complete psychological works of Sigmund Freud*, Hogarth Press, London.

Fromm, MG (ed) 2012, *Lost in transmission: Studies of trauma across generations*, Routledge, London.

Gallos, JV 2005, 'Career counseling revisited: A developmental perspective', *Career Planning and Adult Development Journal*, vol. 21, no. 1, pp. 9–23.

Garay, CMM 2013, 'Follow your heart: An exploration of the somatic knowing of one's calling', PhD thesis, Pacifica Graduate Institute, Carpinteria, CA.

Gerson, J 2004, 'Malinchismo: Betraying one's own', in T Singer & SL Kimbles (eds), *The cultural complex: Contemporary Jungian perspectives on psyche and society*, Routledge, New York, pp. 35–45.

Gill, SD 1996, 'Disenchantment: A religious abduction', in RL Grimes (ed), *Readings in ritual studies*, Prentice Hall, Upper Saddle River, NJ, pp. 230–238.

Gilligan, C 2003, *In a different voice*, Harvard University Press, Cambridge, MA.

Graeber, D 2018, *Bullshit jobs: A theory*, Simon & Schuster, New York.

Grant, G 2005, *Re-visioning the way we work: A heroic journey*, iUniverse, Lincoln, NE.

Graycar, R & Morgan, J 1990, *The hidden gender of law*, Federation Press, Annandale, NSW, Australia.

Guindon, MH & Hanna, FJ 2002, 'Coincidence, happenstance, serendipity, fate, or the hand of God: Case studies in synchronicity', *Career Development Quarterly*, vol. 50, no. 3, pp. 195–208.

Haas, L & Hunziker, M 2011, *Building blocks of personality type: A guide to using the eight-process model of personality type*, TypeLabs, Temecula, CA.

Haas, M 2000, 'The orphan: From complex to archetype', Unpublished master's thesis, CG Jung Institute, New York.

Hall, DT & Chandler, DE 2005, 'Psychological success: When the career is a calling', *Journal of Organizational Behavior*, vol. 26, no. 2, pp. 155–176.

Hamilton, C 2003, *Growth fetish*, Allen & Unwin, Crows Nest, NSW, Australia.

Hamilton, C & Denniss, R 2006, *Affluenza: When too much is never enough*, Allen & Unwin, NSW, Australia.

Harding, ME 1971, *Women's mysteries: Ancient and modern*, Shambhala, Boston.

Hardy, L 1990, *The fabric of this world: Inquiries into calling, career choice, and the design of human work*, Eerdmans, Grand Rapids, MI.

Hari, J 2018, *Lost connections: Uncovering the real causes of depression and the unexpected solutions*, Bloomsbury, London.

Haule, JR 1993, 'Freud and Jung: A failure of eros', *Harvest: Journal of Analytical Psychology*, vol. 39, pp. 147–158.

Henderson, J 1984, *Cultural attitudes in psychological perspective*, Inner City Books, Toronto, Canada.

Heschel, AJ 1976, *Man is not alone: A philosophy of religion*, Farrar, Straus and Giroux, New York.

Hill, J 2015, *Jung's archetype: Emergent and/or pre-existent?* [unpublished work].

Hillman, J 1971, 'Psychology: Monotheistic or polytheistic?' *Spring*, vol. 1971, pp. 193–208.

———— 1972, *The myth of analysis: Three essays in archetypal psychology*, Northwestern University Press, Evanston, IL.

———— 1975, *Re-visioning psychology*, Harper Perennial, New York.

———— 1979, *Dream and the underworld*, Harper Perennial, New York.

———— 1982a, 'Anima mundi: The return of soul to the world', *Spring: A Journal of Archetype and Culture*, pp. 71–93.

———— 1982b, 'A contribution to soul and money', in RA Lockhart et al. (eds), *Soul and money*, Spring, Dallas, TX, pp. 31–43.

———— 1983, *Inter views: Conversations with Laura Pozzo on psychotherapy, biography, love, soul, the gods, animals, dreams, imagination, work, cities and the state of the culture*, Harper & Row, New York.

———— 1989, *A blue fire*, Harper Perennial, New York.

———— 1995, *Kinds of power*, Doubleday, New York.

———— 1996, *The soul's code: In search of character and calling*, Random House, Sydney, Australia.

———— 2005a, 'Peaks and vales: The soul/spirit distinction as basis for the differences between psychotherapy and spiritual discipline', in G Slater (ed), *Senex and puer*, Spring, Putnam, CT, Uniform Edition, vol. 3, pp. 71–95.

———— 2005b, ' "Psychology – Monotheistic or polytheistic": 25 years later', in G Slater (ed), *Senex and puer*, Spring, Putnam, CT, Uniform Edition, vol. 3, pp. 115–148.

———— 2005c, 'Senex and puer: An aspect of the historical and psychological present', in G Slater (ed), *Senex and puer*, Spring, Putnam, CT, Uniform Edition, vol. 3, pp. 30–70.

———— 2010, *James Hillman on archetypal psychotherapy and the soulless society*, DVD, Psychotherapy Videos and DVDs, UK.

Hillman, J & Ventura, M 1992, *We've had a hundred years of psychotherapy and the world's getting worse*, HarperCollins, New York.

Hirsch, M 2012, *The generation of postmemory: Writing and visual culture after the holocaust*, Columbia University Press, New York.

Hirschi, A & Herrmann, A 2013, 'Calling and career preparation: Investigating developmental patterns and temporal precedence', *Journal of Vocational Behavior*, vol. 83, no. 1, pp. 51–60.

Hogenson, GB 2007, 'Reply to Whitmont, The destiny concept in psychoanalysis', *Journal of Jungian Theory and Practice*, vol. 9, no. 1, pp. 39–45.

Holland, JL 1985, *Making vocational choices: A theory of careers*, 2nd edn, Psychological Assessment Resources, Odessa, FL.

Hollis, J 1995, *Tracking the gods: The place of myth in modern life*, Inner City Books, Toronto, Canada.

———— 1996, *Swamplands of the soul: New life in dismal places*, Inner City Books, Toronto, Canada.

———— 2001, *Creating a life: Finding your individual path*, Inner City Books, Toronto, Canada.

———— 2003, *On this journey we call our life: Living the questions*, Inner City Books, Toronto, Canada.

Hurley, D 2013, 'Grandma's experiences leave a mark on your genes', *Discover: The Magazine of Science, Technology and the Future*, viewed 15 October 2019, http://discovermagazine.com/2013/may/13-grandmas-experiences-leave-epigenetic-mark-on-your-genes.

Hyde, L 2007, *The gift: Creativity and the artist in the modern world*, 2nd edn, Vintage Books, New York.

Inkson, K 2004, 'Images of career: Nine key metaphors', *Journal of Vocational Behavior*, vol. 65, no. 1, pp. 96–111.

Inkson, K & Amundson, NE 2002, 'Career metaphors and their application in theory and counseling practice', *Journal of Employment Counseling*, vol. 39, no. 3, pp. 98–108.

International Association for Educational and Vocational Guidance n.d., *Strategies for vocational guidance in the twenty-first century*, International Association for Educational and Vocational Guidance, Wiltshire, UK, viewed 15 October 2019, www.unesco.org/education/educprog/tve/nseoul/docse/rstratve.html.

Isaac, JL 2008, 'Individuation and the orphan archetype: A phenomenological study', PhD thesis, Pacifica Graduate Institute, Carpinteria, CA.

Jacobi, J 1959, *Complex, archetype, symbol in the psychology of C.G. Jung*, trans. R Manheim, Bollingen Foundation/Princeton University Press, New York.

Johnson, RA 1986, *Inner work: Using dreams and active imagination for personal growth*, HarperCollins, New York.

———— 1993, *Owning your own shadow: Understanding the dark side of the psyche*, HarperCollins, San Francisco.

Jung, CG 1911–12, *Symbols of transformation*, The Collected Works of CG Jung, vol. 5, digital edn, ed. H Read, M Fordham & G Adler, trans. RFC Hull, Princeton University Press, Princeton, NJ.

[All references to The *Collected Works* are henceforth referred to as CW followed by volume number].

———— 1916, 'The transcendent function', in *The structure and dynamics of the psyche*, CW8.

———— 1918, *The role of the unconscious*, CW10.

———— 1921, *Psychological types*, CW6.

————— 1928a, 'On psychic energy', in *The structure and dynamics of the psyche*, CW8.

————— 1928b, 'The relations between the ego and the unconscious: Two essays', in *Two essays on analytical psychology*, CW7.

————— 1931a, 'A psychological theory of types', in *Psychological types*, CW6.

————— 1931b, 'The stages of life', in *The structure and dynamics of the psyche*, CW8.

————— 1933, *Modern man in search of a soul*, Harcourt, New York.

————— 1934a, *The archetypes and the collective unconscious*, CW9:1.

————— 1934b, 'The development of personality', in *The development of personality*, CW17.

————— 1934c, 'A review of the complex theory', in *The structure and dynamics of the psyche*, CW8.

————— 1935, 'The Tavistock lectures', in *The symbolic life: Miscellaneous writings*, CW18.

————— 1938, 'Psychological aspects of the mother archetype', in *The archetypes and the collective unconscious*, CW9:1.

————— 1940, 'The psychology of the child archetype', in *The archetypes and the collective unconscious*, CW9:1.

————— 1944, *Psychology and alchemy*, CW12.

————— 1945, 'The philosophical tree', in *Alchemical studies*, CW13.

————— 1946, 'The psychology of the transference', in *The practice of psychotherapy*, CW16.

————— 1948, 'Address on the occasion of the founding of the C.G. Jung Institute, Zurich, 24 April 1948', in *The symbolic life: Miscellaneous writings*, CW18.

————— 1951, *Aion*, CW9:2.

————— 1952a, 'Answer to job', in *Psychology and religion*, CW11.

————— 1952b, 'Synchronicity: An acausal connecting principle', in *The structure and dynamics of the psyche*, CW8.

————— 1954a, 'On the nature of the psyche', in *The structure and dynamics of the psyche*, CW8.

————— 1954b, *The practice of psychotherapy*, CW16.

————— 1956, *Mysterium coniunctionis*, CW14.

————— 1960a, 'The interpretation of visions', *Spring*, pp. 106–148.

————— 1960b, *Two essays on analytical psychology*, CW7.

————— 1964, *Civilization in transition*, CW10.

————— 1967, *Alchemical studies*, CW13.

————— 1969, *The structure and dynamics of the psyche*, CW8.

————— 1970, 'Two essays on analytical psychology', in *The symbolic life: Miscellaneous writings*, CW18.

————— 1974, *Dreams*, trans. RFC Hull, Princeton University Press, Princeton, NJ.

————— 1989a, *Essays on contemporary events: The psychology of Nazism*, trans. RFC Hull, Bollingen Paperbacks, Princeton, NJ.

————— 1989b, *Memories, dreams, reflections*, trans. R Winston & C Winston, Vintage Books, New York.

————— 2009, *The red book*, WW Norton, New York.

Kakiuchi, KKS & Weeks, GR 2009, 'The occupational transmission genogram: Exploring family scripts affecting roles of work and career in couple and family dynamics', *Journal of Family Psychotherapy*, vol. 20, no. 1, pp. 1–12.

Kalsched, D 2013, *Trauma and the soul: A psycho-spiritual approach to human development and its interruption*, Routledge, New York.

Kaufmann, Y 2009, *The way of the image: The orientational approach to the psyche*, Zahev Books, New York.

Kelk, N, Luscombe, G, Medlow, S & Hickie, I 2009, *Courting the blues: Attitudes towards depression in Australian law students and lawyers, BMRI Monograph 2009–1*, Brain and Mind Research Institute, University of New South Wales, Sydney.

Kimbles, SL 2000, 'The cultural complex and the myth of invisibility', in T Singer (ed), *The vision thing: Myth, politics, and psyche in the world*, Routledge, London, pp. 157–169.

Kipnis, AR 2013, *The midas complex: How money drives us crazy and what we can do about it*, Indigo Phoenix Books, Los Angeles.

Kohut, H 1971, *The analysis of the self: A systematic approach to the psychoanalytic treatment of narcissistic personality disorders*, The University of Chicago Press, Chicago.

Kostera, M 2012, *Organizations and archetypes*, Edward Elgar Publishing, Cheltenham, UK.

Lagan, A & Moran, B 2006, *3D ethics: Implementing workplace values*, Verdant House, Maleny, Queensland, Australia.

Lawson, M, Chan, M-K, Rhodes, F, Butt, AP, Marriott, A, Ehmke, E, Jacobs, D, Seghers, J, Atienza, J & Gowland, R 2019, *Public good or private wealth?* Oxfam International, Oxford, UK.

Lee, A (dir) 2012, *The Life of Pi*, motion picture, 20th Century Fox.

Leonard, S & McClure, M 2004, *Myth and knowing: An introduction to world mythology*, McGraw-Hill, New York.

Lerner, M 2017, 'The psychopathology of the 2016 election', *Tikkun*, vol. 31, no. 4, pp. 5–16.

Loach, J (dir) 2010, *Oranges and Sunshine*, motion picture, See Saw Films & Sixteen Films, UK & Australia.

Lockhart, RA 1982, 'Coins and psychological change', in RA Lockhart et al. (eds), *Soul and money*, Spring, Dallas, TX, pp. 7–29.

Luhrman, B (dir) 2008, *Australia*, motion picture, 20th Century Fox.

Lyddon, WJ, Clay, AL & Sparks, CL 2001, 'Metaphor and change in counseling', *Journal of Counseling and Development*, vol. 79, no. 3, pp. 269–274.

MacIver, R (ed.) 2006, *Thoreau and the art of life: Reflections on nature and the mystery of existence*, North Atlantic Books, Berkeley, CA.

Maguire, A 2004, *Skin disease: A message from the soul*, Free Association Books, London.

Malach-Pines, A & Yafe-Yanai, O 1999, 'Unconscious influences on a choice of a career: Implications for organizational consultation', *Journal of Health and Human Services Administration*, vol. 21, no. 4, pp. 502–511.

Marohn, S 2011, 'The shamanic view of mental illness', in *Natural medicine guide to bipolar disorder*, Hampton Roads Publishing, Charlottesville, VA, pp. 173–183.

Martin, CR 2009, *Looking at type: Your career: Using psychological type to find your best-fit career*, Center for Applications of Psychological Type, Gainesville, FL.

May, R 1989, *Freedom and destiny*, WW Norton, New York.

Mayes, C 2005, 'Teacher as shaman', *Journal of Curriculum Studies*, vol. 37, no. 3, pp. 329–348.

———— 2016, 'Jung's view of the symbol and the sign in education', *Psychological Perspectives*, vol. 59, no. 2, pp. 191–201.

McCreary, WA 2000, 'Money and the care of soul', PhD thesis, Pacifica Graduate Institute, Carpinteria, CA.

McGuire, W (ed) 1994, *The Freud/Jung letters*, Princeton University Press, Princeton, NJ.

McMahon, M 2006, 'Working with storytellers: A metaphor for career counselling', in M McMahon & W Patton (eds), *Career counselling: Constructivist approaches*, Routledge, London, pp. 15–28.

McMahon, M & Patton, W (eds) 2006, *Career counselling: Constructivist approaches*, Routledge, London.

McMahon, M & Watson, MB (eds) 2011, *Career counseling and constructivism: Elaboration of constructs*, Nova Science Publisher, New York.

Meade, M 2010, *Fate and destiny: The two agreements of the soul*, Greenfire Press, Seattle, WA.

——— 2016, *The genius myth*, Greenfire Press, Seattle, WA.

Medlow, S, Kelk, N & Hickie, I 2011, 'Depression and the law: Experiences of Australian barristers and solicitors', *Sydney Law Review*, vol. 33, pp. 771–799.

Metcalfe, AW 2013, 'Sociology teaching as a vocation', *Journal of Sociology*, vol. 49, no. 4, pp. 531–544.

Metzner, R 1998, *The unfolding self: Varieties of transformative experience*, Origin Press, Novato, CA.

Mignot, P 2000, 'Metaphor: A paradigm for practice-based research into "career"', *British Journal of Guidance & Counselling*, vol. 28, no. 4, pp. 515–531.

Mignot, P 2004, 'Metaphor and "career"', *Journal of Vocational Behavior*, vol. 64, no. 3, pp. 455–469.

Moore, T 1992, *Care of the soul: A guide for cultivating depth and sacredness in everyday life*, Harper Perennial, New York.

——— 1994, *Dark eros: The imagination of sadism*, Spring, Putnam, CT.

Morgan, G 2006, *Images of organization*, Sage Publications, Thousand Oaks, CA.

Myers, IB, McCaulley, MH, Quenk, NL & Hammer, AL 1998, *MBTI manual: A guide to the development and use of the Myers-Briggs type indicator*, 3rd edn, Australian Council for Educational Research, Melbourne, Australia.

Myers, IB & Myers, PB 1995, *Gifts differing: Understanding personality type*, Davies-Black, Palo Alto, CA.

Neale, M (ed) 2017, *Songlines: Tracking the seven sisters*, National Museum of Australia Press, Canberra, Australia.

Neumann, E 1994, *The fear of the feminine: And other essays on feminine psychology*, Princeton University Press, Princeton, NJ.

Norris, DJ 2015, 'Embracing the orphan archetype: A creative and imaginal approach to developing the abandoned self', MA thesis, Pacifica Graduate Institute, Carpinteria, CA.

Noyce, P (dir) 2002, *Rabbit-proof fence*, motion picture, Miramax Pictures, Australia.

Okiishi, RW 1987, 'The genogram as a tool in career counseling', *Journal of Counseling & Development*, vol. 66, no. 3, pp. 139–143.

Otto, R 1958, *The idea of the holy*, Oxford University Press, New York.

Palmer, PJ 2000, *Let your life speak: Listening for the voice of vocation*, Jossey-Bass, San Francisco.

——— 2004, *A hidden wholeness: The journey toward an undivided life*, Jossey-Bass/ Wiley & Sons, San Francisco.

Parsons, F 1909, *Choosing a vocation*, Gay & Hancock, London.

Patton, W & McMahon, M 2006, *Career development and systems theory: Connecting theory to practice*, 2nd edn, Sense Publishers, Rotterdam, The Netherlands.

Payne, J 2006, *The language of the soul: Healing with words of truth*, Findhorn Press, Findhorn, Scotland.

Pearson, CS 1991, *Awakening the heroes within: Twelve archetypes to help us find ourselves and transform the world*, HarperCollins, New York.

Perkins, M & Boseley, M 2018, 'Older women, migrants swell the ranks of Australia's homeless', *The Sydney Morning Herald*, viewed 15 October 2019, www.smh. com.au/national/older-women-migrants-swell-the-ranks-of-australia-s-homeless-20180314-p4z4c9.html.

Pratt, C 2007, 'Initiation', in *An encyclopedia of shamanism*, vol. 1, Rosen Publishing, New York.

Pryor, RGL & Bright, JEH 2007, 'Applying chaos theory to careers: Attraction and attractors', *Journal of Vocational Behavior*, vol. 71, no. 3, pp. 375–400.——— 2009, 'Game as a career metaphor: A chaos theory career counselling application', *British Journal of Guidance and Counselling*, vol. 37, no. 1, pp. 39–50.

——— 2011, *The chaos theory of careers: A new perspective on working in the twenty-first century*, Routledge, New York.

——— 2014, 'The chaos theory of careers (CTC): Ten years on and only just begun', *Australian Journal of Career Development*, vol. 23, no. 1, pp. 4–12.

Ramos, DG 2004, 'Corruption: Symptom of a cultural complex in Brazil?' in T Singer & SL Kimbles (eds), *The cultural complex: Contemporary Jungian perspectives on psyche and society*, Routledge, New York, pp. 102–123.

Rilke, RM 1986, *Letters to a young poet*, trans. S Mitchell, Vintage Books, New York.

Roeg, N (dir) 1971, *Walkabout*, motion picture, 20th Century Fox, UK and Australia.

Romanyshyn, RD 2007, *The wounded researcher: Research with soul in mind*, Spring Journal Books, New Orleans, LA.

——— 2010, 'The wounded researcher: Making a place for unconscious dynamics in the research process', *The Humanistic Psychologist*, vol. 38, pp. 275–304.

——— 2013, 'Making a place for unconscious factors in research', *International Journal of Multiple Research Approaches*, vol. 7, no. 3, pp. 314–329.

Rosen, D 2002, *Transforming depression: Healing the soul through creativity*, Nicolas-Hays, York Beach, ME.

Rothenberg, R-E 1983, 'The orphan archetype', *Psychological Perspectives*, vol. 14, no. 2, pp. 181–194.

Rowland, S 2002, *Jung: A feminist revision*, Polity Press, Cambridge, UK.

——— 2010, *C.G. Jung in the humanities: Taking the soul's path*, Spring Journal, New Orleans, LA.

——— 2012, *The ecocritical psyche: Literature, evolutionary complexity and Jung*, Routledge, Hove, UK.

Rusiti, E 2015, 'The true cost of suicide: A very personal story', *Law Society of NSW Journal*, no. 18, pp. 36–38.

Russell, D 2012, 'Lost for words: Embryonic Australia and a psychic narrative', in C San Roque, A Dowd & D Tacey (eds), *Placing psyche: Exploring cultural complexes in Australia*, Spring, New Orleans, LA, pp. 120–150.

Sabini, M (ed) 2002, *The earth has a soul: C.G. Jung on nature, technology and modern life*, North Atlantic Books, Berkeley, CA.

Salman, S 2000, 'The wisdom of psychological creativity and *amor fati*', in P Young-Eisendrath & ME Miller (eds), *The psychology of mature spirituality: Integrity, wisdom, transcendence*, Routledge, London, pp. 77–86.

Samuels, A 2004, *Jung and the post-Jungians*, Routledge, London.

San Roque, C, Dowd, A & Tacey, D (eds) 2011, *Placing psyche: Exploring cultural complexes in Australia*, Spring, New Orleans, LA.

Sardello, RJ 1983, 'Money and the city', in RJ Sardello & R Severson (eds), *Money and the soul of the world*, The Pegasus Foundation, Dallas, TX, pp. 1–29.

Savickas, ML 1997a, 'Constructivist career counseling: Models and methods', in GJ Neimeyer & RA Neimeyer (eds), *Advances in personal construct psychology*, JAI Press, Greenwich CT, vol. 4, pp. 149–182.

———— 1997b, 'The spirit in career counselling: Fostering self-completion through work', in DP Bloch & LJ Richmond (eds), *Connections between spirit and work in career development*, Davies-Black, Palo Alto, CA, pp. 3–25.

———— 2002, 'Career construction: A developmental theory', in D Brown & L Brooks (eds), *Career choice and development*, 4th edn, Jossey-Bass, San Francisco, pp. 149–205.

———— 2005, 'The theory and practice of career construction', in SD Brown & RW Lent (eds), *Career development and counseling: Putting theory and research to work*, John Wiley & Sons, Hoboken, NJ, pp. 42–70.

———— 2011, 'Constructing careers: Actor, agent, and author', *Journal of Employment Counseling*, vol. 48, no. 4, pp. 179–181.

———— 2012, 'Life design: A paradigm for career intervention in the 21st century', *Journal of Counseling and Development*, vol. 90, no. 1, pp. 13–19.

———— 2013, 'Career construction theory and practice', in SD Brown & RW Lent (eds), *Career development and counseling: Putting theory and research to work*, 2nd edn, John Wiley & Sons, Hoboken, NJ, pp. 147–183.

Savickas, ML & Baker, DB 2004, 'The history of vocational psychology: Antecedents, origin and early developments', in WB Walsh & ML Savickas (eds), *The handbook of vocational psychology*, 3rd edn, Lawrence Erlbaum, Mahwah, NJ, pp. 15–50.

Savickas, ML, Nota, L, Rossier, J, Dauwalder, J-P, Duarte, ME, Guichard, J, Soresi, S, Van Esbroeck, R & van Vianen, AE 2009, 'Life designing: A paradigm for career construction in the 21st century', *Journal of Vocational Behavior*, vol. 75, no. 3, pp. 239–250.

Selig, JL 2011, *Cultural complexes*, audio podcast, Pacifica Graduate Institute, Carpinteria, CA.

Sells, B 1994, *The soul of the law*, Element Books, Rockport, MA.

Shaffer, SH 1999, 'A thread of meaning: Depth psychology, work, and vocation', PhD thesis, Pacifica Graduate Institute, Carpinteria, CA.

Shalit, E 2002, *The complex: Path of transformation from archetype to ego*, Inner City Books, Toronto, Canada.

Singer, T 2010, 'The transcendent function and cultural complexes: A working hypothesis', *Journal of Analytical Psychology*, vol. 55, pp. 234–241.

Singer, T & Kaplinsky, C 2010, 'Cultural complexes in analysis', in M Stein (ed), *Jungian psychoanalysis: Working in the spirit of C.G. Jung*, Open Court Publishing, Chicago, pp. 22–37.

Singer, T & Kimbles, SL (eds) 2004, *The cultural complex: Contemporary Jungian perspectives on psyche and society*, Routledge, New York.

Sipiora, M 2012, 'Liberating the work instinct from the economy', paper presented at the Reimagining, renewing, reinventing leadership conference, Pacifica Graduate Institute, Carpinteria, CA, 8–10 June.

Slater, G 1996, 'Surrendering to psyche: Depth psychology, sacrifice, and culture', PhD thesis, Pacifica Graduate Institute, Carpinteria, CA.

———— 2008, 'Numb', in S Marlan (ed), *Archetypal psychologies: Essays in honor of James Hillman*, Spring Journal Books, New Orleans, pp. 351–367.

———— 2011, 'Archetypes and the collective psyche', lecture delivered 13 January, Pacifica Graduate Institute, Carpinteria, CA.

———— 2012, 'Between Jung and Hillman', *Quadrant: Journal of the C.G. Jung Foundation for Analytical Psychology*, vol. XXXXII, no. 2, pp. 15–37.

Smart, N 1999, *Worldviews: Cross-cultural explorations of human beliefs*, 3rd edn, Prentice Hall, Upper Saddle River, NJ.

Somé, MP 1994, *Of water and spirit: Ritual, magic, and initiation in the life of an African shaman*, Penguin, New York.

Spoto, A 1995, 'The strange case of the inferior function', in *Jung's typology in perspective*, Chiron Publications, Wilmette, IL, pp. 75–107.

Stoknes, PE 2009, *Money and soul: The psychology of money and the transformation of capitalism*, Kindle edn, Green Books, Devon, UK.

Susskind, A 2010, 'Resilience initiative tackles depression from the top down', *Law Society Journal*, vol. 48, no. 3, pp. 22–25.

Tacey, D 1993, 'The Australian psyche: Archetypal process down under', *Psychological Perspectives*, vol. 28, pp. 32–43.

———— 2003, *The spirituality revolution: The emergence of contemporary spirituality*, HarperCollins, Sydney.

———— 2009, *Edge of the sacred: Jung, psyche, earth*, Daimon Verlag, Einsiedeln, Switzerland.

———— 2011, 'The Australian resistance to individuation: Patrick White's knotted mandala', in C San Roque, A Dowd & D Tacey (eds), *Placing psyche: Exploring cultural complexes in Australia*, Spring Journal, New Orleans, LA.

———— (ed) 2012, *The Jung Reader*, Routledge, Hove, UK.

———— 2014, 'James Hillman: The unmaking of a psychologist. Part 1: His legacy', *The Journal of Analytical Psychology*, vol. 59, no. 4, pp. 467–486.

Tarnas, R 1991, *The passion of the western mind: Understanding the ideas that have shaped our world view*, Ballantine Books, New York.

Teague, K 2013, *Money and life*, documentary, Stormcloud Media, US.

Terszak, M 2008, *Orphaned by the colour of my skin: A stolen generation story*, Verdant House, Maleny, Queensland, Australia.

Tocher, M & Simon, A 1998, *Brave work: A guide to the quest for meaning in work*, Canadian Career Development Foundation, Ottawa, Canada.

Turner, G 2014, *Is global collapse imminent?* MSSI Research Paper No. 4, Melbourne Sustainable Society Institute, The University of Melbourne, Australia.

Turner, V 1969, *The ritual process: Structure and anti-structure*, Aldine Transaction, London.

Van Gennep, A 1960, *The rites of passage*, The University of Chicago Press, Chicago, IL.

Verrender, I 2015, 'Under 30 and out of luck: The age of entitlement truly is over', *The Drum, ABC News*, viewed 15 October 2019, www.abc.net.au/news/2015-08-10/verrender-under-30-and-out-of-luck/6684382.

Volf, M 1991, *Work in the spirit: Towards a theology of work*, Wipf and Stock Publishers, Eugene, Oregon.

von Franz, M-L 1995, *Shadow and evil in fairy tales*, Shambhala, Boston.

———— 2008, 'CG Jung's rehabilitation of the feeling function', *Jung Journal*, vol. 2, no. 2, pp. 9–20.

Waddell, T 2019, *The lost child complex in Australian film: Jung, story and playing beneath the past*, Routledge, London.

Walker, SF 2002, *Jung and the Jungians on myth: An introduction*, Routledge, New York.

Walsh, WB & Savickas, ML (eds) 2004, *The handbook of vocational psychology*, 3rd edn, Lawrence Erlbaum, Mahwah, NJ.

Weber, M 1930, *The Protestant ethic and the spirit of capitalism*, Charles Scribner's Sons, New York.

Weiss, JW, Skelley, MF, Haughey, JC & Hall, D 2003, 'Calling, new careers and spirituality: A reflective perspective for organizational leaders and professionals', in ML Pava & P Primeaux (eds), *Spiritual intelligence at work: Meaning, metaphor, and morals*, Emerald, Bingley, UK, pp. 175–201.

Whitmont, EC 1991, *The symbolic quest: Basic concepts of analytical psychology*, Revised edn, Princeton University Press, Princeton, NJ.

———— 2007, 'The destiny concept in psychotherapy', *Journal of Jungian Theory and Practice*, vol. 9, no. 1, pp. 25–37.

Whyte, D 2001, *Crossing the unknown sea: Work as a pilgrimage of identity*, Riverhead Books, New York.

Wrzesniewski, A, McCauley, C, Rozin, P & Schwartz, B 1997, 'Jobs, careers, and callings: People's relations to their work', *Journal of Research in Personality*, vol. 31, no. 1, pp. 21–33.

Yakushko, O & Nelson, E 2013, 'Making a place for unconscious factors in research', *International Journal of Multiple Research Approaches*, vol. 7, no. 3, pp. 295–305.

Zweig, C & Abrams, J (eds) 1991, *Meeting the shadow: The hidden power of the dark side of human nature*, Jeremy P Tarcher/Putnam, New York.

Index

Note: case studies are listed under case studies by name. Page numbers in *italic* indicate a figure on the corresponding page.

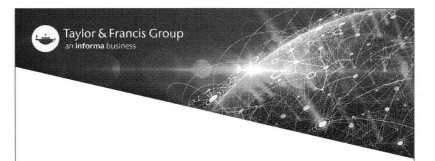